CLEAN FOOD, Messy Life

Clean Food, Messy Life
A food lover's conscious journey back to self.

Jamie Truppi, MS, CNS

This is a story about my life through the lens of food. While it's told from my perspective and most names, places, and events are as accurate as I remember them, some names and details have been modified or changed.

Clean Food, Messy Life © Copyright 2022 by Jamie Truppi
All rights reserved. No part of this publication may be reproduced, distributed, or transmitted in any form or by any means, including photocopying, recording, or other electronic or mechanical methods, without the prior written permission of the publisher, except in the case of brief quotations embodied in critical reviews and certain other noncommercial uses permitted by copyright law.

Although the author and publisher have made every effort to ensure that the information in this book was correct at press time, the author and publisher do not assume and hereby disclaim any liability to any party for any loss, damage, or disruption caused by errors or omissions, whether such errors or omissions result from negligence, accident, or any other cause.

Adherence to all applicable laws and regulations, including international, federal, state, and local governing professional licensing, business practices, advertising, and all other aspects of doing business in the US, Canada or any other jurisdiction is the sole responsibility of the reader and consumer.

Neither the author nor the publisher assumes any responsibility or liability whatsoever on behalf of the consumer or reader of this material. Any perceived slight of any individual or organization is purely unintentional.

The resources in this book are provided for informational purposes only and should not be used to replace the specialized training and professional judgment of a health care or mental health care professional.

Neither the author nor the publisher can be held responsible for the use of the information provided within this book. Please always consult a trained professional before making any decision regarding treatment of yourself or others.

For more information, email jamie@jamietruppinutrition.com.
ISBN (paperback): 979-8-88759-340-1
ISBN (ebook): 979-8-88759-341-8

Download Your Free Guide!

Imperfection can be delicious. Create simple, mouthwatering meals with whole foods while transforming yourself into a health-conscious kitchen badass. This bonus guidebook is jam-packed with the most practical, delectable, nutritionist-approved advice for cultivating ease-and-flow with your food
(without sacrificing your wellbeing or sanity).

Download **"The Mindful Meal Guidebook: 5 must-have recipes + tips to reinvent healthy eating, reduce meal-planning overwhelm, and renew your kitchen confidence."**

You can get a copy by visiting:

https://www.jamietruppinutrition.com/clean-food-messy-life-freebie

To my mama,
whose life has been messy, too,
who cleans often and eats well,
and who has always wanted to write her own book.

To everyone on a path toward awareness of your true self
while navigating complex relationships with food
layered in life circumstances & relationships
and nourishing your mind-body-spirit.

"Daily, our eating turns nature into culture, transforming the body of the world into our bodies and minds."
—*Michael Pollan*

"Keeping your body healthy is an expression of gratitude to the whole cosmos—the trees, the clouds, everything."
—*Thich Nhat Hanh*

"Every experience of love, bliss, belonging, inspiration, and insight provides a steppingstone back to your true self."
—*Deepak Chopra*

Table of Contents

Prologue..13
Chapter 1: Recipe for Drinking Rituals...............19
Chapter 2: Recipe for Dreaming.......................27
Chapter 3: Recipe for Doing It.......................35
Chapter 4: Recipe for Dinner Parties.................45
Chapter 5: Recipe for Diplomacy......................53
Chapter 6: Recipe for Driving South of the Border....61
Chapter 7: Recipe for Discovering Differences........67
Chapter 8: Recipe for Design.........................73
Chapter 9: Recipe for Dependence.....................83
Chapter 10: Recipe for Divisiveness..................91
Chapter 11: Recipe for Distaste.....................101
Chapter 12: Recipe for Doing My Own Thing...........105
Chapter 13: Recipe for Dieting......................115
Chapter 14: Recipe for Different Folks..............127
Chapter 15: Recipe for Distinguishing Values........135
Chapter 16: Recipe for Dietetic Advice..............143
Chapter 17: Recipe for Decision Making..............151
Chapter 18: Recipe for Dark Days & Dishes...........161
Chapter 19: Recipe for Depletion....................171
Chapter 20: Recipe for Deliverance..................179
Chapter 21: Recipe for Death........................185
Chapter 22: Recipe for Depression...................195
Chapter 23: Recipe for Disillusionment..............203
Chapter 24: Recipe for Disconnect...................213
Chapter 25: Recipe for Disagreement.................225
Chapter 26: Recipe for Disappointment...............233
Chapter 27: Recipe for Determination................245
Chapter 28: Recipe for Data Collection..............255
Chapter 29: Recipe for Dixie Debauchery.............261
Chapter 30: Recipe for Desire.......................267
Chapter 31: Recipe for Disaster.....................275

Chapter 32: Recipe for Driving Everyone Nuts 283
Chapter 33: Recipe for Despair 293
Chapter 34: Recipe for Depth 299
Chapter 35: Recipe for Dramatic Moments 305
Chapter 36: Recipe for Dutch Oven Baking. 313
Chapter 37: Recipe for Disagreements 321
Chapter 38: Recipe for Divine Intervention 327
Chapter 39: Recipe for Detoxification 337
Chapter 40: Recipe for Divorce 345
Chapter 41: Recipe for Dissolution. 349
Thank you! 361

Recipes

Chapter 1: Conscious Cocktail 26
Chapter 2: Mindful Merriment 34
Chapter 3: Saucy Tofu with Veggies 43
Chapter 4: Elk Chili 51
Chapter 5: Building Bridges Burgers 60
Chapter 6: Tailgate Fish Tacos 66
Chapter 7: Low-Lactose Cheese Grits 72
Chapter 8: Vegetarian Thai Green Curry & Rice 81
Chapter 9: Hanoi Croissantwiches 89
Chapter 10: Shakshuka 100
Chapter 11: Portabella Mushroom Burgers 104
Chapter 12: Vegan Chocolate Chip Cookies 114
Chapter 13: The Best Vegan Chocolate Pie (Tofu-free) . . 125
Chapter 14: Salad for Everyone 133
Chapter 15: Swiss Chard with Cannellini Beans & Pancetta (Meneste) 141
Chapter 16: Homemade Healthy Mac & Cheese 149
Chapter 17: Indian-Spiced Lentils & Asparagus 159
Chapter 18: Easy Peasy Pesto 169
Chapter 19: Polenta with Arugula, Beans, Shrooms & Sun-Dried Tomatoes 178
Chapter 20: Carrot Raisin Spice Muffins 184
Chapter 21: Panzanella 194
Chapter 22: Dragon Bowls 201
Chapter 23: Nature Nutrition 212
Chapter 24: Cinnamon Rolls & Coffee 223
Chapter 25: Classic Caesar Salad 231
Chapter 26: Sourdough French Toast 243
Chapter 27: Nutty Spicy Date Balls 253
Chapter 28: Quinoa, Broccoli & Bean Bowl 260
Chapter 29: Cajun Beans, Sausage & Collards with Rice . 265
Chapter 30: Bananas Foster 273

Chapter 31: Leprechaun Smoothie 282
Chapter 32: Road Trip Bento Boxes 291
Chapter 33: Simple Quiche 298
Chapter 34: French-Inspired Charcuterie Board 304
Chapter 35: Sunshine Frittata 312
Chapter 36: Dutch Oven Blueberry Coffee Cake 319
Chapter 37: Stovetop Popcorn with 3 Toppings 326
Chapter 38: Muddy Waters 336
Chapter 39: Vegetarian Detox Soup 343
Chapter 40: Dutch Babies 348
Chapter 41: Triple Chocolate Brownies with
Peanut Butter & Sea Salt 359

Prologue

I slipped into the Medical Intuitive session merely because it fit into my volunteer schedule. I certainly was not there because I believed in clairvoyance or that some deity worked through mortals to diagnose and heal. I was feeling quite well, thank you, so I was attending the annual Sun Valley Wellness Festival out of pure curiosity. Plus, my boss at the gallery was a donor and patron, so she encouraged me to leave work for an hour here and there to participate.

Open to a good story about a profound experience, I was intrigued by the concept of "intuition." First, I wondered if I had any, and second, I wanted to understand how any human could find clarity in messages transcending space-time and defying logic.

The speaker, a modest psychotherapist, had a gift. She claimed she had been working with a patient one day when suddenly she saw the other woman's aura—an energetic field of color supposedly emitted by all living things. By learning how colors corresponded to different ailments, the intuitive began unlocking the roots of her patients' problems. And now this healer was telling a room of primarily post-menopausal women (and me) that we, too, could tune into our bodies and "just know." No lab tests. No diagnoses. Just a knowing energy, an innate wisdom.

Hmm. Skeptical, yet inquisitive, I bought her book despite the ironically hideous patchworked baby blues, pastel pinks, and sage greens of the cover. I assumed they were aura colors, though I'd imagined a more vivid spectrum. I felt a pang of guilt for judging the book cover after the enlightenment she'd just imparted, and quickly chalked up my criticism to the contemporary art education I'd been absorbing at my day job.

And though I had no specific medical issues to resolve, there was a restless ache deep inside me that I could neither pinpoint nor define. An emptiness, a longing I couldn't identify or quench despite my explorations into the emotional, analytical, sexual, and psychedelic in attempts to, you know, find myself. Only a year prior, after returning from overseas (again) searching for something to fill me up, I'd landed in this small mountain town. I'd figured my Idaho life would be as temporary as the last few places I'd lived—northern France, Seattle, the small college town of Pullman, WA, plus Italy and France (the first time) while studying abroad. So what happened next made me wonder whether I'd been beckoned to that moment and place by a force I could not yet understand, and whether the "something" I was seeking was intangible.

The medical intuitive signed my book, looked up at me and said, "Well, your aura is the easiest one to read in the entire room. You're lactose intolerant. What do you think about giving up all dairy for a few weeks, just to see what happens and how you feel?"

Lactose intolerance was my disorder? *Dairy? Thank goodness it wasn't alcohol or coffee!* Since I was mostly vegetarian, I was accustomed to dietary modifications and ingredient inquiries at every restaurant and dinner party, anyway. Plus, already I didn't drink milk (ugh, the taste) or eat ice cream (oy, the gas), so giving up dairy altogether shouldn't be too hard, right?

That evening while preparing a quiche with butter in the crust, milk whisked into the eggs (because baked milk seemed fine), and topped with aged white cheddar, I wondered how I could possibly enjoy meals without butter and cheese! Questioning whether eliminating dairy could really make a

PROLOGUE

difference, I realized it was myself I doubted. From the outside, it probably looked like I put myself first, always flying by the seat of my pants, seeking pleasure in adventure, academics, and a robust social life. Inside my head and heart, though, I postulated that focusing on my body was egotistical and vain. I preferred experiences focused on other people and the world around me.

As I popped the quiche into the oven, I wanted to believe in the intuitive's suggestion as an effort to help me become a better version of myself. I was tired of the reckless me. Mostly, I thought a three-week food project might provide some insight into how my body *functioned*. With knowledge to gain, I had nothing to lose.

Except that I was obsessed with cheese, which led to trying to figure out whether goat cheese was considered dairy. What the heck would I eat for breakfast alongside my sliced tomatoes besides cottage cheese? And no yogurt? *Wait, are eggs dairy?* (Yes, I, an intelligent human, asked that question once.) This was before the internet offered an infinite amount of often-conflicting information about health and preceded the Googleplex of dairy-free recipe blogs. Going dairy-free wasn't mainstream when I was in my early twenties; I mean, milk did our bodies good—we all believed that.

At the time, even our tiny local health food store carried only one dairy alternative—soy. It tasted like crap as yogurt, but the sweetened vanilla-boxed-beverage alternative was great. I always drank my lattes frothed with soy milk—the only viable non-dairy option at coffee shops, too. But with no way to internet-verify what I'd heard about cancer-causing estrogens, diving into soy yogurt, soy cheese, and soy ice cream seemed unwise and unnatural.

The first few dairy-free days were akin to the self-flagellation of fasting. I was perpetually hungry, and my stomach had taken on a life of its own, calling out audibly for something in a lactose language I couldn't decipher.

Uncertainty and self-questioning permeated my mind-body, and I picked up poor habits (like extra caffeine) to combat the super-stress as I pined over what I might eat for the next snack, then lunch, then after my run, then dinner. I was already picky about meat—but adding dairy to the restrictions meant I was becoming a pain-in-the-you-know-what dinner party guest. Would others regard this experiment as a "diet" and judge me for weight issues, the way I'd judged myself since I was a teenager?

By day five, I was utterly bored with eggs or granola for breakfast. But mostly I was exhausted, and my body felt heavy, like sandbags tied to my legs and shoulders. I couldn't sleep enough, and I even canceled my plans one night (so not me) because I could hardly drag myself out of bed to my closet to find something to wear. Instead, I stayed home and thought about food. *Do croissants have dairy in them? What about dark chocolate?*

By day seven, I wandered up and down the two aisles in the health food store, scouting out inspiration. Directionless and dazed by the aroma of ginger juice and fresh herbs, I had no idea what I was looking for. I felt more lost in that tiny shop than I'd ever felt exploring unfamiliar markets in foreign countries or trailblazing in the woods.

I settled on what I thought my body was telling me to buy: the sweet-salty-fatty comfort of trail mix, which would become my invariable go-to snack for the next several weeks. As I filled my bags from the bulk bins, I fixated on healthy food, but not from a health perspective. I did not yet understand the implications of dairy on those who were lactose-intolerant, nor did I consider nutrition, nor a need to replace calcium or zinc in my meals for my body to remain replete. No one seemed to talk about that.

Like many women, I'd given up some foods for ethical reasons, and adopted extreme cabbage soup and grape diets to fit into a mold I'd envisioned. At 16, I'd sworn off meat after participating in the slaughter of our chickens (which we'd raised to eat), and because the dog across the street feasted on my pet rabbit, and because I loved the sweet, long-lashed beef cow we'd co-raised (to butcher).

Yeah. After that, my senses kicked in. The presentation of any animal on my plate was as appetizing as hairless roadkill; meat infiltrated my mouth like a salty gristle bomb; and gnawing on dead flesh was not a texture or conscious act that appealed to me. After thinking about it, the same was true of milk. I gagged at the silky, watery texture, sour flavor, stinky aroma.

Prologue

In tandem, my body rejected milk with what equated to ample bloating. Let's just say I avoided eating dairy around cute guys but until now, hadn't explored the true effect dairy had on my mental state, gut function, or metabolism. No one discussed those things, either.

Nevertheless, three weeks after giving up dairy—including all goat products (which, I learned, are dairy)—I was a different human. Not only had I lost 10 pounds (mostly around the middle) without changing anything else in my diet or my exercise regimen, but I also had more energy than I'd ever imagined possible. I felt *alive*. For the first time in years, I wasn't afraid to move my body. In fact, the craving for sweet-salty-fatty-food morphed into a craving for movement. It was as if the energy pent up for years behind inflammation and self-criticism had emerged. I felt comfortable in my skin.

That summer, I set out on trails intent on being as bad-ass as the 50-something women with rockin' bods who, just that spring, had kicked my 23-year-old butt running effortlessly uphill around switchbacks at 6,000-feet elevation. Desperately trying to appear at ease, I hacked and shuffled along the trail while twinkling aspens encouraged me. The challenge was beyond acclimating to elevation and party-hardy singles recreation. Turns out, my inability to digest dairy also had kept me from endless energy that correlated with my age.

Until that no-dairy experiment, it never occurred to me how food mattered viscerally or energetically. I'd survived adolescence, my undergrad years, and a couple of stints in Europe thinking I'd had a grasp on healthy eating. Even my college girlfriends pegged me as a "health nut," simply because I refused to eat conventional meat (overlooking that I was simultaneously an alcohol and caffeine addict, neither of which epitomized health nor sustained my pre-college pant size).

I felt sure the medical intuitive worked her magic on me in other ways. Her single, simple suggestion allowed me to trust the unknown and to notice the interconnectedness of all things. Importantly, I began to consider food as something more complex than just fuel. It was the essence of life.

Now dairy-free, I was more "in my body" than I could remember. That freedom nudged me to settle into mountain life with renewed gusto. I awoke each morning feeling fresh (even when hung over) and exhilarated by the cool, crisp air and savory scent of dew evaporating off the wooly sagebrush. Feeling tall in my shoes and light in my heart, I greeted my southern belle roommates with a bit more poise, though nothing comparable to theirs. I functioned at the gallery with ease and confidence.

Alongside my newish friends, job, and trail shoes, I was a revitalized human. For the first time, perhaps ever, I felt *free* in my mind-body.

Maybe a little too free.

CHAPTER 1
Recipe for Drinking Rituals

I can package my college years into a bottle of cheap alcohol. Not neat, nor top shelf. The experience was somewhere between bland Busch Light and sweet Strawberry Hills Boons permeating most social gatherings I attended for four destructive years. That stretch wasn't inferior like the booze or efficient like the ice beer, yet equally irresponsible and totally messy.

Washington State University is located in the middle of the pea-and-lentil capital of the world, so there wasn't much to do but drink (and study, I suppose). Every event in our robust "Greek" system centered around drinking. Ranking as the nation's third biggest party school was our celebrated accolade.

Like thousands of others new to a life centered around beverages, it consumed my life. Even as a poor college student, it was easy to manifest cheap and easy liquid intake. I balanced alcohol with caffeine by intentionally working in a coffee shop on campus several mornings a week. Other hydration just sort of happened between caffeine and beer, though I shunned soda and all forms of high fructose corn syrup.

During my junior year, when I studied abroad in France and Italy, cheap wine was readily available. In the Loire Valley, Beaujolais Nouveau was the most affordable. In Tuscany, magnums by the case topped our weekly grocery list. In both countries, table wine was a staple.

In the year following college, I explored happy hour life in Seattle. Drinking under the drizzle was inextricably tied to single life there, and I readily plunged into craft cocktail culture. By the time I left again for France with my friend Naomi, alcohol had been a long-time resident in my veins, so imbibing seemed the most natural way to meet locals in our new town (and drown my fear of foreign language mistakes).

Naomi and I had arrived in Europe only a few days before the bombing of the Twin Towers, which changed the trajectory of foreigners' work life in northern France. Unable to obtain a visa (a new rule while the US was working out the details of 9/11), I walked dogs and worked in cafés until they asked for paperwork. I pieced it together, holding out for something more. In my frustration and to feel grounded, I planned dinner parties for Naomi (who had obtained her teaching visa before leaving the US) and me and our entourage of international friends, who brought lots of wine.

When my job offer to run a bed and breakfast in the south of France was given to a married couple instead of to me and the photographer I loved in Seattle who was set to come, I gave up and promptly returned stateside the following week. But the Pacific Northwest no longer felt like home—not the city, the burbs, or my folks' house farther out. And the man I loved was off in Mexico (with another woman), so in my gut-wrenching sorrow I ended up (drinking) at a friend's house party where a man I'd loved *before* the photographer showed up. He handed me a sealed and stamped package ready to send to me in France. Inside was a love letter.

It was too much. I had to get away.

I headed east from Seattle with an empty wallet and tearful eyes in my 1989 BMW. A college roomie said I could crash on his couch, and he'd help me find a job, so I fled to the Idaho mountains in a freakish, two-day blizzard. I arrived in the small town of Ketchum where four dudes and two dogs shared a 3-bedroom, 1-bath house. *What the heck am I doing here?*

I found work immediately in a coffee shop—my go-to place of employment each time I moved. The job came with morning discipline, breakfast and lunch, and beverages I could control (ristretto shots, honey instead of unnatural syrups). I earned enough in tips to invest in the night life and my hyper-cautious spending helped me calculate evening beverage choices. I knew I could *not* drink tequila (thanks to one fateful night in Mexico) or stout beers (which tasted like bong water blended with robusto coffee grounds). I'd sit at the bar wondering what I'd feel unapologetic about spending my money on. In my hesitation, drinks were often bought for me. Otherwise, I found my pocketbook and tastebuds easily saying "no" to the fairly flavorless array of liquids with loads of refined sugar. In doing so, an unusual thing occurred: my palate developed refinement. I wanted a *good* drink.

Busy bartenders were irritated with my indecision and incessant questions. But those who were chatty (and good at their jobs) offered samples and, for once, I slowly sipped shot glasses of microbrews on tap, middle-shelf liquor and, of course, house wine before deciding how my gustatory sensors would resonate with an entire drink. I made a few good bartender friends who possessed patience and knowledge, and I avoided the others.

Soon, I felt slightly more sophisticated when ordering Maker's Mark instead of a well drink. Visually, the crimson wax that dripped over the cork and the squarish shape of the bottle made it seem like an educated choice from a southern library of libations; but really, it was the balanced caramel and spice compared with the whiskeys (hidden inside paper bags) I'd consumed in college. I decided not to bother with soda mixers. What, then, would pair well with Maker's that wasn't Coke, artificial cherry, or white sugar? Rocks? Seriously, *just ice?*

My penchant for bourbon was officially inaugurated when my new friends introduced me to Old Rip Van Winkle's fine bourbon. Not yet highly sought after yet already legendary Kentucky bourbon—and their family's legacy—offered me a portal into antiquity, tradition, and pleasure that would transform my drinking life.

At their rental condo, one of the triplets, granddaughters of Pappy Van Winkle, walked over to the cocktail bar. Even at 22, the girls had a dedicated bar atop a buffet with select bottles displayed on vintage trays, accompanied by the basic mixing tools. The setup, an image of the American South, was as foreign to me as the books I'd read about folktale spirits in the bayou.

Selecting a small pear-shaped glass with a heavy bottom that begged for pursed lips at its tapered top, Carrie uncorked a bottle of 20-year-old Special Reserve and poured a small amount into the glass—no ice. Four of us—two of the triplets and their close friend—settled on the stairs, sipping. I felt their eyes casually fixated on me. As the gilded liquid touched my lips then tongue, and the soft bite of maple syrup and vanilla transported me to a leathery cigar lounge I'd never set foot in, a crackling fire that warmed me to the bones, and a hankering for a nutmeg-and-cashew-cream custard that maybe never existed. *What is this stuff?* The girls looked amused—it was more than just their family drink. More than a ritual. It was their life, and they'd just ushered me into the secret of existing in their past-present.

But more than that, they introduced me to notions I'd never associated with drinking: the pleasure of taste; the enjoyment of doing nothing else but savoring each sip; being present with friends instead of all over the map; and tuning into the moment as if it were the first and last of its kind. It was magic.

When we moved in together, Carrie and Louise shared all the Pappy bourbon vintages available at the time, gifting me with an understanding of refinement, tradition, and sense of place. I swore never go back to well drinks. In fact, that special bourbon had convinced me I should never again consume anything substandard. It helped direct the course of my life.

The enlightenment also exposed me to more than just a small town: there was sustenance, depth, richness in the working folk who served owners of grandiose log and modern homes and countless vacation condos. Sure, the traditions were brought in from elsewhere, but then I didn't have to go to Kentucky, New York, or even Amsterdam to find them. Maybe I, a lonely rootless globetrotter from a severed, middle-class family, could

Recipe for Drinking Rituals

absorb rituals that were not stale and mainstream, but poignant and meaningful.

Despite improving my drinks, the party life ensued. My habits were somewhat disastrous. Like other working locals, I spent countless hours in sticky bars, noodling to bluegrass music, and inhaling lines in dirty bathroom stalls with rolled up cash. I hadn't quite connected quality consumption with recreational activities—I was very much "outside myself" in those moments. Obviously not thinking straight. "Going out" was synonymous with recklessness. It's what I'd groomed myself to do, and I'd convinced myself the night life eventually would unearth something deeper.

After all, the après-work and mountain social life is what brought us 20-somethings together. Whenever there wasn't a live band, theater show, fundraising event, or free chamber music, there was a costume party, birthday party, ugly sweater party, or just a few friends gathered at the bar to party. Like pinballs, we'd bump into someone we'd met the night before at Dollar Night or last week at the Irish pub. There was always someone new in town who knew someone you knew. Small gatherings turned into open invitations for our closest 40-or-so friends. Someone else on the street invited you somewhere for "just a few minutes," and then you rallied on to the next joint with another friendly face.

Before you knew it, you were an hour or so late to the party you'd actually RSVP'd to attend, so you and your entourage would flock there until it was time to catch the headliner you remembered about because the tickets fell out of the back pocket of your jeans when you relieved your bladder the first time that night. On fire, you'd close down the venue, rationalizing you didn't have to be at work 'til noon on Sundays, so, *YES!* you'd love to come to the after-hours party for another beverage and another weary but profound conversation.

At least, that was how I rolled.

On those subsequent hangover mornings, I hid from the sunshine, shamed by the revelry, not knowing how I got home, and the sense that life was one, fantastically fleeting celebration. With a pulsating head and a hankering for hash browns, I chastised myself for overdoing it. Again. I'd peel myself out of bed, find my roomies on the couch—wide awake, post-exercise—reading *People* magazines, poised and coiffed, nourished. They had the personal integrity to know when to stop and come home for a good night's sleep (they were raised to be dilettantes, after all). I was the crazy hippie with unfathomable stories and a partying problem. I knew my lifestyle was unsustainable and (unsurprisingly) contributed to my going in circles instead of anywhere useful.

Thankfully, the endless summer days and a new job provided a daily reset. I'd dress smartly in thrift-store skirts and flats, a fresh coat of mascara, and present myself at the art gallery. Mostly on time and quasi-refreshed, I was re-energized by connecting clients with artwork, shuffling sculptures, organizing artist events, helping to curate shows. By 6:00 pm I'd perked up enough for an in-town hike or short trail run to sweat out the drugs and alcohol. By dinner, a drink or two seemed as curative as my grilled tuna-and-sprouts sandwich with roasted veggies, and I was too-often lured out on the town.

I was very much aware of the fleeting life I'd created. As the nights grew longer and tourists and second- and third-home owners retreated, giving us back our town, trails, and parking spaces, fewer events brought pause and an invitation to retreat inside. With a bourbon on ice, and a twist of citrus, I reexamined my life. Up to then, following my heart had turned into one wildly experimental bust after another.

During the quiet "Slack" time between summer recreation and winter skiing, I was frustrated and antsy. But quite unlike myself, I resolved to find peace in just being there. Swathed in a colorful vortex of energy from the shimmering golden aspens, the Valley promised the chaos of summer was on the exhale and the respite of autumn on the inhale. Sunshine was deceiving—nothing warmed up until late morning. We zipped up puffy coats to walk outside 10 steps to start the car, our senses intoxicated by layers of frosty sage, wet leaves fallen upon clay, burning wood from a neighbor's chimney, and exhaust fumes hanging low in the frigid air. Those mornings, I had only to close my eyes to be transported back to the French countryside, beyond the wilted, frozen fields of sunflowers and distant chateaus, where old men sat in smoke shops drinking cognac together in their heavy coats and work boots. I was there and everywhere.

Admittedly, I loved the simple life. I was ready to shelve the past chapters of my adolescence; the pudgy, shapeless college years; unproductive studies and travels; menial jobs just to scrape together another experience to remember; one broken heart after another.

Without direction or agenda, I found freedom in the woods, comfort with other young adults who also found solace in simplicity. I glimpsed the extreme wealth that supported our town; found confidence in the contemporary art world and gratitude in the middle-aged gallery women who took me under their wings. This new world held me like a comfy fleece blanket. Somehow, at 23, I was filled up by the ease of small-town life. It curbed my carelessness while encouraging my free spirit.

Even the photographer (who had broken my heart) noticed the difference. I'm not sure why he came—I assumed it was a great excuse to travel to the mountains for a fall photo shoot and not to apologize—but still, he came. Charlie looked at me with new eyes, with reawakened appreciation and respect. He said what I felt, "The mountains are good for you. Stay here." Of all the things he said to me (and didn't), Charlie knew my soul. He helped me escape the urge to move again.

As we lay (fully clothed and sober) under blankets in a circle of aspens one clear night, marveling at the Milky Way, I sensed belonging. Yet my comfort was imbalanced by something essential that was missing. Something meaningful. Direction? Guidance? An avocation or life pursuit? An epiphany would have been lovely but apparently that's the easy way out.

Though I couldn't say it out loud to myself or to Charlie, I wanted someone to cradle my soul and remind me that life's little pleasures were meaningful. I wanted that, but without being constricted by the idea that another human could fill me up. He gave me both. So why did I feel so alone?

A few weeks later, I was flying over the Pacific Ocean to join Charlie in Singapore.

RECIPE for DRINKING RITUALS

Make your first (or only) drink of the evening a conscious, joyful choice. Savor it. A good quality drink, sipped slowly, makes for a truly memorable moment.

Conscious Cocktail
Yield: 1-2 drinks
Time: Timeless

Ingredients
- Your favorite, high quality alcohol
- Accoutrements such as bitters, simple syrup, and citrus
- Ice cubes
- A glass you enjoy holding
- Good company
- Time
- Water

Instructions
1. Mix up your favorite cocktail. My favorite is a true Kentucky bourbon with a hint of orange bitters, a splash of simple syrup, and an ice cube (call me old fashioned…).
2. Be one with your beverage. Smell. Sip. Savor.
3. Be present with your company. Look them in the eyes. Don't multitask.
4. Drink water. Even 4-6 ounces is a good idea. Add a twist of lemon if you'd like.
5. If celebrating with friends, consider whether a second drink in that moment is a good idea or not.
6. If having a second drink, consume the same type of alcohol (trust me, I've tested this), yet feel free to mix up the cocktail ingredients so you start again with pure enjoyment during round two.
7. More water. Don't skip this step!
8. Tune into your body and habits. Do you really need a third drink? How about bourbon in your lemon tea? Have you moved on to another activity and are no longer paying attention to your beverage intake? Be truthful and mindful. Just sayin'.

CHAPTER 2

Recipe for Dreaming

A few weeks in Southeast Asia with a platonic companion brought me new perspective about home—Idahome. If I were going to stay put for a while, I needed to prioritize my work and finances, maintain a healthy social life, and simultaneously find a legit excuse to remove myself from potential all-night situations.

A part-time night job pouring wine would do the trick.

Back then, Ketchum had exactly one farm-to-table restaurant. It wasn't called that—this was before the farm-food revival—but it was committed to sourcing local food and cooking from scratch. It also boasted a well-crafted wine list.

Set in a converted cabin, The Evergreen was a rare place where we common folk communed with the 1%-ers (more like 0.01%-ers) with relative equanimity in select settings. A few famous actors and musicians with palatial vacation homes brought their guests via private jet to play anonymously in our secluded valley—and to dine at The Evergreen. We catered to important politicians, CEOs of top corporations, and trust-fund heirs to old-world American and foreign money. Also, well-off tourists arrived in obnoxious fur coats and Italian leather boots, but we liked them, too. Mostly, locals of all ages came for the food and wine, of course, and everyone stayed because they were treated like family—and because high expectations were met by staff who actually gave a hoot about impeccable service, ambiance, and fantastic food.

I was recruited to recommend wine pairings with the braised something-or-other cut of well-pastured dead animal bathed in buttery wild morels over local Idaho potato puree, then another wine to follow it up with something perfect for *crème brûlée* yet before espresso. In between, I was to help ensure tables were "crumbed," silverware replaced, waters refilled, and napkins refolded each time a guest got up from the table. I was an adept multi-tasker, surely; but I'd never worked in a fine dining establishment. And it showed.

The head sommelier, a friend of mine, was impressed with my "palate" during a casual tasting of several vintage, old-world reds. He wanted me on his team. Apparently, my drinking hobby in Europe had provided me a discerning sense of terroir, and he had a reputation for hiring female protégés without certification or official training. Since I also spoke French and a bit of Italian, and felt comfortable conversing with anyone from anywhere, I was a good fit.

I was not, unfortunately, given a full job description, which I soon discovered included side work, bussing tables, cleaning the espresso machine, and 700 other tiny details contributing to the restaurant's allure. The nuances were why every single diner felt doted on and beamed about their eating experience. It was well orchestrated, overwhelming, and over my head.

Still, I knew I was capable. At the gallery, for instance, I'd learned about 50+ artists and their careers, techniques, personalities and also how to sell to artwork enthusiasts on a shoestring or with a $40K monthly art budget. Even my boss, Gail, was happy for me to supplement a night job where, conveniently, our art collector clients feasted. Since my own drinking and eating habits were shifting toward more intentional, higher quality meals, I naively felt ready to master the role.

The wining-and-dining learning curve was steep. Besides a petite café in Brussels, Belgium, where I fumbled with tableside language and caught my hair on fire with a candle, I'd worked only in casual coffee shops. To become a knowledgeable wine steward, I would need to study like mad, drink a lot of wine, and fake confidence while facing an onslaught of restaurant chaos that dizzied me.

I relied on my knowledge of people—I had no qualms about interacting with individuals of any pedigree or demeanor. Often, I knew the artwork they'd just purchased while visiting; I'd been inside their remodeled vacation condo, tasteful mega-mansion, or heritage mountain lodge. I'd helped curate or install artwork for their bedrooms, bathrooms, trophy rooms, and guest quarters. In some cases, I'd met their kids, grandkids, dogs, and cats.

I figured the Massachusetts couple who'd just written a $67,000 check for a pop-art triptych I'd helped install in their swanky pad might go for a bottle of Chateau Mouton Rothschild (spoken with an almost-perfect French accent). The young California family remodeling a 1970's ski townhome had thoughtfully purchased a couple of mountain birds on cigar boxes for a stretched total of $5000, so a bottle of Talley Pinot Noir would be the perfect accompaniment to their rack of lamb. The newlywed art enthusiasts from Texas who hadn't yet started a collection would be thrilled with an affordable Cayuse Syrah.

Perhaps too regularly the guests invited me to bring another glass for myself, adamant that I take a few minutes to sit and sip with them. With a thirst for experience and a zest for human connection, I loved those gestures, but my co-workers pegged me as lazy, too social, and unsupportive. I tried to make up for it by staying late and going the extra mile to polishing 155 delicate glasses, but that didn't benefit the heat of the dinner rush.

Unlike at the gallery where I rocked it most days, I was quite useless to my restaurant co-workers. According to those busting butt, I wasn't pulling my weight. Proper training and clear expectations would have been helpful amidst whispers that I "should have been experienced" before being considered for hire. Well, shoot. Wine sales were through the roof; camaraderie was in the pits.

I persevered and, over time and over wine, found true friendships with the staff—the only way people last in the food biz. Many times before, drinking had helped me feel as though I wasn't running away from myself, but instead, accepting myself just as I was. Now, in place of mock escapism, alcohol was leading me, like a good wine pairing, to association with others.

At the restaurant, I was in a rhythmic drinking-working environment with the sobering reminder that the gallery work I also enjoyed was only a few hours away. Tuscan red hangovers were tolerable, thanks in part, to purple Peruvian potatoes and Caesar salads, but also because they afforded me good company in a dreamlike state, instead of unrestrained bar foolishness. I felt deeply entwined with people over their stories, heightened by drinking. Though I felt alive in forests, at festivals, at dinner parties, and during travels, pairing those places alcohol highlighted the good times and kept me feeling free. Every night presented new faces, narratives, and experiences I could choose to expand or not. I could stay for another glass or go home to my roomies and warm bed. Definitely I did not need the obligation of the same company every night, someone else's schedule dictating mine, or a routine that would drag on day after day. *Why would I, when I was living so spontaneously?*

Drinking also was my justification to temporarily couple-up, then brush it off as an "in the moment thing" while in an altered state. Nothing serious. Fleeting passion. No one got hurt. Usually. Except me. Unfortunately, like a rich *mousse au chocolat*, alcohol was a double-edged knife that brought momentary bliss, with gluttonous shame.

My life appeared simply dreamy. Before then, the scale teetered heavily toward evading the status quo. I would never have imagined life in the Idaho mountains would open my eyes to the potential to be myself *and* stable. Idaho—where my mother's family had settled five generations earlier and where I'd always been embarrassed to call home. In some ways, this life was a return to my childhood growing up in the pristine backcountry when our family co-owned a 160-acre dude ranch deep within the Frank Church River of No Return Wilderness. I'd been imprinted by the comings and goings of guests amidst something innately natural and rare. It was unusual and idyllic. I had no way of foreseeing the impact Idaho mountains would have on my psyche.

Now, I was entranced by nature bliss that attracted many other people just like me—including a lot of men. The joke was they all had "Peter Pan Syndrome"—never wanting to grow up—which worked for me because I certainly didn't want to be tied down. It was refreshing to be in a town full of single freedom-seekers and I loved my fly-by-the-seat-of-my-tie-dye-pants life; I believed in it more than I believed in life-long love.

But beneath the single life glow existed a shadowy side: following the buzz of hot parties lurked cold, lonely nights. Even those dark spots kept us humans longing to move through cycles along with the rotting leaves. I cycled through men, mostly appropriately, and always appreciating moments with them—the leaving moments too. Like the perceptive mandolin player who worked for the forest service and brought me wildflowers in a jar and farm-stand berries. Wildflowers and berries! I could see us falling asleep in the woods, sharing trail mix on mountaintops. But then I invited him to attend the Hemingway Writers Awards ceremony—I had "placed" for my short story about the photographer. It was too graphic, and perhaps too recent. He left. I was alone again, newly shaken from the pulse of something suddenly gone flat.

The pattern repeated itself. I was unable to love the men who wanted me, and I was uninvited to love the ones I wanted. I found the in-betweens, reasoning that my independence was of utmost importance to me…until one fateful day when I met someone I would never have expected to fall for.

One Thursday, I biked from the gallery to a front-of-the-house staff meeting with our new restaurant manager. It took a while to recognize everyone in street clothes. Then I saw him. He didn't work with us. *Who is he?* Tall. Olive skin. Jet black hair. A prominent nose like one you might find on an Arabian knight. Leaning against the buffet, shoulders slouched slightly, the button-up shirt tightening across his back, arms crossed casually. You know the type. Dreamy.

Only he was not arrogant or aloof. His eyes were joyful, accompanied by a somewhat shy demeanor. An unusual mix of confidence and kindness. Not the same energy of any of the guys I had loved and left. I caught him looking back at me. As fate would have it, we met later that night at Whiskey Jacques, a bar infamous for coupling. (I apologize here to my Catholic relatives—and especially my grandmas, rest their souls—who might have *assumed* we met elsewhere.)

Anyway, after a Western-themed costume-dinner-birthday party and plenty of alcohol (and maybe some recreational drugs), I was lit up! In my second-hand cowboy boots, chocolate corduroy skirt, and "naked shirt"—a gift from one of my matron moms that (unbeknownst to me) was hard to distinguish between my summer skin color under dim lights. He was ignited too, with his shirt off (not so shy, after all). He danced like he'd taken lessons from a hip-hop artist, commanding the dance floor to the likes of Outkast and JT. My dude friends stood at the bar, mouths agape, clearly astounded that I'd be into *that kind* of man. (Envious, maybe? Guarding me? Whatever.) They were just *standing* there, watching life play out in front of them. This guy was, at least, actionable.

Of course, he'd been drinking too. It was "Dollar Night" so drinks were a-flowin', and at least two (typically three, I later learned) drinks were a requirement for this guy to bring his inner self onto the dance floor without worrying what others thought of him. I was cautiously enamored.

And since my roomies and I were hosting an after-hours party, naturally, I invited Tall Dark Handsome and his friend (a girl, but not *his* girl) to join us. They came. She caressed my legs. *Huh?* He spoke French. *Unusual.* His accent was terrible, and he told me he learned the cheesy phrases from his ex-wife. Oh. *Ex-wife.* No wonder he was so vivacious—newly single. Free. Well, his enthusiasm was captivating.

And so was the rest of the night and next morning. I was cat-sitting for a gallery friend; he came with me. We played at the piano, mused amongst her artwork, adored the two Siamese kittens and each other. I was surprised at how easy it was to love that man for who he was. No excuses. Yes, okay, I might not have been thinking straight, but isn't that what *love* does to us?

Still, I broke two of my recently declared rules (an attempt to make smarter decisions): 1. I brought home someone I'd met at a bar; and 2. I had intimate relations with someone whose last name I didn't know.

Even though the night was dreamy, I knew I'd fucked up. I felt all the things I tried to avoid—guilt, self-reproach, ugliness inside. I was a good person, but I felt otherwise. I washed away those thoughts as I downed some electrolytes (to remedy my mini hangover) and pulled myself together for work. Coffee with honey and soy milk as a pick-me-up remedied the lack of sleep.

The next day, I met Last Night's Mistake at the coffee shop next to the gallery. I'd planned to apologize for my behavior and impulsiveness—something that never seemed necessary with my previous acts of contrition. I read aloud to him from my journal—about the loveliness and shame. Without knowing his full name, I half-joked, "Chris, I guess you'll have to marry me."

And then he confessed he had a girlfriend. He said they'd broken up before the weekend, before we met, that he wasn't intentionally out drinking to look for anything close to the magic we'd experienced. He'd just wanted to have fun. He apologized to me (and later to her). We went our separate ways.

Over the subsequent weeks, friends and co-workers convinced me he was just (another) one-night-stand. I convinced myself the same, yet I knew he was different. Or, perhaps, the incident had reawakened love inside me with a vision that I, too, could coexist with a man who was equally footloose and fancy-free.

I could be filled up and rounded out, like good legs on a glass of old-vine wine.

RECIPE for DREAMING

One more drinking recipe to highlight a favorite pastime of my '20's, with a side of personal integrity, and a natural hangover remedy, to boot. All good evenings go awry when you drink too much, so be mindful. If you have addiction or liver issues, please seek help from a mental health therapist and nutritionist (who can work in tandem to help you heal).

Mindful Merriment
Yield = 1 serving
Time = seemingly endless

Ingredients
- 750-ml bottle of white or pink wine
- 750-ml bottle of red wine
- At least 1 other person or, perhaps, a roomful
- A smattering of appetizers: cheese, bread, meat, olives, nuts, grapes
- Recreational drugs, optional (typically I endorse the nature-derived)
- Water (remember!?)
- Costume (comfortable; required)
- 1 16-oz bottle of Kombucha, coconut water, and/or electrolytes
- Strong, French press coffee with honey & creamer of choice (optional)
- Protein (required) with your greasy breakfast of fats and carbs

Instructions
1. Create a reason to celebrate life with friends.
2. Commit to an imaginative theme for the night.
3. Dress up in clothes and accessories that transport you to another time and place.
4. Start with a glass or two of light-colored wine.
5. Drink water.
6. Next, red wine. Start with lighter reds (pinot noir) before uncorking a cab or syrah.
7. Consume foods that complement the vintages. Be merry.
8. Hydrate. Even a sip of water here and there.
9. Responsibly recreate in other ways (totally optional).
10. Pause to enjoy your friends and the wistful event you created.
11. Go to sleep before you think you're ready (and without another drink).
12. The next day, wake up on time. Don't take ibuprofen or aspirin (NSAIDs can contribute to gut issues). Instead, opt for natural relief like kombucha.
13. Drink more water. Coconut water is ideal—electrolytes help.
14. Eat protein—eggs are easy. Add salt (an electrolyte). Maybe toast.
15. Once nourished and hydrated, you may drink coffee. Embellish with your fave natural ingredients.

CHAPTER 3

Recipe for Doing It

I needed to get my head on straight. Since the dairy experience, I believed in clairvoyance; since the glimpse of fate and love, I ached to open myself to more possibilities.

That's why, when I bumped into to a woman at the local bookstore who can open up Akashic records, I scheduled a reading with her. I hoped she would provide insight into what was next in my life. But I missed my appointment because, unfortunately, I was throwing up (too much cabernet followed by port thanks to a visiting gallery artist). I made certain not to miss the rescheduled session (for which I was slightly hungover).

For an hour the psychic opened up my Akashic record—the vibrational reading of my soul's journey past, present, and future (crazy, right?). A few pivotal points surfaced: 1. Perhaps I was drinking too much; 2. I was attracting the wrong men (and did I even like them?); 3. I needed nature and the ocean close at hand, but also a city (out West, a port city, perhaps) to support and stimulate me.

Geez. How little I truly understand myself.

I thought about my drinking, which had never felt like an insurmountable problem. Yet as I considered nature and men, I saw that booze was dualistic—it brought inner freedom yet bound me to a cycle of self-destruction. Nature was boundless, with literally zero negative associations. Men…?

I recalled the men currently in my life: the designer who called the gallery to ask for my cell number; the man I'd met at a Chicago coffee shop; the blue-eyed river guide up north who was also journeying to find himself; my client's brother-in-law who made a pass at me at the Irish pub (while I was with another man); the bike mechanic who braved a dinner party at my house; my co-worker with the curly locks who flirted with me yet made me feel unworthy. And, of course, the boys we invited to dinner. I had plenty of male friends, yet no lasting intimate relationship.

Alrighty, time to rethink everything. Since I wouldn't meet my match for some time—years, according to the records—I needed to focus on what was calling to me…. But other than hiking, social connections, and wine, I was totally unsure.

One night, instead of working at the restaurant, I sat in the wine bar intending to read my book and sample a new Salice Salentino. The elegant woman who designed the interior of The Evergreen was also there, solo, with a slender glass of Cliquot. As we conversed about life, she said, "Jamie, create a vision. Then, just *do it*. Push. Don't let anyone tell you otherwise."

"Yes!" I agreed. It was time to paint a new picture of my life.

Then she asked, "What are your goals?" *Dammit! I hate that question.* I'd relinquished my goals years before, the day I dropped out of architecture school. Ever since, I'd been meandering.

I said, "I am going to *do it all*." (Because, of course!)

But "doing it all" was not a goal; it was a vague notion. *What, exactly, am I going to do?* This required introspection. An inner adventure. Perhaps by way of the city? *Yes!*

In early November, after the first dusting of snow, I packed up for a month-long trip (Back East because, for some reason, I wasn't ready to go West)—first to Boston, then New York, followed by a jaunt to the Berkshires for a yoga and meditation retreat. I figured two weeks focused outward in big cities with lively people followed by nine days in the woods with mindful people would help me tune into myself, define some aspirations, and reset.

All packed up, I popped into the bar where Carrie and Louise worked and many of my friends convened. I never ate there—it served quintessential dive bar food with deep-fried everything (even pickles and, surely, the fry oil had never been changed)—but it was my watering hole.

As soon as I walked in, I saw Tall Dark Handsome sitting at a table with a girl (not the leg-caressing girl) and a guy I didn't recognize but who addressed me by name. Nervous and knowing I had no choice but to say hello, I sauntered over. We made small talk for a few minutes before I excused myself to meet my friends. I grabbed my mug (number 123) from the hook on the ceiling, asked for a two-thirds-full Fat Tire, then bounced from pool table to booth to learn where other locals were headed during fall Slack.

Someone tapped me on the shoulder. I turned to meet hazel eyes inviting me to take a matchbook from his hand. Chris was headed to California but would be back in early December, and could we please hang out then? His number was inside the matchbook.

Phone number in a matchbook. *Is that cliché or hot?* Cheesy meant an excuse to walk away; sexy meant pursuit. My hand trembled; my heart swelled, though I waited until I was home to open the book to pore over his handwriting. Plus, I wasn't supposed to meet my true match for some time.

The next day, I woke early to hit the road before dawn. The heat went out in my Beamer so my teeth chattered in three-degree weather as I headed south, then west across the Camas Prairie. I was warmed only by my coffee and the anxiety of potentially skidding off the icy road. Then, two flat tires—*two!*—and a frozen can of Fix-a-Flat. I caught a ride to a gas station with a couple of missionaries; was rescued by man with a woman's name, feathered hair, an orange-tinged goatee, and two tires for my BMW. But my battery was dead, too. When I finally arrived at the Boise airport, I was running late and (while running) I twisted my ankle, fell, and watched in horror as my yoga mat, snack bag, boarding pass, and driver's license went flying.

Instead of helping me, the security team rummaged through my massive food bag: homemade egg-and-arugula sandwich, apple, orange, nuts & seeds, energy bars, dark chocolate, tea bags, vitamin C powder, my favorite local molasses cookies—but no explosives. They also searched every pocket in my camera bag—no hazardous materials. By then, my ankle was swelling, and tears were streaming. I was going to miss my flight.

The security lady called to hold my plane and, declining the offered wheelchair, I ran-limped through the terminal, out onto the tarmac, and up the metal stairs. Through blurry eyes I found my seat at the back of the plane, huffing-puffing-sweating, chilled, embarrassed. A complete wreck. By then, my ankle was the size of a softball. The flight attendant brought ice. I accepted her offer of a drink (whiskey, though I wanted bourbon), but politely refused the anti-inflammatory medication (because, confessing here, my Catholic upbringing told me the ankle issue was *mea culpa*).

What is going on? Are these signs that I'm headed in the wrong direction, after all?

My friends in Boston were inviting, but Boston was not. It was dreary, bone-chilling, and wet. The food—hoagies and chowder—was terrible and the best coffee I could find was at Dunkin' Donuts. I definitely belonged Out West.

I caught the bus in Chinatown and headed south to take a bite out of The Big Apple. My ankle still recovering, I hailed cabs to make the most of my limited time: museums by day, gallery openings at night, clubs into the wee hours. An artist I represented had an opening at a posh photo gallery on the Upper East Side. He invited me to the swanky Indian food dinner, then cocktails next door. Women with face lifts, in stilettos and sequins, swooned over the rogue photographer. He drank it up and, under his Jack Daniels breath, thanked me for being authentic and down to earth. *If he only knew.*

The next night, I met up with a party friend from Idaho who had just moved back to his birthplace for a job organizing events at A-list night clubs. In Tribeca, we shared a bottle of La Segreta Sicilia Rosso at Max Restaurant. Typically, I opted for vegetarian meals when eating out (because, you know, I wanted to know what the meat I was eating had been eating) but I opted for salty, dead pig (prosciutto) along with marinated eggplant, heirloom tomatoes, true buffalo mozzarella and, of course, house-made pasta. The meal called me back to my Italian roots in the city where my dad's family had landed only two generations before. But I felt estranged in the city and, therefore, an impulse to end the night after that amazing meal. But no. My friend insisted I come with him to a rave. I'd never felt so fashionably un-chic or out of place as I did that night. Other than people-watching, I don't remember much. Physically and biochemically intoxicated to the point of blacking out (oops), I woke up in the wee hours in a high-rise condo with a couple of German guys I didn't know and somewhere far from the introspection I was seeking.

You'd think an intelligent person on her way to a yoga and meditation retreat would choose more sensible activities while in New York, or that someone so picky about food would, at least, fixate her adventure around nourishment. But back then my choices echoed my activities everywhere: escapist, irresponsible, and without limits. Obviously, I'd learned nothing from the Akashic reader, the Tall Dark Handsome experience, or listening to my intuition.

How I found my way back to Brooklyn and my things that morning was a combination of kindness, luck, and innate sense of direction. My friend from France, up early with her infant, handed me a waffle as I grabbed my bags and jumped into a cab. Miraculously, I made it to Penn Station and sprinted (on my mostly healed ankle) to catch my bus to the Berkshires. Surely smelling of booze and bars, alternating states of nausea and loose bowels plagued me during the four-hour bus ride. I cursed my lack of preparedness—not a crumb of my trusted morning-after healing foods or beverages. An empty food bag.

I arrived at Kripalu Center for Yoga and Health with a pounding head, grumbling gastrointestinal organs, and a shitload of frustration with myself. I pretended I was prone to motion sickness, dehydration, and migraines. Now I was a liar too. At a yoga center.

Still, I was blessed with time to shower and nap before a dinner of plain basmati rice, Bok choy, and naan with garlic butter. Orientation was a shock, however: I learned the meditation retreat I'd signed up for was a *silent* retreat. *Whaaaa?* I was hoping to make friends with peaceful yogis and wise humans, perhaps meet someone interesting while focused and sober. Instead, I took the vow of silence and wore the badge: "In loving silence."

Silence meant more than no talking. The rules were clear: no music, no reading, no journaling. Only when prompted in class or during chanting could we make noise with our mouths. My identity and my personality were stripped! *This is going to be the longest five days of my life!*

As when I gave up dairy, I longed for something I couldn't have—this time, connection with others. Oh My God, I was addicted to socializing! The potential was everywhere around me, yet out of reach. No one spoke to me; or they glanced at my badge before acknowledging me with their eyes or a silent smile. With little to do except *Be Silent*, I was forced to adapt to a schedule beginning at 5:00 am—the same time I'd sauntered into the Brooklyn apartment after partying the previous day.

We were given the bare necessities for inner work: a warm bed, healthy food, support, space, time, breathwork, movement, chanting. Thankfully, the vegetarian food was familiar and lovely. Otherwise, like dieting—no, like detoxing—I was forced to let go of what no longer served me. Cold turkey, I was obliged to give up much of what I'd subsisted upon—caffeine, alcohol, people, and running away from myself. This slap-in-the-face experience forced me to turn inward.

It was, I reminded myself, exactly why I'd come.

By the third day, I was lonely and experiencing emotional overload. With two daily yoga sessions, six hours of meditation and three meals, we had one hour of free time. I took to nature. There was a labyrinth on the south side of the property, and I walked there daily, then farther to the edge of a lake. The atmosphere amongst hundreds of yogis inside was solemn, but these solo walks outdoors allowed me to process what the hell was going on.

The chatter in my head, at first intensely berating, slowly morphed into hope and possibilities for what might come from clarity juxtaposed with doubt—I was unsure I'd ever really listened to myself before. As the headaches subsided and my gut neutralized, the need for substances beyond nutrients shifted from desire to angst to self-assessment. The drinking obviously had to stop, but what else?

As I neared the heart of the labyrinth, a flash of images surfaced: Catholic Sunday school, high school Christian Youth discussions, and the cultish chanting at my sister's Confirmation. The absence of God/divine in my life. *Oh, no. Stop. I'm not ready for that journey.*

In the afternoon session, our meditation guide proffered that God lives in each of us. It's something we need to feel. The power of Om—the energy of the world. *Has she read my mind?*

Like the intuitive, the Akashic reader, and the interior designer, the meditation guide shared something unsettling about me. She asserted life would be easier for me if I were like others who were satisfied by malls and movies, those who go through the motions, accepting all they are taught. But I was on a different path, more difficult and probably more confusing. She saw my earnestness to experience and to go to great lengths seeking understanding. She called it beautiful. She hoped to teach me one thing: that all energies in the world are one divine energy that cannot be defined yet is everywhere, all the time. If I could truly understand that, I might accept the perfection of each thing in and of itself.

Like tofu. Yeah, tofu. It was the next tangible thing on my plate, so I fixated on the energy of the world in my marinated tofu.

Our evening meditation work centered around mindful eating. This concept, as new to me as the Oneness of all things, was both frustrating and intriguing. Gathered in a room and isolated from the rest of the guests and staff, our silent group sat shivering in the gray, rainy light edging in from the only window. Hands folded in our laps, we eyed the tofu on our plates in front of us. Fearing my meal was getting cold, I tried to focus on calming my breath—as we'd been instructed to do numerous times—and simply notice and accept the feeling (annoying as it was) to obey this lesson in Cultivating Patience.

We were also cultivating *awareness*: "Take one small bite of food, put down the fork, close your eyes, and move the food around in your mouth *without chewing.*" To my relief, the tofu was still slightly warm, and the marinade was delightfully tangy, sweet, spicy, and salty! Concentrating on the texture and flavor of the food, I chewed *slowly,* while counting to 40 (as instructed). *Is it possible to masticate one bite of tofu 40 times?* Apparently, yes.

The soft, supple chewiness of the tofu was surprisingly sensual. I marveled at the perfect textural combination, that it was neither crispy nor oily, not dry nor crumbly, far from styrofoamy. Immediately, I sent a mountain of mental gratitude to the chefs-in-training for nailing it—I'd eaten my fair share of spongy, airy, and rubbery tofu, but this iteration was likely *the best*. Before that moment, I hadn't considered whether I even *liked* tofu and was surprised to find that I did!

Energetically, I felt my body tingle from the idea of the chefs imparting love on our food, which, in and of itself, was nourishing. But what about before the tofu swam in marinade? Was it made in-house (and was that possible?) or did it arrive encased in plastic packaging? Was it farmed nearby, or in middle America from seeds derived in a lab by a major corporation? *Do the answers to those questions even matter?* Yes.

There was a sensation in my body that my tofu and me were energetically aligned. And another sensation was telling me I needed to feel that aligned relationship with everything I put into my body. The essence of food might hold the key to the essence of everything else. Like, perhaps, God?

Who'da thought that in just a few days I'd go from hitchhiking in freezing Idaho, to passing out on the subway in New York, to meditating soberly on tofu at a silent yoga retreat in Massachusetts? Yet, there I was, just…doing it all.

And that was when my real food journey took root.

RECIPE for DOING IT

No need to marinate your tofu, but the sauce is key. A recipe like this will have even meat-eaters enjoying a plant-based meal. Pair with veggies and rice. Share with your carnivorous friends and meditate on their feedback.

Saucy Tofu with Veggies
Yield = 2-4 servings
Prep time = 10 minutes
Total time = 40 minutes

Ingredients
- 1 lb firm tofu
- 3 tbsp coconut oil or peanut oil
- ¼ c low sodium soy sauce or tamari
- 1 tbsp water
- 1 tbsp rice wine vinegar
- 1 tbsp peanut or almond butter
- 2 tsp coconut sugar
- 1 tsp toasted sesame oil
- Hint of siracha (optional)
- Steamed or sauteed veggies of choice
- Rice or noodles (optional)

Instructions
1. Cut tofu into cubes or triangles.
2. Heat 1-2 tablespoons of peanut or coconut oil in a cast iron skillet on medium heat to coat the skillet.
3. Add tofu in a single layer. Allow to cook at least 5 minutes before turning. This is a great time to prep and steam veggies.
4. Check the tofu. When the bottom side is brown, turn each piece over to brown the opposite side—not all sides have to be brown. Ensure there is enough oil to keep the other side from sticking to the skillet. Fry 5 minutes more.
5. Make sauce. In a glass measuring cup or small bowl, whisk together tamari, water, vinegar, nut butter, coconut sugar, sesame oil, and siracha. (If the nut butter is hard, try heating it in a microwave for 10 seconds). Taste the sauce then adjust flavors and consistency.
6. If you feel like frying other sides of the tofu, do it! Otherwise, remove from skillet and serve while warm, ideally with veggies over noodles or rice.
7. Pour sauce over your meal and enjoy!

CHAPTER 4

Recipe for Dinner Parties

Just before Thanksgiving, the opening weekend of ski season, we locals trickled back into town. Our intimate evening gatherings resumed as we anticipated long, dark days of working around the clock during the impending onslaught of winter wonderland mayhem over Christmas and New Year's. I struggled to integrate back into a life that previously had grounded me, while resisting the lure to resume where I'd left off. I felt different, but had I changed?

As I pondered who I was and who I might become, I eyed the matchbook atop my dresser. I wasn't ready to call Tall Dark Handsome—I'd see him at the restaurant soon enough.

A few weeks later when our shifts overlapped, I watched him glide through the kitchen and dining room with confidence and ease, but not cockiness. Intriguingly, Chris genuinely enjoyed describing to diners the origin of sumac, how spices were roasted on cast iron and then ground by hand in marble mortars, that our chefs were adamant about locally procured tomatoes, slow roasted in-house. His pitch-perfect knowledge of wine and pairings wasn't what impressed me most, nor the way his focus seemed to wrap around the glass as he viewed the color and considered the profile. Rather, he could recommend a vintage based on the guests and their preferences, because he kept a black book with their names, dietary needs, what they'd enjoyed (and didn't) about their last experience, who was the decision-maker, who paid the bill, and how much money they liked to spend. He memorized not only the nuances of the menu, but every guest's order changes, how they liked their venison cooked or the garlic held from the sunchoke puree. Waiting tables was not a side job; it was his profession.

I, on the other hand, had been demoted to coat-check and dessert girl. *Huh? They want me in the coat room and kitchen instead of on the floor selling $200 bottles of wine?* Okaaaay. I checked my ego at the door and spectated the well-orchestrated fine dining experience, witnessing Chris in his flow—checking every detail at each table, rescuing co-workers who were in a jam—and experiencing the comfort everyone felt around him. He radiated "gregarious virtuoso foodie."

Outside the restaurant sphere, I had my own venues of self-confidence—the gallery, of course, and the trails (now covered in the white stuff I loved and loathed) and…dinner parties. Yeah, my other favorite pastime was planning or executing shared meals, whether I was hostess or guest. With many others in our dinner circle, we ladies ensured cocktail hour included goat cheese and cucumber bites and that the huge pot of homemade chili was accompanied by fresh-baked cornbread and a smattering of simple garnishes like avocado, lime wedges, and cilantro. Dessert was a must, and we took turns baking apple pie with lattice crust, Derby pie with pecan crust, or pumpkin bread with fresh whipped cream. Simple and hearty, intentional and meticulous, the collaborative effort and execution of dinner parties was the window into my soul.

Perhaps Chris was too nervous to notice my passion for parties during the first dinner he attended at my house. Yes, I'd fretted over my outfit—flattering, yet casual (I didn't want to look like I'd put too much thought into it). Plus, I didn't have time to prepare mentally because I hadn't *planned* to invite him to dinner; it just sort of happened. Still, I remember Chris walking up the stairs with a 6-pack of IPA, seemingly relieved to see people he knew—some of the Southern boys worked at the restaurant, too. We ate, drank, and made merry, and I thought

Recipe for Dinner Parties

everything was lovely. Later, I learned he felt completely out of his comfort zone.

That January, we had our first real date, sledding in the fresh powder (with one of his ex-girlfriends). We quickly took to one another. It was refreshing to be with someone who prioritized nature-based activities over drinking. Then, we hooky-bobbed out one of the winding roads, holding the rope and hitting freshly plowed berms as his friend artfully swerved the truck alongside the frozen creek. We soaked in hot springs. We snowshoed. Soon, he came with me to the different houses where I dog- or cat-sat. He kicked my butt at Scrabble. I kicked his at cards.

Naturally, I invited him to more dinner parties. My girlfriends and I hosted them at least weekly. The boys hosted less-fancy but equally tasty and occasional "grill-outs", and often invited me over before dinner to *coiffure* shaggy heads before their parents came to visit. In exchange, they made delicacies like elk-heart-and-morel stroganoff, with bonus haircut payments in wild game, weed, or wine.

Those dinners resonated with me deeply—they were like the blood force of an expanded family. Our gatherings vibrated with our devotion to each other and to good food. Eating together meant time together to hear about the crazy shit we'd endured that day—or in life—to become who we were in that moment. Our table talk dove into uncertainties about personal issues and musings about both existential and trivial things. For me, every step of the process was nourishing, whether I was prepping the table decor, creating new recipes to share, or helping to organize exactly who would bring which ingredient, drink, or side dish.

Chris came with me sometimes on nights he didn't work. And everyone thought he was great! He seemed to get along with the other guys; he drank beer and bourbon with us; his smile was warm, he was polite and charismatic, and he always helped wash dishes. Soon, though, I noticed he was more relaxed and chipper when he *couldn't* make the dinners. Many times, Chris made plans with his own friends, instead. Valid. Separate lives were totally healthy.

Eventually, when Chris had avoided dinners for months, he confided that he simply didn't understand why the guys just stood around drinking—why they weren't *doing* something, like tossing a frisbee or a football, or playing yard games. I never noticed because I never stood around—I was helping with food, setting the table, or getting drinks. Besides, the dinner party *was* the activity, right?

He, on the other hand, grew up playing yard games with his dad and brothers while grilling. Putt putt with beers in hand bonded them like food, drinks, and cooking bonded my friends and me. "So, bring games!" I suggested.

"No," he replied. "I'm not the kind of person who brings games to someone else's house."

I didn't understand. Wouldn't that be a contribution to the evening? He could be known as the fun-loving dude who always brought games!

One night, when it was just the two of us, Chris washed dishes fervently, passed me on the way to the bathroom without making eye contact, forgot to put toothpaste on my toothbrush, and curled up on the couch instead of picking up my guitar. He didn't seem to notice when I turned down the lights, didn't touch me when I sat next to him. He said he was tired and just wanted to go to bed, so when I went to take out my contacts, he climbed under the covers without me. I knew.

A strange jolt had coursed through my veins once before this, the time I *first* realized we had lifestyle differences: Chris and I were alone in the kitchen while 10 of our (my) friends were in the living room eating Rice Krispies treats I'd made (for his sake), when he shared something his friend had said: "You'd better get used to social functions if you're going to date Jamie Truppi."

What he shared that night was more disturbing: he wasn't a social person and simply didn't like dinner parties. It occurred to me I'd never asked him if he *wanted* to come to the fish taco party, nor did I tell him I'd suggested fish tacos because they were his favorite. I figured he'd become friends with the other guys, and soon would be biking and running trails with them.

Quite the opposite. Chris said, "I don't enjoy big groups of people, and I don't belong with your friends.... Truppi, I wash the dishes at parties to *escape* everyone." Yikes. Chris then suggested I host or attend dinners on nights he worked so I could still enjoy them, and he wouldn't have to come, and I wouldn't have to worry whether he was having a good time. Though my heart had deflated somewhat, his compromise seemed like a reasonable solution.

We still spent plenty of time together, sometimes drinking wine with our co-workers after work. On mutual nights off, we'd camp—just the two of us—or gather with *his* friends in smaller groups. On the nights he worked, I led my own life.

And that was our balance.

The next fall, gallery clients from Chicago asked me to caretake their home where they resided only a couple of weeks at a time, several times a year. I'd have my own apartment, and my duties would be to water plants weekly, help coordinate landscapers, contractors, chefs, the cleaning service, and others who needed to get inside. No cooking, cleaning, laundry. They offered me a monthly rate that would cover the mortgage on the condo I'd just purchased. Naturally, I accepted.

The isolated 25,000-ish-square-foot house (it was palatial, and we called it "The Palace") was only 10 minutes north of town. My neighbors were the deer and elk who were reprimanded by the homeowners for consuming the expensive landscaping. About a month after moving in, I asked if my boyfriend could join me. The family knew Chris from the restaurant, and obliged because he was kind and professional. Also, they thought it was a good idea for a man to help with some of the bigger projects, like installing a 20-foot Christmas tree.

Chris moved in and rented out his own condo. He still worked five nights a week. I hosted small dinners in the small apartment. Sometimes I'd invite my closest girlfriends. Other times, I curated invitations for three to five guests, ensuring that none of us knew each other well but that we'd collectively make for an interesting group.

Plus, The Palace was the epitome of what we loved and, paradoxically, detested about our valley—excessive and exquisite. With an excuse to offer something a little different at dinner parties, I'd leave the green curry simmering on the stove or the tubers roasting in the oven, ensure everyone had a drink in hand, then usher my guests into the dark hallway between the apartment and the house, close the door to create blackness, then…turn on the lights. *Oooh! Ahhh!* The entire home lit up at once, illuminating the spaciousness from one end of the hall to the other—a quarter mile away—through the guest bedrooms, kitchen, sitting room, dining room, great room, spiral stairs leading to the tower, to the far master wing. It was a spectacular look-but-don't-touch revelation of art and elegance to awe us before dinner.

Rarely did my friend-life and Chris's friend-life intersect. It was the wrinkle of imperfection in our otherwise perfect relationship.

RECIPE for DINNER PARTIES

Chili is perfect for a gathering because you can prepare it before people arrive; it can be modified for dietary preferences; it allows each guest to bring something—a simple side or drink, or a more elaborate salad or dessert; and allows you to hang out with your guests instead of cooking. Ideally, you've soaked and cooked the beans (to, um, you know, reduce gastrointestinal gaseousness). My favorite accompaniments are a garlicky kale salad and cornbread.

Elk Chili
Yield = 10 servings
Prep time = 45 minutes
Total time = 1 hour 45 minutes

Ingredients
- 2 tbsp extra virgin olive oil or avocado oil
- 1 ½ lbs ground elk
- 1 large yellow onion, diced
- 2 tbsp chili powder
- 1 tbsp each ground cumin and dried oregano
- 2 tsp sea salt
- 1 head garlic, peeled and minced
- 3 green bell peppers, chopped
- 1 c red table wine
- 12-15 Roma tomatoes, chopped (or two 29-oz cans of diced tomatoes)
- 2 bay leaves
- 6 c stock (veggie, beef, or mushroom)
- 3 c cooked kidney beans (or two 14.5 oz cans)
- 1 c dried quinoa, rinsed (optional; makes for a thicker chili)
- Garnishes: cheddar cheese, avocado, cilantro, lime, plain yogurt

Instructions
1. Prep all veggies, cook beans (or open cans and strain), and measure quinoa.
2. In a large pot with a lid, heat oil on medium and crumble elk into the pot. Stir.
3. When elk is mostly cooked through, add onions. Cover. Stir every minute or so.
4. When onions are translucent, add spices, garlic, salt, and green peppers.
5. Add wine, tomatoes (and their juices), and bay leaves. Let simmer 1-2 min, covered.
6. Add stock, beans, and quinoa. Heat to a boil, then reduce to a simmer. Cover and cook for about 60 minutes, stirring every 10-15 minutes, until everything becomes soft, unified, saturated with spices and herbs, and tender.
7. Enjoy time with your dinner guests as they arrive with garnishes and side dishes, and a glass of wine.
8. Serve chili hot with your favorite toppings and sides.

CHAPTER 5

Recipe for Diplomacy

The uncertain social energies around Chris and me seemed buffered by our devoted inner core. We were electromagnetically charged with all the sweet stuff and withstood the sour. But often we faced a gap between us and the world around us.

Or a vast chasm. Like opposing food ideals or political ideologies. Intermixing either of those was like oil and water, giving a false sense of unity. Or causing an inflammatory response, like too much baking soda in the *clafoutis*. Or fermented beyond palatability, like when kombucha becomes vinegar.

Or like a free-spirited Idaho Liberal visiting a Republican family in Southern California. We headed south together for sunshine, yes, and to Chris's hometown to visit his family.

I was anxious—not to meet the fam, per se, but to eat with them. For me, food had surpassed necessity. Now a bona fide trail runner with a palate for farm-to-table food, a mostly curbed drinking problem, and a slightly deeper connection with myself, food was absolute nourishment. With enough money finally to spend on finer things, I chose exceptional food. It was the best investment I could make in myself, for the earth, and for farmers and chefs with aligned ideals about not just quality, but food the way nature intended. Still mostly vegetarian, I'd dabbled in eating chicken (because TrailRunner magazine told me it would help my runner's game), but local sources were limited and, ultimately, I didn't love the taste, texture, or weight on my conscience.

I entered the home with what I thought was an open mind and stomach. Quickly I realized eating in someone else's home requires going with *their* flow and being respectful, while figuring out how to honor our own needs.

I failed at both.

Their food was markedly different, making it impossible to avoid the food topic. I'd never before witnessed how food can bind or divide families. For some, food is spiritual; for me, food connected me to Mother Earth and my body's wellbeing. I didn't grow up with religious teachings of the true essence of God-given food (though often I wish I had). I mean, unleavened wafers and grape juice as the body and blood of Christ? *Please, y'all, at least give us crusty, traditional sourdough and real wine.* But I found myself suspended between Chris's family and my deeply value-driven and highly personal food issues: emotional, physical, and mental, with a side of economic and environmental.

Unfortunately, food is also annoyingly, undeniably political. The link between politics and food became apparent to me during my college years when I was introduced to publications such as Adbusters (vengeful) and Mother Earth News (helpful). I grew angry and frustrated with the abominations of global food destruction in production and appropriation.

My personal family food story was mostly idyllic. As Idahoans, we lived part of each year within the Frank Church Wilderness—the largest roadless area in the lower 48 states. With Italian immigrant roots mixed with Finnish stock-rancher blood, food brought us together. For example, after my parents married in 1970, my mom spent nine months back east driving a school bus in NYC and her side-job was learning to making my dad's favorite foods: Gramma Truppi's sauce from scratch, spinach and ricotta ravioli, meatballs, and stuffed shells. Mom was cautioned to avoid pasta *fazool* and eggplant *parmigiano* (my dad's least faves). I'd heard that Gramma Truppi scoffed, at first, when my mom comingled her Idaho flavor into the family meals—elk sausage in the meat sauce, trout on Good Friday, and Idaho-potato gnocchi. Her own mama, Gramma Day, was pleased.

As a young adult moving beyond family traditions to discover food's effects on my body, eating became a more sacred experience and food became the gift of my new life. I grew disheartened with convenience and fast food, and began to judge that most American meals were devoid of tradition. Even national holidays were bastardized with crappy, non-food icons (like hot dogs) washed down with sodas and cheap beer. I started to see symbolic American food as scraped together remnants and mass-produced iterations of the cheapest commodity crops (corn, soy, wheat) that no longer resembled food from the earth.

To my astonishment, hot dogs—the most politically incorrect food on the planet, in my view—were Chris's father's favorite food. In addition to the several Bud Lights Chris's dad consumed before breakfast on non-workdays, amazingly, he was not overweight. Both facts blew my mind, not from a cultural perspective but because he was so *active*. Bill woke at 5:00 am daily to ride his bike or kayak for a couple of hours before working as a contractor, a very physical job. Maybe he needed the extra calories and hydration or, perhaps, there was something metabolically different about drinking in the morning after exercise versus my method of drinking at night (and then dragging ass while trying to motivate to exercise the *next* morning).

Now that I'd been consuming fresh, clean food that made me feel healthy inside, the salty, "dead-flesh" food made me lethargic, thirsty, inflamed. Hot dogs were at the pinnacle of that category, and everything about them made me shudder. The bland white buns stuck to the roof of my mouth unless smothered with ketchup gritty with sugar (*I mean, why?*) and mushy from relish juices.

I'd come a long way from the kid who preferred baloney and mustard on Wonder Bread to PB&Js. I was befuddled by how American food had strayed so far from real food cultivated not too long ago by pioneers who immigrated from lands bursting with farming, fishing, and cooking traditions. Or how we *preferred* seemingly simple foods processed in complex factory machinery.

So much nourishment had diminished during the quarter century of my own lifetime. Born under President Carter, a former farmer who pushed for environmental preservation, I was raised under Reagan, who unraveled many environmental policies. Democrats and Republicans continue to out-voice the other side's view, stuffing it categorically with economics or technology; but never with food—too politically sensitive! *Can't we all just agree that without trees, clean water, and biological diversity we'd all be dead?*

No. There was clear—and perhaps intentional—disconnect politically between American eating habits, which stemmed from mass food production and environmental demise. This became a debate in SoCal, with a family who loved nature and grew their own tomatoes. I grew tired of defending my choices, and I reproached myself because I couldn't easily draw upon data or specific laws or examples to defend benefits of fresh, local, and seasonal food.

One night after dinner, though, while writing about my frustrations, a piece of paper fell out of the back of my journal. On it, I'd written, "A society is defined not just by what it creates, but also by what it refuses to destroy." It was a quote from a lecture I'd recently attended to hear two-time Pulitzer Prize winner E.O. Wilson speak. He described the precariousness of nature and mass extinctions due to the destructive relationship between humans and the natural world. That quote reminded me I was not alone in my ideals.

Unfortunately, the food debate wasn't the only challenge during our trip to Orange County. I had no idea every member of Chris's family was a staunch Republican, so it didn't occur to me that visiting during the final days of the 2004 Presidential election would become an issue. But my political standing—and theirs—became a thing. Over dinner.

John Kerry, on the ballot that year, lived part-time in Sun Valley, dined at The Evergreen with his wife and entourage, and seemed genuinely kind and approachable. George G.W. Bush's close friends also ate at the restaurant—which I learned after inadvertently mouthing off about Bush's politics while sitting in the wine bar next to his friends. *Oops.*

Nonetheless, I voted for Ralph Nader. An environmentalist.

Recipe for Diplomacy

On election night at Chris's folks' house, we ate pasta (a peace offering between processed meat and vegetarianism), drank beer, and watched the results scroll across the bottom of the TV screen. As state after state went Republican, the IPAs and my increased frustration made me more vocal. Actually, I was cursing loudly and disrespectfully. *(I'm Italian, remember?)* But nothing excused the fact that I was in *their* home; I had just met these lovely people, and I was acting l like a total asshole.

Bush won.

I let his family gloat (they were silent, really). But it was much more personal than politics. I was ashamed by my behavior and uncertain how to mend the relationship. I wanted this family to know the real me—the me that cared about people so deeply that my concern for our planet was rooted in my concern for the future wellbeing of humankind (and, I thought, the outcome of the election). I wanted Chris's family to know I had Republican friends and family members, too, (lots of them—duh, Idaho), and that I loved them in part *because of* our differences.

At first, it seemed we might repair our divide through food, as Chris's Italian stepmom, Catherine, and I found common ground over our favorite meals. Like my Gramma Truppi, she was a devout Catholic who loved to cook. I was genuinely interested to read her hand-written family recipes and see how they were different from the Truppi's collection. We bonded over coffee, baking, and *limoncello*, which she made from the fruit of the Meyer lemon tree in her back yard. I had brought ground elk to share, and we made meatballs the way I was taught (and she loved them). It seemed like election-night recovery might happen, one meal at a time.

Among the brothers and Bill, beer was our neutral ground. Our Switzerland. Our bridge over troubled waters. Beer—a manmade substance derived from Earth's bounty, by the way, and quite possibly the true reason for modern agriculture—still made me feel dang good, and I enjoyed the steady increase in dopamine as I worked through a pint of microbrew. Drinking turned out to be one of the five things Bill and I had in common, and beer helped me chill the F- out so I could focus on the friendly competition of tennis-golf, frisbee, and other such beer-drinking lawn sports.

Unfortunately, things digressed when I offered to prepare a "thank you for your hospitality" dinner. I envisioned preparing food in their outdoor kitchen, anchored by the grill, and flanked by the kegerator with hand-built custom taps. Bill was uncomfortable accepting an entire meal from me, so we compromised with the promise of a meat-focused menu for which he would be grill-master.

For some time, I'd been adamant the only meat I would eat was wild game. But, since it was illegal to buy it, and wild fish scared me (too much mercury and wasn't the industry destroying the oceans?), I reverted to Plan B: locally raised sustainable meat. Sadly, I could find exactly zero local sources (in California, an agriculture state). Naturally I searched the internet for health food stores, which were surprisingly difficult to find considering the dense population I'd pegged as obsessed with their health.

My idyllic vision of Orange County with lush, endless orchards—a thing of the past—was supplanted by tract neighborhoods, shopping centers with a Starbucks on every corner. The manicured parkways were beautified by the very irrigation systems once used to grow oranges upon which the parkways now spread above ground, like man-made roots.

I was further surprised by my failure to locate a farmers market or community supported agriculture program to locate a pasture-raised meat source. So, I drove to the only health food store located within a 30-minute radius (in a massive strip mall). Mother's Market: a breath of fresh air smelling of herbs, essential oils, and carrot juice! After spending an hour perusing every shelf on every aisle for other goodies I coveted, it took me another hour to settle on locally farmed, pasture-raised ostrich burgers (for an exorbitant sum), and organic fixin's. I hadn't set out to create an exotic meal, but that bird was more affordable than bison from Montana, giving me enough change for a 6-pack of not-too-fancy yet small batch pale ale for Bill.

Back at the house, I stowed granola, date bars, and raw nut mix into an unremarkable small brown bag behind the coffee pot on the counter. I tucked hummus, carrots, and a portabella mushroom into a little corner in the fridge, behind the box of almond milk Catherine thoughtfully purchased for me. (I was grateful for her gesture, though I noticed right away, and kept to myself, that it was neither organic nor non-GMO). I vowed not to think about the depleted almond farms just north of LA that sucked massive amounts of water from reservoirs and dammed-up rivers and, instead, I thanked her.

Bill asked me, "How long do I grill the ground bird?" (as if I knew how to grill) and, "Is it supposed to be cooked through or pink inside?" (as if I'd thought to look that up). We guessed and it turned out deliciously! I felt a sense of peace from eating food that was relatively well-produced, as local as possible, seemingly mostly toxin-free, and met the dietary preferences of each of person at the table. Everyone else appeared to enjoy it well enough. The meal seemed to epitomize tactful relations. *Whew.*

Later, I was informed the meal was "too complicated" for this "simple" family.

During that first visit, Bill pegged me "Earth Muffin"—for him, an endearing nickname that described my intrinsic values more than other potentially descriptive words about my obtrusive behaviors. Laughing on the outside, inside I was bothered by how doing what I felt was right for myself somehow felt wrong in someone else's home. My goals were nourishment and respect, though even preparing my separate side dishes for a few family meals made me feel unappreciative. Were my organic products offensive, or was it a relief they didn't have to spend extra money on my food preferences?

I was sure Bill and Catherine were relieved when I'd gone. Despite all their efforts, I was misunderstood. Despite all my efforts, I was terribly undiplomatic. And so, for peacekeeping, we'd learned to skirt around the issues.

RECIPE for DIPLOMACY

The most important thing about meals shared between different folks is intention. Diplomatic dinners date back to the beginning of time, offering a taste of local, seasonal cuisine while considering different cultures and building connections among diverse people. I implore you to do the same. This recipe gives an example of what I consider when creating a meaningful, American meal to share.

Building Bridges Burgers
Yield = however many are coming to dinner
Prep time = 20 minutes + time to procure ingredients
Total time = 45-60 minutes depending on side dishes

Ingredients
- Local meat, fowl, fish, or veggies in the form of a "burger"
- Buns or rolls from a local bakery or made by someone you know
- Fixin's that conjure of a sense of place such as
- Sheep cheese from the local dairy
- Seasonal produce (tomatoes, sliced zucchini, or microgreens from the farmer down the road, greens from your own backyard, etc.)
- Condiments to accentuate the burger patty
- Sides that complement your event, your culture, the season, and always your guests' dietary needs (or all of the above)
- Beverages to align with the season, the time of day, the terroir, and which reiterate that you've paid attention to your guests' preferences

Instructions
1. Inquire—in advance—about how to cook the burger
2. (if it's new to you).
3. Add spices or embellishments to the burger "meat".
4. Prep cheese, greens, and other toppings.
5. When guests arrive, invite them into your kitchen to help prepare side dishes that will take longer than grilling burgers. It's a great way to connect over food.
6. Don't be a meal Nazi. Instead, choose which component of the meal means most to you and own it.
7. Then, to provoke camaraderie, give guests full or partial reign (depending on their comfort level) over another part of the meal. Ask if they'd make changes, or how they do it at home. They might have a great story there….
8. Make drinks for everyone, pause meal prep and toast together. Cheers!
9. Cook burgers; assemble the meal; sit down to eat; toast again.
10. Be polite about others' food preferences that may not match your own. In six months, each of your diets may change.
11. Wash the dishes. Together.

CHAPTER 6

Recipe for Driving South of the Border

Back in Idaho, we were met with a heavy early snowfall, though I felt lighter in my own space, where I could speak and eat freely. Though Chris and I had regained our routine, I felt stagnant and longed for action, something to organize and execute, an event to plan. Dinner parties had become stagnant and with virtually no cultural food in town, I found myself in a state of creative food deprivation.

Thankfully, a gallery trip to Miami reminded me that food-centered cities do exist. In December, Gail and I and a few other staff members traveled to the melting pot of Florida to check out Art Basel. Clients scooped us up, exposing us to an incredible array of Cuban coffee, ingenious combinations in noodles and sushi, and incredible street food luring us with spiced chimichurri, lime-sprinkled ceviche, and baked plantains. It had been too long since my last exposure to food edification or ethnic artistry. Our small town in Idaho—and even the farm to table restaurant where I worked—fulfilled my hunger only for intentional Idaho food, and the recent California jaunt had yielded little in the gastronomical department.

Inspired, I set to work planning the spring mud-season trip to somewhere neither Chris nor I had ever been, but where we could afford to stay for a couple of weeks while sampling local food: a road trip to Baja California.

April couldn't come quickly enough! We drove south, said hello to Chris's family, then crossed the border at Tijuana and into the unknown. After the unnerving chaos of the world's largest border town, our shoulders relaxed a little and, as we paused to inhale the sea breeze, we were caught by the aroma of deep-fried-fish from a roadside taco stand. We devoured an insanely satiating combination of crispy, soft, crunchy, smooth deliciousness, which stimulated our quest to find the best fish tacos in Baja.

I'm not naturally drawn to fish, the sea, or hot, dry places, but I am a zealot for open markets and artisan food. As co-pilot and map reader, I fixated on finding towns where fresh fish vendors might exist and where handmade tortillas would be plentiful for tailgate happy hours. But 2004 was before 5G towers, international cell service, and Google Maps, making driving down the peninsula nebulous, getting around small towns a lesson in patience, and identifying landmarks outlined by guidebooks a downright necessity.

Naively, I thought that because I spoke French and a bit of Italian, I'd be fine fumbling through Spanish. I'd previously learned one key phrase: *no camarones, por favor* (because I hated shrimp). Chris knew Spanish kitchen lingo and a few food terms because most of the prep staff and dishwashers in our valley's restaurants were Latino. But more concerning than communication in touristy Ensenada was the pickpocketing. In San Quintín—strangely quiet for a wine-tasting town—Chris's Spanish skills proved helpful when we needed a *cuchara* for the guac.

South from there, we saw few outsiders and almost no cars. There were times we thought we'd run out of petrol. In Guerrero Negro we questioned whether a side jaunt to a surfing beach was wise or worth the effort, but our minds were made up *(definitely no!)* when we stumbled into what we believed to be a cartel restaurant to ask for directions and order some *chilaquiles con dos huevos*. We were advised to stay on the main highway, but

Recipe for Driving South of the Border

not informed about the military checkpoint where a band of young soldiers spoke no English and were adamant that Chris was Mexican. They inspected our coolers, my long legs in short shorts, and Chris's Maxim magazine (which we gifted to them in exchange for our safe passage).

We remained on the anxious precipice of "anything could happen." Informed that we could camp wherever we wanted we shrugged off safety concerns, though I kept my Swiss army knife at bay. The population was sparse, places of interest were far apart, and regulation turned out to be sketchy. On the beach at Bahia del los Angeles—a side trip we shouldn't have taken—seven or eight soldiers and their automatic weapons woke us from our slumber in the back of the truck. *No, we haven't seen the man you are searching for.*

We blew out of there immediately, only to find ourselves in fog so thick we struggled to make out the roadside saguaro cacti, looming like mystic creatures watching us pass. The further south we drove, the more ominous, like moving deeper into the heart of darkness in a Joseph Conrad novel. It was the loneliest road we'd ever driven. We turned off our road trip music, opting for silence to focus on being so far from anywhere familiar. No one knew our location. My stomach was in knots, perhaps from hunger, but more likely from freaking out.

Petrol and tacos became the only reasons for stopping. Something about roadside taco stands plucked us from our fearful illusions and into the reality that we were safe. The vulnerability of the open road shifted as we held warm tortillas in our hands and bit into the salty fish, crunchy cabbage, and spicy salsa. Though we were inept at carrying on a decent conversation with the vendors, there was solace simply in *being seen*. We were real. And, hey, the tacos were *good*, though, to my stomach's dismay, many were fried—at one stand, the entire taco was like a deep-fried version of a calzone. The burritos in Machaca brought on gut issues, so from San Ignacio to Mulegé, we resorted to trail mix and electrolyte powder. Anxiety eased dramatically as we neared civilization again—in Baja, that simply means small towns grouped slightly closer together. We wandered the few streets, peeked inside old churches, sought out small grocers for bottled water, fresh vegetables, herbs, and citrus.

Relaxation finally set in when we reached our planned destination, the beaches at Bahía Concepción, south of Santa Rosalía on the west coast of the peninsula. Each day our comfort increased as we camped amongst American hippie vans that dotted the otherwise empty beaches. We nestled the truck between two trees that shaded our tailgate "kitchen." By early afternoon on our third day, three young men—late teens or early 20s—rolled up in a tiny hatchback beater with Vermont plates. They were fragile and fearful, having also encountered the aforementioned militia (or uniformed cartel). They had driven the entire central peninsula in 24 hours, taking turns at the wheel, and feeling relieved to have arrived in one piece.

When the sun was just shifting into its happiest hour, Chris set up our makeshift kitchen, placing cutting board, bowls, and a knife on the tailgate, while I reached for the cooler. Only a dozen feet away, the young trio pulled out a pot, a jug of water, a single Bunsen burner, and Styrofoam cups of Top Ramen. "Ramen for two days," they mumbled as they eyed our guacamole ritual. As Chris mashed avocados and sliced limes, I prepped fresh nameless fish, shredded cabbage, and opened a couple of Coronas. The boys' eyes widened, and they stopped eating altogether, plastic forks suspended in midair.

Finally, I asked, "Why the hell are you eating *ramen* in Mexico?" They said they didn't really think about stopping for groceries. Realizing they needed a quick lesson in road-trip cooking and local cuisine, we invited them to join us, provided they help cook and clean. They scrambled over so fast they practically kicked sand in the guac. We showed them our bins of necessary kitchen materials, spices, plan B canned beans, quick rice, and coconut water. We described our list of fresh food essentials to procure in each town. I'm not sure how much of the lesson they absorbed, but they ate the tacos with gusto.

The next day Chris and I explored other pristine beaches off the beaten path via a couple of rough side jaunts littered with smashed cans, plastic bags, and other debris. The roads were practically unnavigable, uncomfortable, and the opposite of thrilling. "I hate off-roading," I grumbled, fearing we'd pop a tire, run out of gas, and be rescued by a psycho who would rape and kill us. I gritted my teeth. For a trusting person, I had little trust in the middle of nowhere (flashback to an unpleasant

Recipe for Driving South of the Border

hitchhiking experience in rural Alaska with a bear trapper in boxer shorts drinking a Corona, of all things).

Chris parked the truck (as level as possible) on top of the nearest hill (more of a bump), with the best view (not much, really). He rerouted my worries and complaints with a daiquiri, using the small blender that plugged into the cigarette lighter and a mixture of Malibu and Captain Morgan rums. We peeled a mushy mango, added coconut water from our emergency stash (*this* emergency was my sanity), and the last of our ice cubes, which tasted plastic like the cooler. I jumped when the blender's motor raced, speeding up my heartbeat and echoing across the desert. At high noon, the stiff drink eased my mind only somewhat; my soul was ready to head home.

RECIPE for DRIVING SOUTH of the BORDER

I have been warned to neither drink the water nor eat fresh produce or fish in foreign countries, for fear of bacteria (ahem: diarrhea). But what the heck were we supposed to eat in Baja? I say, bring electrolytes and a complete tailgate cooking kitchen set-up because tailgate tacos are a delicious outcome of forethought, local food, and enjoying the easy life.

Tailgate Fish Tacos
Yield: Enough for yourself, your travel partner + leftovers for hungry college students
Prep time: Timeless

Ingredients
- Cerveza and lime wedges
- Avocados, tomatoes, cilantro, jalapenos
- Onion and garlic
- Salt, pepper, cumin, oregano
- More lime
- Local fish (the smaller the better, for mercury-related reasons)
- Avocado oil
- Black beans
- Cabbage, cactus (nopales), or other local veggies
- Cotija cheese
- Handmade tortillas
- Cortado (if you can find it)
- Chipotle sauce

Instructions
1. Locate the nearest fish market and purchase the smallest fish available (to minimize methylmercury intake). If you speak Spanish, ask about fish that matches your taste preferences.
2. Seek out local everything. Source Mexican cheese, veggies, and handmade tortillas (often stored in coolers, ironically, to keep them warm).
3. Wash produce with water you brought with you; or boil local water first for a couple of minutes, to eliminate potentially harmful bacteria and bacteria foreign to your body.
4. Crack a beer. Add lime. Sip. Ahhh...
5. Make guacamole.
6. Warm the beans.
7. Fry the fish with oil, spices, and lime on medium low. Add beer to the skillet. Cover. Poach. If the fish is thick, flip it over after a few minutes and cook thoroughly.
8. Prep veggies and garnishes. Shred cabbage. Crumble cheese. Slice limes.
9. Warm the tortillas.
10. Assemble tacos. Pile all the fixins on top. Sip cerveza. Enjoy!

CHAPTER 7

Recipe for Discovering Differences

On the road, we had been well-balanced companions and, upon returning to the Valley, Chris remained steady as we navigated poignant and unnerving life circumstances—my parents' divorce, my dad's head injury, a friend's near-death experience. Emotionally, I felt safe, but somehow also tethered. Mentally, those pivotal events unearthed thoughts about the preciousness of life—my own life—and a reminder that I was on a modest path that opposed my nature. There was something else I was meant to do. Someone more I was meant to be.

At the gallery I had been promoted to Associate Director. Amidst the chaos of eccentric artists (whom I admired), privileged clients (whom I envied), a fastidious boss (whom I respected), and the ever-changing contemporary art world, an inner voice whispered my fears that staying—in that gallery, in that town, and even in my relationship with Chris—would be *settling*. This *status quo* prophesied cessation of adventures, an end to experiencing the world outside the bubble, limiting my dreams! "No more world out there waiting for me to experience" seemed suddenly lonelier and more alarming than Baja roads in ominous fog.

I started analyzing the usefulness of my life: I sold beautiful artwork to foster artists' passions and uplift clients' collections; I volunteered haphazardly with environmental groups, wrote letters to the Idaho state legislature, and replaced plastic Gallery Walk cups with biodegradable ones made of the same corn used to make ethanol. But was I making a difference in the world, even in our small town?

My efforts seemed insignificant. The days droned on as mountain town fun wore off and my friends paired off. Crazy nights out had long been replaced with quiet nights at home. My responsibilities had supplanted passion. I was exhausted from working around the clock—at the restaurant and pet-sitting, too—and could hardly force myself on short jaunts in the woods. I lost social enthusiasm and, anyway, found little to say to others outside of work. Was I *that bored*? Or had I become boring in the normalcy of coupling and routine?

People stopped inviting me to grill-outs, campouts, concerts, drinks, trail runs. Dinner. Nights Chris worked at the restaurant and I didn't, I sat home eating chips and salsa, studying wildflower books, too tired to write in my journal or cook new recipes. I'd stare at the under-used, clean kitchen—it begged me to make just a simple appetizer or one-pot-meal.

Strangely, Chris seemed perfectly happy with our life. Perhaps, even…thriving. *Can I live happily this way? Can we coexist harmoniously with disparate needs?* I loved him, so I tucked those sentiments aside and dug elsewhere to uncover the source of my discontent.

Knowing I was the keeper of my happiness, I reached out to socialize and find new creative outlets to bring joy. My friend Katie and I started meeting weekly at the Starbucks in a historic brick building on Main Street, for lattes and haiku-writing sessions. I made hula hoops to sell at her lemonade stand. I attended the annual Writers' Conference for inspiration by poet laureates, and with hopes of finding my people. I took a figure-drawing class. I started a "creative ladies" night so my girlfriends and I could convene monthly to make theme-based food and crafts. I sketched out the details of an earth-focused,

RECIPE FOR DISCOVERING DIFFERENCES

community-centered café I'd previously envisioned opening in Seattle with four coffee-loving girlfriends.

Creativity was time-consuming. To continue exploring I'd need to give up my job at the restaurant, the last morsel of my nourishing food life—and time with Chris at work. To remain with Chris, I needed time and energy to find my own joys and my people again.

Then suddenly, The Evergreen unexpectedly closed for good after more than two decades. The owner-founder had decided to let go of *his* creative side project. For me, it was a sign I was on the right path. For Chris, it was devastating. He'd found his place after working for a decade in every other quality restaurant in the Valley—a classy five-star resort restaurant; a high-end private golf club restaurant; an intimate cabin with a talented chef and a reservation list six months out. Where would he go next? His friends shifted into the wine world, but stocking wine on grocery store shelves was not enticing to him. I encouraged Chris to explore another field entirely, but being a professional server was his jam. It was flexible, so that he could ski all day in the winter, trail run or mountain bike in the summer, with two Slack/Mud Seasons for down-time. It paid well, he ate great food, drank great wine. It suited him. He worked to live, versus living to work.

But what now? The Valley was small, and he'd exhausted his options. He was ready for a change (and *obviously* so was I). The end of the era of fine dining had brought Chris lack of direction. For different reasons, we both felt the urge to bypass the difficult shit (our inner voices) with the distraction of setting up camp elsewhere. Starting over again. A new venture!

Naturally, I suggested the foodie city of Portland, Oregon. A *port* city, out *West*. With creative food people—*um, yes!* Back then, PDX was still both weird *and* cool. Chris was game to visit, and we arrived during an unusually sunny week in February—the cherry blossoms bloomed, the sun illuminated the river and bridges, the pulse of the food scene brought new life into our hearts and heads. By bus and light rail, on bike and on foot, to each destination we arrived with attention on the legendary foodie world. A couple of my friends offered us the grand tour of running trails, the coffee scene, the craft brew world, food cart hubs, and glimpses of the dark, hushed-up life of the homeless and transients.

Portland attracted a different breed of wait staff—instead of mountaineers, they were artists who worked to afford tattoos and trendy single-speed bikes, with side gigs as drummers, filmmakers, or distillers. There were few "serious" servers, yet the chefs and restaurateurs were passionate, articulate changemakers. The movement was idyllic, a sometimes hair-brained frenzy of effort based on environmental stewardship, sustainable farming, and revival of artisan cheese-, bread-, beer- and bacon-making. Sometimes just weird. Sometimes just *too* cool. Many of these efforts blossomed into successful artisan businesses with big personalities. I wanted in.

Deep down, I hoped we could find a new social circle, too. Not his, not mine. Ours. No history, no baggage, and certainly with anticipation (at least on my end) of a united social group. In Portland, perhaps our inherent differences might be less pronounced. Perhaps we'd both find purpose. I was betting a lot on this move.

We made an appointment with a real estate agent, and after a bidding whirlwind at the peak of the market we landed a historic condo in the heart of the Alphabet District. It took just one day to sell my condo in Sun Valley, and we planned to rent out Chris's condo.

Now I had something to look forward to, a plan to formulate, a vision to elicit. A food city to discover! With our move on the horizon, I was also motivated to make the most of our transition specifically to prepare for a career change.

But first, I traveled to Virginia to be a bridesmaid in my friend, Margot's wedding. Chris, not surprisingly, didn't feel like attending (they were "my" people, after all). Flying solo, he missed my conceding to taste true Southern fried chicken (I was either bribed or imbibed), and cheese grits (yikes, dairy!) with Cheer wine (not-so-fancy Coke). Needing a distraction from wondering what kept Chris from sharing such joyful experiences with me, I drank irresponsibly and flirted confidently with the southern single men there because, of course, I was "taken."

Mostly, I was preoccupied with preparations for a big overseas experience that I'd hoped would change the trajectory of my profession. Chris, uninterested in attending, drove to California to stay with his folks and work with his dad. To remain hopeful about us, I decided it was not the time to fuss over our differences. I simply accepted traveling on my own.

RECIPE for DISCOVERING DIFFERENCES

Cheese grits are all about celebration and comfort food (so says a non-Southerner). A non-dairy girl, I am wary about eating traditional grits in the company of others lest my digestive tract go haywire. But cheese grits taste amazing, so I've experimented with a low-dairy version so I can enjoy them without abdominal pain!

Low-Lactose Cheese Grits
Yield = 6-ish servings as a side dish
Prep time = 2 minutes
Total time = 25 minutes

Ingredients
- 2 c broth of choice
- 2 c unsweetened plain soy milk (or 2 more c of broth)
- 1 ½ tsp garlic powder
- 1 c old-fashioned grits (not instant)
- 4 oz plain goat cheese (chèvre)
- 4 tbsp grass-fed butter
- 2 tbsp olive oil
- ¼ tsp smoked paprika
- ¼ tsp ground black or white pepper
- Salt to taste

Instructions
1. Bring the broth and milk to a gentle boil in a medium pot. Immediately reduce the heat to medium-low.
2. Whisk in the garlic powder.
3. Slowly add the grits, stirring constantly. Then, cook for about 20 minutes, uncovered, until the grits have absorbed the liquid and are tender, not crunchy. Stir often to keep the grits from scorching.
4. Remove the pot from heat. Stir in the cheese, butter, oil, paprika, and pepper. Taste, then season to your liking with more paprika, pepper, or salt.
5. Enjoy with fried chicken (humanely raised) and roasted local veggies, perhaps some mushroom gravy and, of course, Cheer Wine.

CHAPTER 8

Recipe for Design

Our Idaho exit revolved around a permaculture and design course taking place in Thailand that November. Christian, the spearhead person of the project—whom I'd met years prior in Thailand through of my high school besties, Sarah—had found a devastated mango plantation in the northeast to transform into a food forest and permaculture education center. Not only had I contributed financially to purchasing the property, but also I knew I'd need some field experience to help me enter the environmental scene in Portland come spring. The permaculture course presented an ideal opportunity for my transition.

Though I'd never been particularly interested in sciences like biology or chemistry, understanding nature had become as intriguing in terms of preservation and conservation. I was pumped to grow and harvest tropical fruit and vegetables, learn to cook Thai food, and share meals with others equally passionate about living harmoniously with the earth. I was beyond ready to embark on a soul-searching adventure in outdoor education, community living, and vegetarian nourishment.

So, after the Virginia wedding, I flew to Orange County to meet Chris and reorganize my belongings before my trip.

On departure day, Chris took me to eat one more American meal together: In-N-Out Burger, his favorite joint, conveniently located off the interstate en route to John Wayne Airport. Previously, I'd succumbed to eating there—another peace flag with his family to soften the big stink I carried around with me about my food quality standards. But I felt like I was selling my soul when ingesting that so-called food. I chewed uninspiring veggie burgers—literally just iceberg lettuce, a tomato, and yellow mustard on white bun—and a few fries. For lactose and dairy industry reasons, I often skipped the milkshakes.

In-N-Out, a wildly successful fast-food chain that gave people who were not like me exactly what they wanted, was for me another limbo location that challenged me to ask what I was doing there and why. I was with a man I loved in a sterile joint teeming with my contra-crowd. As I looked at Chris, I realized he took me to eat at *his* happy place, perhaps because he wanted palm trees, sunny yellow, and pretend smiles to mask his fears. He was transporting me to embark on an exploration that resonated through every layer of *my* complicated human form and spirit, but which did nothing for *him* personally. I was traveling halfway across the globe to meet 20 or so passionate earthy people, yet I was already a world away.

Yes, the meal was tasteless and lacking the nutrients I needed for travel, and memorable because my worries were deeper than not enjoying the food. Before loving Chris, traveling had been an excuse for me to end relationships or to avoid getting into them in the first place. This time, I was somewhat assuaged by Chris's pledge to join me in Thailand at the end of the program. But what would transpire before I saw him again, four weeks later? *Might my parting from Chris in that moment mean leaving him forever?*

After some tears during the first leg of the flight, I regained the sense that I was doing what I needed—to care for some part of me that required nurturing. To help revive a piece of land destroyed by agriculture was also symbolic. Like the mangos that fruited despite pesticides and the razing of the vegetation at its roots, I'd blossomed into someone now yearning to bring nourishment to the world, despite myself having been raped and depleted when I was ripe for the taking. I'd been shaken and, since, had been uncertain, unstable, unable to locate solid

Recipe for Design

ground inside or out. My relationship with Chris had given me stability to reexamine my passions and choices.

I hoped the intentional adventure in Thailand would invigorate my self-worth; moreso, I wanted to learn something useful to help safeguard nature from more pillaging. My now-past mountain town life had reconnected me with woods, trails, rivers, elk, woodpeckers, peaks and valleys, and endless wildflowers. There, I wanted to protect the ecosystem so people who came to bike or ski wouldn't inadvertently ruin the natural beauty while simultaneously appreciating it. Most Idahoans recreated in harmony with Mother Earth. A few felt it was their right to thrust their ATVs and dirt bikes over lichen-encrusted rocks, delicate purple flowers, and tiny insects, leaving scars of tire tracks, ammo casings, and empty beer cans.

Surely, I could do more than pick up trash and write letters about preserving pristine wilderness. In the permaculture course, I'd be using my hands and body physically to help transform the damaged soil into a flourishing food forest. The property, adjacent to an existing permaculture farm to the west, and backed up to government-protected land to the north and east, had become the perfect regeneration project for a group of Earth-conscious activists and a globally renowned teacher.

It would be my third time visiting the Land of Smiles and, in addition to loose cotton clothing and mosquito repellent, I brought a notebook, a sleeping bag, and a purpose. I was doing what I loved most—adventuring. Only, this time, I'd be doing what I loved second most: absorbing information through hands-on experiences by experts and in community.

Arriving at Bangkok Airport at 12:39 am, I joined other sleepy travelers—mostly Thai—sprawled out on metal benches in the new terminal, to await the 5:00 am express bus into Bangkok. As I stepped off the bus, I was bombarded by with the intensity of street food grills clinging to the humidity, a waft of chili pepper that made my nose itch, and a lingering hint of sweat emanating from bodies all around me (and my own). In the moments of noticing and finding my bearings, I sensed my navigational north inside me somewhere. As foreign as Thailand felt, I also sensed I'd come home to myself.

The freedom was immediately met with disorientation. I felt simultaneously lost inside. I'd traveled alone many times before—in Europe, parts of Southeast Asia, and, of course, within the United States. I'd always been content in my solo wanderings. But after traveling to Baja with someone I loved, loneliness overtook me. I wanted Chris there with me! Mostly, I wanted him to share my passions. He just didn't.

I pondered our differences in the 12 hours I had to check out a couple of temples and buddhas in various patinas and postures. I lamented the burden of my heavy pack (why did I bring colored pencils and three camera lenses?) as I schlepped it around the hot, dirty city. I witnessed an unusual number of young military men perhaps keeping the peace, the constant humdrum of people weaving through each other like ants, and weather-worn Thai men and women carrying long poles across their backs with hanging baskets filled with papaya or beans.

I was hungry, but it was too hot to eat spicy noodles. I bypassed street-meat-on-a-stick and other such unidentifiables. Even fresh pineapple followed by fried tofu with red sauce and crushed peanuts did a number on my gut. I hoped a chocolate crêpe would help soothe my insides but, of course not. By 6:25 pm, I'd arrived at Hua Lamphong Station—the Grand Central Station of Bangkok—way too early to check in for the overnight bus headed north, too weary and uncomfortable to do anything other than sit (near the bathrooms) and become present to the distinctions in culture and climate.

Finally, I arrived in Chiang Mai in the wee hours and shared a tuk-tuk with two Swedish travelers to a hotel near the eastern gate of the old city. The girls let me shower in their room and I felt like a million Thai bahts as I ventured to a Westerner-focused internet café to relay my safe arrival to Chris via email. Famished again, I couldn't stomach the runny yogurt and spongy orange rolled-up sandwich they handed out on the bus. Alas, the café had run out of croissants by 8:00 in the morning.

With a couple hours until being picked up, I wandered down the street to the temple, recalled long-ago high school dreams of designing a '50s diner and menu, musing now about a more purposeful temple-like building, with food as the shrine—a place to offer nourishments for our own corporal temples (bodies).

Recipe for Design

I wanted to create a healthy space for community to gather. Perhaps something like that would be my calling to gather earth-conscious people?

When Christian arrived in an ancient clunky truck, he retrieved me and a couple of others who'd shown up with their gear. We perched on metal benches in the back of the truck and bumped along toward the property for the next two hours.

We toured the land together. Others were hard at work preparing the space for the arrival of us trainees. They'd built structures for sleeping, eating, eliminating, and cleansing. The main *sala* was the central space for cooking and eating, learning, and hanging out when class wasn't in session. An upstairs loft was where several of us would sleep. However, I pitched a tiny tent down by the creek, buffered underneath from the rain with corn husks. The tent fit only me, my sleeping bag, my mosquito spray arsenal, my pack, and the headlamp required to inspect every inch of the tent for spiders and scorpions. We washed our clothes in the creek with natural soap. Outdoor male and female showers, fed by buckets of water we'd haul up from the creek, were a necessity in the heat and humidity of the tropics.

Awakened by the 6:00 am whistle, we practiced yoga in the common space (while providing breakfast for the bugs). I was part of the first-day kitchen crew, so by 7:00 I was making rice pudding with bananas, accompanied by leftover stir fry and veggie soup. To help everyone make meal decisions according to their needs, I pined over lovely signs indicating "egg, peanut, dairy, soy" and other such descriptive ingredient labels for our vegetarian meals.

One imperative was to know how our food affected our motility—runny or stinky? frequent or urgent?—so our collective poop would direct how we designed meals. As such, we recorded descriptions of our poop in the log outside the two thin-walled adjacent compost toilets. Poop talk lightened the mood of these private activities conducted in close proximity.

Our community was organized into teams with rotating daily schedules: foraging (for bananas, papayas, and firewood from the surrounding area); cooking (assisting in meal prep and clean up); *metta* (spreading loving-kindness in creative ways); and down-time (rest and relaxation every fourth day). We also worked collaboratively during specified timeframes, dividing projects like installing drinking mug hooks, setting up a shower curtain as the screen for our teacher's slide show lectures, and painting signs indicating why only organic soap was to be used in outdoor showers and the creek. Local students translated the signs into Thai.

Our Thai cook, Gai, coordinated all the meals. When she showed up that afternoon with an impressive abundance of fruit, veggies, tofu, and sweets wrapped in banana leaves, I immediately volunteered to join her on her weekly visit to the market. I was grateful for Gai's patience as she attempted to teach me Thai words for both familiar and unfamiliar foods and cooking terms. And whenever people went to town to mail letters, visit temples, stock up on coffee, coconut cream and other supplies, I joined them, as well. I mostly observed, inhaling the mixture of smoky dry season air entwined with flowering plants, incense, and coriander. These intense aromas transported me back to other evocative travels: Tangier's street market on 9/11; Istanbul's wool rugs and coffee during an unexpected American tourist ban; Singapore's fried food and gutters after a monsoon. My senses were invigorated.

My team helped Gai prepare a feast to welcome our instructor, Geoff, who had arrived from Saudi Arabia, to celebrate the beginning the course, and to announce the birth of a new way of living for all of us. The protégé of the founder of permaculture, Geoff was pleasantly surprised to be among our hodge-podge group. He admitted that if he hadn't committed two years prior, he probably would not have come (he was in high demand). But what struck me personally was his not-so-funny joke about teaching us how to deal with parents and partners who may never understand the power or workings of permaculture. Sometimes, he mentioned, their lack of desire to know—or too much insistence from our side—resulted in divorce.

Interesting. It was like he had articulated my fear of finding a new path without Chris, not only in permaculture and being in community with others, but even in doing something helpful for humans and the earth. I watched, somewhat enviously, as Sarah and her partner managed to balance the energies of the group by finding projects just the two of them could work on together. They moved together, relaxed together, grew together.

Recipe for Design

I kept my distance from the single men, feeling pangs of guilt even to express appreciation for their zest for our project or to find interest in their passions for skill-building, working with their hands, planting seeds. I was not concerned about loving them; rather, I was concerned about discovering more disconnect from my own partner.

My mind was busy enough with unexpected enthusiasm for the scientific concepts behind intentional, thoughtful design of *the land*. In high school, I'd pursued physics over biology (I was good at math) and during undergrad, opted for botany as my science prerequisite (thinking perhaps someday I might grow *Cannabis*). But this immersive nature-science took me back to my freshman year in architecture school, where I noted during Functional Design that surprisingly few contemporary structures are created in harmony with Earth.

In contrast, my art history courses had revealed patterns and symbolism fundamental to the earliest purposeful plans and ritualistic objects. Functional cities like Pompeii were carefully organized around practicality, use, access, and making sense of otherwise chaotic systems. Humans and nature had co-existed for thousands of years until mankind took too much without giving back. Permaculture, on the other hand, offered a cooperative and regenerative approach, giving humans a platform to understand the *elemental interweavings* of nature, and to create abundance *with* nature.

What an enlightening perspective! Observe patterns in the natural world, then apply them to the built environment. What a brilliant nature-first concept of reorganizing terrain to create an ecosystem where both Earth and humans can flourish. What a refreshing shift from man's coiffed, contrived landscaping—and structures that jarred against a landscape's fluidity—to outcomes grounded in unassuming esthetic and multi-purposeful functioning. *This is it! Permaculture's human-and-Earth symbiosis is the core concept to direct my life choices.*

My mind and heart expanded exponentially during those few short weeks, and I felt immense satisfaction in the many little tasks that had already made noticeable differences. Something I'd once read surfaced in my mind: "What you do each day is an indication of what you do in life." My days on the permaculture farm consisted of practicing yoga, eating a simple breakfast of locally grown plant-based foods, witnessing the progress of seed starts, turning compost piles, meditating while working garden rows, washing laundry in the creek, reading expansive books, showering under the open sky, preparing fried fish soup and sweet rice, and retiring to my tent with utter satisfaction. All this, in a like-minded community working toward a common purpose.

Despite finding deep meaning in our work, I had so little to contribute beyond my physical efforts and participation, which were welcomed despite my lack of skills. My attempt to build a box for the projector using the metric system failed. I took thousands of photos documenting the process and which never left my hard drive. Others played music, were adept builders, danced, sang, and more. All worked as part of the team, so each of us was integral. Despite a gamut of personality differences, we were welcomed for who we were.

One day, as I walked to the village for Thai iced tea and to buy sesame treats to share, I considered what gifts I truly had to offer the world. Once in Portland, I wanted to work with a company making a beneficial mark on this planet—but doing what? I wanted to help heal our Mother Earth—she who birthed all life—yet, how? Further, I feared Chris would not be on board for this newfound passion. In fact, I knew he would not care about the process at all—he loved nature, but it wasn't in his nature to want to save it. He simply wanted to enjoy it.

These thoughts gnawed at me daily while in class in the *sala*; while no-see-ums chewed at my legs; while digging swales on the hill until my shoulders ached; while purchasing fruit trees and reconstituted solar panels in the village; while zipping up my sleeping bag alone each night. Every day there was visible, empowering progress on the outside, while my own vision-scaffolding was taking shape on the inside.

RECIPE for DESIGN

I never mastered Thai cooking. Instead, I focused on improving a few recipes, including green curry. Authentic ingredients are not always available, making every meal slightly different from the last. However, homemade curry paste is key! Switch up the veggies and protein, sure, and always make paste.

Vegetarian Thai Green Curry & Rice
Serves = 6-8 servings
Time = 45-60 minutes

Curry Paste Ingredients
- 2 stalks lemongrass (use only the inner core of the bottom sections)
- 1 large jalapeño pepper, minced
- 2 small shallots, minced
- 3-4 cloves fresh garlic, minced
- 1" piece of ginger (unless you're lucky enough to find galangal), minced
- Zest from an organic lime (or 4 kaffir lime leaves, if you have access to them)
- ½ tsp each sea salt, ground coriander, ground cumin

Green Curry Ingredients
- 2 c rice of choice
- 1 lb extra firm tofu, cut into cubes
- 1 head broccoli, cut into florets
- 1 c green beans, tips removed then cut in half
- 1 tbsp coconut oil
- 13.5 oz can of full fat, unsweetened coconut milk (BPA-free can)
- 1 c veggie broth or stock
- 1 tbsp tamari
- 1 tsp coconut sugar or succanat
- ½ c bamboo shoots
- ½ c fresh basil leaves, cut into ribbons
- Juice from 1 lime

Instructions
1. Make the rice according to instructions.
2. Make the paste by preparing all ingredients, then adding them to a bowl and mashing together well.
3. Prepare the tofu and veggies.
4. Melt coconut oil in a large, heavy bottomed skillet on medium heat. Add half the curry paste and mix into oil until well combined.
5. Add coconut milk and stir to blend with the paste.
6. Stir in veggie broth, tamari, and sugar.
7. Add tofu and veggies and cook, about 10 minutes or until broccoli and beans turn bright green. Stir every few minutes. Add more broth if it becomes too dry. Taste the sauce and add more paste if you'd like more flavor.
8. Add bamboo shoots, basil leaves, and lime juice, then cook for another few minutes.
9. Enjoy hot, served over rice and with a bottle of Singha.

CHAPTER 9

Recipe for Dependence

In the days after the permaculture course ended, I focused my physical and mental efforts on fruitful farm projects. Without daily gatherings for class, I began distancing myself from the few of us who remained. Though I felt more confident with my hands-on skills and was eager to continue the transformative work we'd started, I held back from showing up fully. I ached to see Chris and show him the farm, even as our teacher's words of warning loomed: Chris might never understand. Uncharacteristically, I sought solitude.

At the end of the week, I trekked down to Chiang Mai to meet Chris at the airport, my heart jumping out of my chest as I tried to even my breath. His loving smile turned my fears to happiness, reminding me I was safe with him. Loneliness waned as I relaxed into the arms of the man I trusted. Within minutes, I felt like we hadn't been away from each other at all.

We hailed a *song tao* and the driver toured us through the city. I'd booked a private room, thankful to be off the hard ground and away from spiders for the night. We took a cooking class, hiked to temples, and headed northwest to Pai—then a relatively unknown and sleepy, hippie town. We rode rescue elephants, met new friends while spinning poi balls, drank mango smoothies, and held each other close under the mosquito nets until the sticky humidity forced us to separate. It was a blissful reuniting, the perfect balance of my knowing the local ropes and our experiencing Thailand in ways that were new to both of us.

I was excited to show off the now-quiet farm where only six people remained. Much had transpired in the week I was away, including the completion of a new cobb dwelling, dubbed the "honeymoon suite." Chris and I kicked out the scorpion squatter and became the first humans to christen the curvy, earthy abode lit only by candles.

It seemed like a sign from above that our daytime task was brick building. Chris's father was a masonry contractor, and Chris grew up helping lay foundations, mixing mud, and cleaning sponges. Together, we kneaded clay, sand, and water with our feet in a bathtub-like-pit in the bottom swale. We added corn husks and stomped around some more. It was "thick enough" when the mixture didn't collapse upon lifting our feet. Using the bucket brigade method, we transported mud to the molds. In about two hours, we had built 20 bricks. Estimating it would take 3500 bricks for the shop/shed/parking structure, it would take us 44 days, working eight hours per day! We recruited our neighbor, the green-building guru whose theory was, "If it's too much work, you're not doing it right." We ramped up to 124 bricks in an hour and a half.

Secretly, I hoped this satisfying work was the ticket for Chris to fall in love with permaculture, as I had; or, at least, to appreciate it enough to affect the unfolding of our Portland life. I envisioned us sowing seeds and creating systems that would flourish from the fruits of our labor and function like clockwork. We'd start by growing herbs at the condo, then buy land.

But that's not what happened.

As much as he enjoyed our days on the farm—the intention circle, hiking in the jungle, showering under the full moon, the pineapple-cucumber-avocado salsa—Chris was uninterested in living off the grid. That was hippie life, and not his personality. *But it's mine. Isn't it? Can we intermix modern living within the permaculture matrix?*

With my vision blurred, Chris and I ventured on from the farm. Over the next weeks, as we traveled through southern

Recipe for Dependence

Thailand and into Malaysia, I spoke of permaculture with every new person we met. On touristy Krabi, on remote islands, in the southern border town of Kota Bharu, and on Pulau Pangkor in northern Malaysia. I was spreading the gospel of faith in our future while discussing the condition of the planet; how human health and reparation of the land will become a priority; and how permaculture would reinvigorate the earth to save everyone from imminent desolation. I felt Chris rolling his eyes as I preached permaculture's philosophy to be unique to each geographical location based on climate, vegetation, and inherent needs. I caught Chris frowning as I spoke fervently about "all the people who were screwing up our environment," reminding other travelers of the garbage we'd witnessed floating in the ocean. In truth, as passionate as I was about the potential of permaculture, I struggled to remain optimistic. Our planetary situation was dire.

On Christmas Day, amongst luscious tea fields of the Cameron Highlands, with the snip-snip-snipping of tea leaves echoing through the rolling hills, our differences exploded into our first big argument. He'd had enough! "Can't you just *shut up* about it?" he cried out.

Shoot. All that time, I had been trying to convert him. But it was abruptly clear our together-life would not include oneness with the land.

Deep breaths. All day. After some tears and frustration, inside I conceded. We still loved to hike, camp, and eat seasonal food together, so we had plenty of nature-loving going for us, right? I'd have to figure out another avenue for bringing permaculture into my life. Surely in Portland, the mecca of tree-hugging-metro-hippies, I would befriend bee-keeping buddies, pick fruit in a community orchard, work for a company with a rooftop garden and a pack of science geeks.

That night, in an ex-military-bunker-turned-hostel, we met a couple from Portland—the first Americans we'd met since the farm! They were living in Singapore while the wife, Michelle, fulfilled a contract as a water guru. Michelle was looking forward to pasta making upon return to the States. Art was into crushing grapes and beer brewing. They were designing a chicken coop. The best part was, Chris hit it off with them, too! These were the first friends we'd made *together*, and they were to become our bike-tour and wine-tour guides around Portland when we all returned.

See? The universe delivered.

By the time we descended the mountains with newfound hope, we'd found each other again in the shadows of Kuala Lumpur's Petronas Towers, dreaming up plans for our own restaurant in Portland. It would be a version of the café I'd been thinking about for years, but with ingredients procured locally and a menu that reflected world cuisine in simple, palatable vegetarian dishes.

"No way," Chris argued. "Meat eaters buy more beer." He insisted the only way to make money in the food industry was with alcohol sales, so a strictly vegetarian restaurant was *out*.

"Do meat eaters *really* drink more?" I pouted. "Vegetarianism is just more *earth friendly*," I argued. Didn't matter.

"The restaurant biz is hard enough. We'll need steady sales in microbrews and wine." Chris debated.

"Can we, at least, serve organic wine?" I inquired. The Willamette Valley was famous for its wine, yet I had no idea about its earth consciousness.

"Why muddy it all up? Just serve what people will buy—wines with the best reviews," he said.

"But…the impact? Don't we want to entice customers who care about the earth?" I implored.

"No, we want to draw people who will come back again and again. Spend money."

"Fine." I huffed, but I was not going to give up my composting endeavor, *nor* plans to make every sauce and dressing from scratch.

"That's all you, baby."

Thankfully, Chris was on board for my human-powered smoothie-bike idea that would raise money to donate to small farms or artisan food purveyors.

Over the next few weeks in Vietnam, Cambodia, and back to Thailand, I survived prawns in supposedly "vegetarian" Gỏi cuốn wrapped in rice paper, cockroaches in a morning-after watery cocktail, and nine-hour bumpy-dusty bus rides with chickens—but no toilets or stops. We mapped out a business plan and recorded our favorite meals in Hanoi, Siem Reap, and Koh Chang (the not-so-touristy one). I documented meals I enjoyed—noodles and veggies with eggs and basil; vegetable soup; coconut rice; banana, chocolate, or coconut milkshakes—and every meal I couldn't possibly serve—shrimp won tons (my body inherently said *no* to shrimp), chicken drowning in rice for breakfast. I said yes to Vietnamese coffee and *cao lầu* (rice noodles with bean sprouts and slow-roasted pork), and no to pig skin floating in *phở*. I'd had enough of fried fish with dried chilis, but perhaps we could rotate some local seafood seasonally, such as crab in green curry sauce or squid in clear liquid (to appease customers, though it felt almost too foreign). It would be irresponsible to serve tropical dessert bowls with papaya, pineapple, mango topped with yogurt and muesli, but we could certainly come up with a northwest variation using berries. I could literally taste our future!

Originally, I'd intended to venture back to the farm in January for round three of work, but after our travels, I agreed it was more important for *us* to return home together. We had work to do—and Chris and I had a plan that needed research, staff, a space. We needed to find a holistic chef, aligned suppliers, farmer partnerships, plus define a mission statement and perhaps procure funding. I also had the idea of going back to school for a thorough grasp on nutritional and healing foods. It was exciting, overwhelming....

On our last day in-country, we inadvertently transitioned back to Western life with a French fry hankering at an American joint with good reviews on Khao San Road, a street teeming with newbie tourists, sweaty under heavy packs, checking maps. Others—like us—with unkempt hair and worn clothes, presented an air of ease.

We were returning to the States, though not yet to our new Portland condo. With two months to go until our renters moved out, we headed back to Cali, land of In-N-Out Burger. I had come with a goal of finding my own purpose, and we were leaving with one that suited both of us. Once again, that inner voice whispered about the unknown. *Is the café my calling or his? Is it a good idea to embark on that venture as a couple?*

We'd depended on each other through some scary shit, like New Year's Eve when we found solace in vodka and coconut cream after the Vietnamese government took our passports, and our tour guides left us in the middle of literally-fucking-nowhere (and the locals were roasting a dog). We'd endured Chris's sprained ankle, mosquito armies, the dripping heat of the tropics, language barriers, the gastrointestinal aftermath of too many fruit smoothies, and fundamental disagreements about our differing passions.

For the first time ever, I felt co-dependent. Not in a mental, "I have issues with men and can't be alone" way, but in a trusting, loving way I once judged others for having. Thank goodness, because I was pretty sure my birth control had failed thanks to the tropical heat.

RECIPE for DEPENDENCE

I don't often make this simple recipe but it's deliciously comforting. When we stumbled into the Little Hanoi Café in Vietnam, this meal nourished my waning endurance, reminding me that as soon as discomforts become unbearable, a real-butter French croissant could help everything feel good again.

Hanoi Croissantwiches
Yield = 2 sandwiches
Time = 15 minutes

Ingredients
- 2 croissants (made with real butter, not hydrogenated oils)
- Tuna (or canned mackerel, which is much lower in mercury)
- Celery, finely chopped
- Tarragon, chopped
- Mayo (I prefer mayo with avocado oil)
- Dijon mustard
- Capers
- Avocado, sliced
- Cucumber, sliced
- Microgreens or sprouts of choice

Instructions
1. Procure amazing croissants from the best possible source. It's worth it in the short term (your lunch) and long term (your health).
2. Make the tuna salad. I call it "tuna" but I've long since strayed from eating tuna (after much research on methylmercury) and now opt for canned salmon, sardines, anchovies, or mackerel.
3. Drain excess water (if the fish is packed in olive oil, feel free to use some).
4. Prep the celery and tarragon.
5. In a bowl, add fish, a spoonful of mayo, a hint of Dijon, chopped celery, some capers, and fresh herbs.
6. Mix ingredients together until combined and to desired texture and flavor.
7. Prepare the toppings.
8. Cut avocado into slices.
9. Slice cucumbers (if organic, keep the skin on—it's home to many nutrients).
10. Make your sando.
11. Gently slice croissants lengthwise with a serrated knife, taking care not to cut all the way through—you're making a "pocket"—or to smoosh the croissant!
12. Stuff with tuna salad.
13. Add sliced avocado, cucumbers, and microgreens on top of the tuna, then fold the croissant top back over.
14. Close your eyes as you take your first bite and transport yourself to a place that brings comfort.

CHAPTER 10

Recipe for Divisiveness

We returned from sticky, overgrown tropics and dusty roads to pristine parkways, strip malls and California's mid-winter sunshine. We were painfully broke. We hadn't planned it that way—the sale of our Park City condo had fallen through, my gallery bonus hadn't shown up, and a friend still owed me money from months past. With renters in our condo until April, we were in limbo.

It was unsettling to be a jobless vagabond living in Chris's parents' home within an endless web of uninspiring tract neighborhoods. I was also without a vehicle and could have worked at Starbucks just down the street, though any 2-month job seemed fruitless. Chris resumed work helping his dad on job sites.

Notably, I suck at doing nothing. Working on café plans was tough enough without knowing Portland! So, when my younger sister Jaclyn called to welcome me back to the States and asked if I wanted to come to Costa Rica with her, my soul jumped at the chance! I checked my bank account—my people still hadn't paid me. Still, I could always figure out how to travel and that trip felt extra important because Jaclyn and I hadn't traveled together since she'd visited me during my post-9/11 stint in northern France. She was going through a rough time in her life, which may have prompted my parents to gift me with enough money to buy a roundtrip ticket. It was a generous gesture for my sissy and I, and a much-appreciated birthday present from my folks.

I was packing again. Same sandals, cheap sunglasses and lightweight, cotton clothes (some noticeably tighter) I'd worn all over Southeast Asia. I needed to buy only one new item before leaving: a pregnancy test. I begrudgingly visited the CVS down the parkway, took about 50 deep breaths before entering the sliding doors, and 50 more breaths to the aisle housing pregnancy tests. Somehow, I could calmly navigate a city of 10 million people who spoke another language better than I could navigate big box stores while hyperventilating.

Anyway, I bought the test, which cost the equivalent of five nights' lodging in Thailand. It sat, unopened, on the bathroom counter for two weeks.

Meanwhile, I struggled with my weight gain. None of my new clothes from Hoi An—made for *my* body only a month prior—fit me! I blamed the coconut cream and the lazy life we'd been living. I'd always joked that I was the type of person who gained weight when I ate celery, but that had been a stupid cover-up story for my drinking problem. Now, I had no good lies to tell myself. I didn't feel ill and, other than what seemed like edema and missing my cycle (twice), there were no other signs. Nevertheless, I couldn't bring myself to drink beer with Chris's family, feel comfortable in my skin, *or* take that damned test.

Soon enough, in Costa Rica at the base of Volcan Arenal where lava seeped out of the mountain day and night, so did the blood from my uterus. In a co-ed, shared-room hostel, I woke in the night with cramping and the urge to visit the bathroom. I bled through my clothes, sheets, and all the way to the toilet, then for another hour or more. I spent another two hours cleaning up the room in the glow of my headlamp while trying not to wake anyone.

And that was it. I casually told my sissy and pretended not to care. Mostly I was relieved, and I took the miscarriage as a sign my body was currently unfit to grow a human. In the town of La Fortuna, I felt fortunate the episode wasn't more painful emotionally or physically, though I also felt responsible in some unclear, unspoken way. *Am I malnourished? Did years of fearing*

Recipe for Divisiveness

motherhood and ruminating about the burdens of children cause my body to reject growing one?

It was impossible to know. I decided to celebrate the wisdom of my body instead of focusing on rhetorical questions. By the time we reached a sleepy beach town on the coast of the Nicoya Peninsula, I was feeling more like myself. I'd shed enough water weight that my clothes felt looser, and I was no longer swollen. We basked in the warmth of the hot springs, and I felt unusually replenished by the minerals. I watched in envy as other travelers sipped fancy cocktails I couldn't afford yet felt content with water as an accompaniment to my first *casado*—a hearty lunch of rice, black beans, cabbage-and-tomato salad, mango-onion-potato salad, a fried plantain, half a hard-boiled egg and our choice of meat. I chose the local beef in tomato sauce, thinking I might need iron-rich food upon losing so much blood.

We made our way through the cloud forest jungles and hippie beach towns. We landed in Santa Teresa, named for the patron saint of flowers—not canonized for spreading flowers, but for maintaining her spiritual faith—blossoming despite daily struggles to do so and despite questioning her faith. Hmm, I certainly had avoided placing my faith in something divine, but the simple consideration of how a flower gracefully blooms amidst struggles was somehow comforting to my own unfolding, and despite my own seed not implanting.

The next day, on my 29th birthday, Jaclyn gifted me with a fishing trip complete with local guides. She was the fisherwoman in our family—she'd lived on Idaho's famed Salmon River for more than a decade already, boating, fishing, and living the river canyon life. But not me. I'd fished, sure, in the summers, but when it came to smashing a rock on a fish's head to kill it and take it home to eat it, I faltered. I've never been an animal lover, per se, yet always enjoyed the energy animals brought to our home, to the backcountry ranch, and especially in the wild. I abhorred the notion of trophy hunting and wondered what compelled man to take more than he needed. After a week in the Costa Rican jungles with howler monkeys, a magnificent quetzal, a vivid purple hummingbird, and emerald iguanas, I couldn't fathom how anyone could dismiss these majestic animals while razing the forests for commercial gain.

While I was no longer a strict vegetarian, I was hyper-conscious of the origin of the meat I consumed and against killing anything for sport. Like fishing. I knew we would consume what we caught, yet I grappled with justifying the slaughter in which I was about to participate.

During our five hours at sea, we were air bombed by brown boobies and, at first, we thought the massive school of sardines was a whale until the fish broke through the surface in bunches. We caught a couple of flounders, barracudas, and a Bonita to bait some small tuna, a big-eye jack, a green jack, and a dorado. We released many fish back into the ocean (to my delight) and kept only the fish legally large enough or badly snared. Still, it was too much. We filled the cooler. *What are we going to do with all that fish?* I took the pole only when Jaclyn offered it, reminding me the trip was my birthday present.

I conceded. Tossed in the line. Then, as if Neptune himself sensed my discomfort, my line pulled so tight I nearly fell off the boat. With some struggle and help, I reeled in the most beautiful creature I'd ever seen: a rooster fish, weighing probably 80 pounds. While our guide released the hook, I struggled to hold the massive animal. Its floundering breath pulsated into my veins. The midday sun reflected off its scales, glittering aqua, green, and every possible hue in between. The breeze ruffled its mane, which seemed caught between handsome confidence and defenseless struggle. This was the kind of fish tales were written about and why people believed in mermaids. It was the reason many people learned to snorkel, diving to witness such splendor.

In the land of "pura vida"—a place at odds with itself, where Ticos (locals) simultaneously touted eco-tourism while negligently littering the roads with plastic waste—I had the choice of taking the life of this brilliant fish or releasing it back into its home. Images flashed unbidden through my mind: wild horses trapped by man; exotic animals poached for greed; even a fallen tree I'd once cut for firewood with a chainsaw that had me feeling like I'd robbed the tree of its destiny to decompose and enrich its native soil. I trembled with the enormity of this life-or-death decision, knowing we had more food than we needed without the flesh from the majestic creature in my arms. This fish belonged in its ocean home, not filleted and encrusted on a plate, digested in our bellies, mounted upon a wall.

I burst into tears. Jaclyn stared at me, mouth agape. Everything inside me said keeping this sea creature was wrong. I had to release it.

"Oh, *Jamie!*" Jaclyn called out, clearly annoyed—if not confused—by my decision. She'd paid for this fishing trip, after all.

"I can't do it," I cried.

I sensed a gulf between us. I'd always joked I was the only woman in my family who didn't own a gun, and there I was, hunting fish, desperate not to kill. Would Jaclyn judge me for letting the fish go, just as I judged those who never thought twice about the fate of the food on their plates? (I had judged myself for the same). A chasm widened within me, too, between killing for food and killing for sport. Human vs. Nature. The kind of modern-day struggle that Santa Teresa may have witnessed from wherever people go when they die.

It was a pivotal moment for me. That day, a clear, inner knowing resounded: I needed to be part of the solution, not part of the problem.

My sister wasn't mad, after all—she *knew* me.

That night, Jaclyn offered to make beer-battered fish tacos to share our bounty with the other travelers in the hostel—young people like us from Israel, Slovakia, Germany, the UK, Argentina, and a few more from the States. As sous chef, I was impressed with how my sister effortlessly sliced, patted, and rolled strips of fish first into flour, then into the batter she'd whipped up before placing the fish gently into a pan of hot oil. The result was an ever-so-flaky outer crispiness with subtle spices encasing juicy, soft flesh with a dollop of yogurt-lime sauce and wrapped in warm corn tortillas. Her tacos tasted better than any I'd ever made or eaten—fresh and sustainable—despite my guilt. I didn't know it would be the last time I'd eat fish for years to come.

The meal transformed the casual and quiet hostel into a space of celebration around the dinner aromas, the awed description of the fish flavors and textures, the cracking open of beer bottles, and the metal caps clinking on the floor. I imagined the air of togetherness must be ageless with the gifts of providing food for the benefit of community and to showcase one's culture. In the revelry, the rest of us decided to take turns creating our favorite meals to share. As we signed up for dinners and wrote ingredient lists based on what we could find in the tiny oceanside town, I felt satiated not just from the tacos, but also from the energy created by the willingness to experience a piece of each other's lives through food.

When it was my turn to cook, Jaclyn accompanied me on rickety bikes to the local market with our recycled bags (yes, we'd brought them with us, even back then). I had promised to make Thai green curry with coconut rice and mangoes. Lacking tofu at the small market, my eyes skipped past the meat options to wander from veggie to veggie, thankful green curry wasn't traditionally made with fish.

While prepping dinner, one traveler—a vegan from Portland—seemed extra grateful for the curry. We struck up a conversation about what it was like to live in Stumptown, and I wanted to know more about veganism. To my surprise, he traveled with a DVD about veganism (seriously, who *does* that?). He kindly and unassumingly asked if I wanted to watch it. I did.

In fact, I stayed at the hostel an extra day to watch "Eating," a small budget film that was well researched. It touted the health benefits of a plant-based diet and how almost every disease discovered in the past 100 years may be directly related to diet. With convincing imagery, the film shared data from the USDA on conventional agriculture's depletion and poisoning of the soil. What hit me most was the depth of the environmental impact of eating meat, fish, dairy, and eggs. Eating vegan meant reducing the insurmountable strain of cow, pig, chicken, and fish production on soil, in water, and in the air; reducing the amount of animal cruelty as part of the conventional agriculture chain; and limiting an individual's intake of man-made chemicals, hormones, herbicides, and pesticides required to raise the animals.

The film also provided positive, doable solutions. For example, if each person ate several fewer burgers every year—even smaller portions—we would save thousands of acres of rainforest and offset climate change in noticeable ways. I felt morally responsible that my own choices could help. It seemed blatantly hypocritical to be both an Earth Mama and an omnivore. I decided: veganism would be my ticket to doing more. Multiple times per day, my small choices would add up to big impact.

Recipe for Divisiveness

I knew veganism would be a hard lifestyle to uphold, but I committed. In Portland, which boasted the highest concentration of vegan-friendly restaurants in the US at the time, I would start my total-vegan venture on the first day of Lent, a few days away. A revered season for devout (and non-devout) Catholics, Lent previously had served as a platform for me to become healthier by sacrificing a food crutch or beverage addiction. For example, my senior year in college, I gave up alcohol. While studying abroad in Italy, I'd scratched bread. During my second stint in France, it was pastries. Over the years I'd also given up added sugars (multiple times) and—the most epic form of self-flagellation—coffee. This time, I would give up all animal-derived foods, including honey. I committed to figuring it all out before returning to Chris's parents' house.

After watching the film on my last evening in Costa Rica, the two cute Israeli boys who were enamored with Jaclyn's kitchen skills made one of their home-town favorite meals—*shakshuka*. The recipe was vegetarian, so I graciously accepted (and it was delicious). I wondered whether the eggs—again, the last I'd eat for the foreseeable future—were from the neighboring chickens we heard squawking outside the hostel every day. In the moment, I was glad not to know, to simply enjoy them poached in warm spices and tomatoes.

On the journey home, I ate nuts, dried mangoes, and papayas, and seemingly little else. *What else does a vegan snack on?* I was grossly unprepared for a plant-based life, let alone how I'd navigate that in SoCal. And I certainly didn't think through the dissatisfaction from, well, Chris's entire family.

I'd discovered one way to create a deeper divide between omnivores and vegetarians (or between conservatives and liberals: divide Standard American Diet eaters and earth-conscious vegans. The blank faces were hard to decipher (judgment or incredulity? Perhaps frustration?). Nonetheless, the first few days went relatively well. I offered to cook dinner and brought home a squash so massive it almost broke my bike basket. I made squash soup with cinnamon, coconut milk, veggie broth, and cardamom, served over brown rice. I can't remember whether anyone else liked it, but I did!

For daytime nourishment, I visited a juice bar in the strip mall that served açai smoothie bowls with wheat germ and ginseng (and I caught the owners eating burgers and shakes from Wendy's). For other meals on the horizon, I needed a plan. We were set to have lunch with Chris's grandmother at her favorite Mexican joint. *What will I order?* Then, off to San Diego for a house party. *Is it impolite to ask about ingredients in every appetizer?*

I was utterly consumed by what I would consume. And my meals became fodder for inquiry from others, as well. For once, I found myself fearing debates, which was so un-Italian of me. Never before had I been so adamant about avoiding uncomfortable conversations, criticism, and judgment among family and friends, hosts, waiters, and, yeah, pretty much everyone except other vegans. It quickly become clear I needed more than just meal preparation; I'd need to adopt a positive, non-confrontational attitude around those who were not vegan. My choice was for me—and one not to be advertised.

Quickly I found that veganism is an impossible topic to ignore because American culture is deeply rooted in eating animals.

In the fridge, I was inundated with salami, steak, sausage, jerky, cheddar cheese, Swiss cheese, feta, provolone, cream cheese, and blue cheese salad dressing. I was left with creating a meal out of salsa, balsamic vinaigrette, and pantry staples such as pasta, raw almonds, and kettle chips.

By day nine, my brain was fatigued from thinking about food and, emotionally, I was toast. I'd been reading every label—not just for dairy, anymore, but for all animal-derived products. *What, exactly, should I avoid? Are binders and gums made from cockroach wings, pig bones, sea animals?* Cereal contained honey—and a surprising number of preservatives and artificial ingredients. Olives had an added chemical to retain their color. Mixed nuts listed ingredients I couldn't pronounce. Label-reading was becoming more than a lesson in animal welfare, yet I convinced myself to focus on just animals (for now); it was enough to tackle without considering preservatives, processed ingredients, and chemicals.

Recipe for Divisiveness

Less than two weeks in, my body felt mostly energetic and, except for a hangover or two (most beer is vegan, conveniently), my mind was clear, and my digestive organs (even my liver) were noticeably content. The slight puffiness in my face disappeared and, in fact, it seemed that any inflammation lingering in my body subsided. I didn't crave meat, cheese, or eggs. I looked forward to lighter, fresher food. I felt *clean* inside.

RECIPE for DIVISIVENESS

The spices in this recipe make it one of my absolute favorite ways to consume tomatoes. It can be modified for any diet—sausage and chicken broth for omnivores; eggs and veggie broth for vegetarians; tofu for vegans. And shakshuka can be eaten for breakfast, lunch, or dinner.

Shakshuka
Yield = 3-4 servings
Time = 45 minutes

Ingredients
1 tsp each cumin seed, coriander seed, fennel seed
- 1 medium yellow onion, finely diced
- 5 cloves garlic, minced
- 1 medium red bell pepper, roughly chopped
- 10-12 whole tomatoes, chopped, with juices (or a 28-ounce can whole tomatoes)
- 3 tbsp extra virgin olive oil
- 2 tsp smoked or sweet paprika
- ¾ tsp salt
- 1/8 tsp ground cayenne pepper (if you like it hot!)
- 6 eggs from pasture-raised hens
- Garnishes: avocado slices or labneh, fresh mint, and your favorite artisan bread.

Instructions
1. Heat oven to 400 degrees F.
2. Measure ground spices into a small bowl (including paprika). If using seeds:
3. Add cumin, coriander and fennel seeds to a small, dry cast iron skillet or other type of skillet (but not non-stick, which is toxic).
4. Toast on medium-low for 5-7 minutes, shaking the skillet often to prevent burning.
5. When the seeds become aromatic, turn off skillet and remove from heat. The seeds will continue to cook for a couple more minutes so don't let them burn!
6. Prep onion, garlic, bell pepper, and tomatoes.
7. Add olive oil to a cast iron or heavy-bottomed skillet that has a lid and is oven-safe. Turn to medium heat. Add onions, coating them in olive oil. Cover and simmer, stirring occasionally until translucent, 3-5 minutes.
8. Meanwhile, grind cooled, toasted seeds in a grinder or mortar & pestle.
9. Add spices including paprika and salt, plus garlic to the onions, stirring to coat. If too dry, add more oil. Cook 1-2 minutes and stir once or twice to disperse evenly.
10. Add tomatoes and their juices to the pot. Stir. Cover with lid to retain moisture.
11. Using a ladle, make small holes in the onion-tomato-spice mixture. Crack one egg into each hole. Cover.
12. Bake in the oven for 7-8 minutes, or until the egg yolks are well cooked.
13. Scoop shakshuka into bowls and serve with slices of avocado, a dollop of labneh, and fresh mint. Mop up with your favorite bread.

CHAPTER 11

Recipe for Distaste

Until the lobster incident, I wasn't a 100% certain I had a shellfish allergy. Since my teens, I'd had an aversion to shrimp and prawns, though I'd never landed in the hospital after testing them on the rare occasions they were available. My Gramma Day was allergic to them, so with a genetic predisposition, my allergy was possible. Since my inland hunting, gathering, and gardening family wasn't a "seafood" family, I'd discovered my intolerances only during young adulthood.

At gallery dinners or during travels to new lands where crustaceans were on the menu, I suspected food poisoning on many unfortunate occasions, not knowing about cross-contamination. The Christmas crab dinners seemed to go okay, but as my intuition increased, I purposefully arrived late to crawfish bakes or seafood dinners having eaten already and with dessert in hand to share.

The allergy suspicion culminated one fateful New Year's Eve in northern France with a single, grayish prawn drowning in something that was supposed to make it appetizing—and lovingly prepared by my Swedish friend, Karen. I spent the evening drinking Beaujolais and champagne, eating meatballs and cheese. When the clock struck midnight and Karen had asked me 17 times if I'd tried the prawns, I finally conceded, warning her of my previous episodes. Closing my eyes, I popped the nasty into my mouth, discarded the tail, chewed quickly holding my nose in case I gagged, and choked it down.

Within minutes, my body begged me to exit the party. I kissed Karen quickly on both cheeks, and walked alone down the dark, narrow streets to my 15th century apartment, already shaking inside with flu-like symptoms. Over the subsequent days, I vomited every few hours, retched with abdominal pain while curled up in a ball on our futon, and endured a killer migraine and body aches from severe dehydration.

My roommate, Naomi, was away with her sister, and I'd planned a short trip to Paris. Hence, we had no food in the house except one kiwi in the fridge. Remembering kiwis were full of vitamin C and that vitamin C was good for the immune system, I ate it. I threw it up. Profusely. (For the next two decades, the sight of kiwi made me nauseous.)

On day four, my South African friend knocked on the door. I crawled to the door to let him in. François took one look at me and said, "I know you're going to hate what I'm about to do, but my dad's a doctor and I've seen your condition before. I'll be back in ten minutes." He returned with a bottle of Coca Cola. *You've GOT to be kidding me!* It was no joke. François assured me the sugar in Coke would help restore the sugars in my depleted cells, relieve my migraine, and set me on a path to recovery. He was right, dammit. Brown, sugary soda had alleviated the pressure and the spins.

Without an "official test" the verdict was in: I was allergic to crustaceans with curvaceous spines. Prawns, shrimp. Were there more? Could I enjoy (and keep down) any variety of shellfish? I tried oyster shooters and King crab in Seattle; clam chowder in Boston; deep-fried squid at all those "high-end" chain restaurants in strip malls; mussels on the coast of France; Berberecho clams in Barcelona; octopus in Rome. None of these foods appealed to me; I consumed them to partake in local gastronomy. No enjoyment (no biggie), and no puking (big deal).

But I hadn't cleared lobster. And, unfortunately for Chris's family, the occurrence happened during my first few weeks of veganism, when food tension was already high. A month into

Recipe for Distaste

just "hanging out" at their house post-Costa Rica, the discomfort in taking up space in their home was deepened by my picky diet. It was bad enough before, being particular about meat quality and dairy, but now I grappled with everything from how I would run a non-vegan café we didn't have enough resources to start, to the contention I caused with my rejection of all animal products.

I needed to get out and also give Bill and Catherine space for an evening, so I found a yoga studio thirty minutes away (in their borrowed car) and planned to attend a class, find my center, revel in some much-needed alone time.

But first, dinner. Bill was grilling lobster. I believe it had been a gift from one of his clients and, apparently, wasn't as fancy pants as ostrich burger. It was harvested locally so before veganism I'd have been tempted to try some. Instead, I opted to grill a portabella mushroom.

None of us could have predicted that flipping my shroom on the grill with lobster-tainted tongs would be problematic. As I said, I had no idea about cross-contamination. Nor that my aversion to crustaceans was *that* sensitive. But about halfway through dinner, the purging sensation in my throat and stomach came on so suddenly I almost didn't make it upstairs to the toilet. For the next few hours, I rotated between vomiting and curling up in a ball on the bathroom rug. It was not the alone time I'd been craving.

Everyone felt terrible because I felt so terrible. Even so, there was a subtle shift in the household. It was as if Chris and his family had realized there really *was* something to my food preferences, my tastes, and distastes. Maybe I wasn't just a food-freak after all. Or, at least, maybe my lobster reaction had authenticated some of my food parameters. If only I could determine a less painful method for understanding my food issues.

RECIPE for DISTASTE

Though mushroom allergies are uncommon, many people have an aversion to the taste or texture despite vast variation between different shrooms. All fungi, however, provide that "umami" mouth flavor, which can be incredibly satisfying. Even meat eaters can find satisfaction in a simple, well-made portabella burger.

Portabella Mushroom Burgers
Yield = 1 burger per person
Prep time = 5 minutes
Total time = 20 minutes

Ingredients
- 1 large portabella mushroom per person
- Extra virgin olive oil
- Balsamic vinegar
- Garlic powder
- Freshly ground pepper
- Goat cheese, Manchego, Swiss cheese, or vegan cheese
- Arugula, lettuce, or spinach
- Challah buns or another artisan bun, if desired
- Dijon or stoneground mustard
- Your favorite Mediterranean whole grain side dish, such as one with garbanzo beans, tomatoes, feta, herbs, nuts and/or seeds
- Maybe some grilled asparagus

Instructions
1. Wash and dry the portabella mushrooms, then remove the stems. The stem is edible, but removing it creates a lovely crater in the middle where the cheese melts. (Omnivores may wish to chop up the stems and add them to say, ground meat with breadcrumbs and eggs—think meatballs—then stuff the mixture in the shroom.)
2. Place shrooms in a large, shallow bowl or ceramic dish. Drizzle olive oil and balsamic vinegar, then shake garlic powder and freshly ground pepper over the top. Don't add too much. With your hands, coat the shrooms evenly.
3. Turn on the grill or heat a cast iron skillet on your stove to medium. Place the portabella mushrooms crater side down and grill for about 5 minutes. Then, turn and spoon remaining oil/vinegar/garlic/pepper mixture in the crater. Grill 3 more minutes. Turn off grill and leave burgers on grill to keep warm.
4. Lay cheese of choice over the crater side of the burgers and let cheese melt slightly.
5. Prepare buns and/or condiments on each plate along with side dishes. Just before you're ready to eat, place a mushroom atop the bun (or if bun-less, atop the grain dish). Top with greens and serve immediately (they're better when hot).

CHAPTER 12

Recipe for Doing My Own Thing

April in Portland can be sheer misery under the grey weight of wet air, but instead spring welcomed us with vibrant trees bursting with fragrant blossoms intermingled with the aroma of roasted coffee. The greenbelts and bridges were alive with bike commuters, runners, and the homeless. And we had a place of our own to settle into. Between painting walls and setting stone in our historic northwest condo, we broke for short runs in Forest Park, to sample microbrews, to locate a vegan food cart or three, and to hunt for jobs. It took all of five minutes for Chris to land a job at one of the original farm-to-fork restaurants in town, a short walk from our condo. Wildwood was an epicenter of local food culture where elegant people, farmers, and foodies came to eat.

For me, landing a job was not as easy. I sought something in an earth-conscious field, one that would help protect nature, and give me other tools and connections we'd need for our café. I applied to assist at one of the farmers markets, an environmental non-profit organization, and even an eco-building supply company. I interviewed a lot. Juice bars, the co-op, and food trucks were hiring-a-plenty, but none of those felt right. And each offered starting wages of $8-$10/hour. Boo.

Portland is one of those places where you must *know someone* to get your foot in the door or you must be the shining star with the ideal résumé for an unusually hard to come by and coveted gig. You've got to be either talented, popular, or unique before starting your own café, so we placed our business plan on the back burner.

I wasn't one to settle or make decisions lightly, yet the pressure was on. Desperate, I began applying everywhere. But I was underqualified for the curator position at Portland Art Museum. The famed Powell's bookstore never called me back. Guiding wine tours meant long commutes each direction (and we had one vehicle to share). I couldn't stray from my vision by becoming a salesperson at Restoration Hardware or Williams and Sonoma, only a few blocks away (and hiring).

In my attempts at networking, I attended NW VegFest, permaculture meetings, "Green Drinks" events, and the city's job fair. Continually, I was defeated with my niched skills consisting of art sales, organizing, and managing a small team. I had little else to offer except my enthusiasm. I was a dime a dozen in the city, and penniless.

My fruitless efforts soured with an unforeseen economic crisis. Remember the real estate boom followed by the crash in 2008? Yeah, well, that was happening, and like everyone else, Chris and I had purchased a few places at the peak of that crazy market—Sun Valley, Idaho; Park City, Utah; Kauai, Hawaii; and now Portland, Oregon. We thought investing in real estate would be the smart way out of working until we were 85. We hadn't anticipated a major recession. Hence, I was insanely anxious about our finances.

One Saturday at the downtown farmers market, while eating a vegan muffin, a friend's brother asked me what job I was looking for. As I explained all the jobs I didn't want, he politely stopped me and said, "Jamie, what if you start talking about jobs you *do* want?"

I looked at him blankly, realizing I'd been fixating on all the wrong things. He continued to describe The Law of Attraction.

Recipe for Doing My Own Thing

"When you ask for what you want—and even visualize it—it will happen. So…what do you want?"

I knew I was expected to reply with a detailed description, but with frustration, I responded, "Well, I don't really know. I want to be useful, stimulated, and challenged in an environmental food organization making a difference in the natural world. Whatever that means."

Like when asked about my goals in life, once again I was unclear. I vowed to stop focusing on the fact that I hadn't worked anywhere for more than four years because I was busy traipsing around the world and, therefore, had no résumé of interest. I tried to stop cringing at those who gave me shit for not yet having "it" all figured out, reminding myself I also didn't want a job in a cubicle or another preordained societal box. My college degree in English with minors in French and art history did absolutely nothing to point me in any direction or equip me with marketable skills.

For clarity and comfort, I called my Haiku friend, Katie, who happened to be a feng shui consultant. I wasn't sure how feng shui and the Law of Attraction comingled, but both were energetic and intentional and, obviously, I needed guidance. Katie helped me understand energy centers of the home, so I declared to Chris that we needed to repaint our entry blue (to stimulate my career space), the kitchen red (to energize the prosperity space), and move the desk to the guest room (it was in a misaligned spot). Chris responded with his version of extreme annoyance, refused to let me re-paint or re-arrange, and stated that my job search had whittled down to witchcraft.

Ugh. No faith in just trying something new? Maybe his lack of supporting my energetic endeavors was part of the problem? So, to find middle ground, I scrubbed the front door and the walls that flanked both sides. I washed away cobwebs sticking to pots on the front porch and planted a blue delphinium. I bought coat hooks that spelled WATER (which symbolized the color blue). Okay. My career center was set, and my mind refreshed.

And *it worked*.

Of course, it wasn't what I was expecting. I must have been focused on my recent adventures while preparing the house because a traveling job opportunity came to my attention from three different people, three times, within three days. Three is a magic number, right? It was not a high-paying job and, unfortunately, it was not a Portland-based company. But I'd be *touring* and guiding active trips, with time in-between to come home. As excited as I was about living in Portland, I wasn't anchored there. I know I was told to go West, to water and a city—*but my soul still yearned to be on the road.*

I had totally forsaken that my anchor was my partner—we'd always just done our *own* thing, balanced by our *together* thing. Our first home together still didn't feel quite real or grounding. And Chris didn't plead for me to stay. Was it because he knew how much I loved to travel? Or did he know it wouldn't matter—I'd do my own thing anyway? This travel job was, at least, *something* to raise my spirits! Plus, I could make it temporary—just through the summer.

I scraped together just enough to travel to a two-day interview in Salt Lake City. And *wow* was it competitive! Everyone seemed on edge, unusually nervous, or overly confident. My French language skills may have tipped the decision: I got the job with Backroads, which started immediately. I stayed in Utah for the three-week training.

The leaders said the European staff was all set, cautioning us not to get our hopes up for an overseas placement. I listed France as *le numéro un* anyway (not thinking it would manifest) and *mon dieu!* I was placed there. I would be leading biking and hiking tours in Brittany and Normandy, off-the-beaten-path, where history pulsed through every weather-worn structure, weeping beech tree, and mysteriously placed stone. While polishing my French language skills and drinking wine with guests. I was elated! For about two minutes.

Uh, oh. What now? Chris and I had left our cozy mountain town to start a new life *together*. We bought a condo, and he landed a job that suited him. In just two months of searching, my enthusiasm to save the world through the environmental food movement seemed to have evaporated into the ether. Could I really leave him alone in Portland and run off again? My heart loved a man; my soul loved traveling. I was equally exhilarated and sick to my stomach. *What am I doing?* Caught in a whirlpool of indecision, I pictured his face. Going overseas at this point surely would tear us apart.

I declined the assignment in France. Immediately, I received a warning from "the top." My new boss relayed, "Why would you apply for and accept a traveling job only to decline your number one destination?"

Thankfully, I was reassigned to the San Juan Islands of Washington, near my ol' high school stompin' grounds and close enough to hop to Portland between tours. It seemed like a good compromise. It was still West, and coastal. See? Everything seemed to be lining up.

One of my tasks as a trip leader was to prepare food for daytime excursions and ensure guests' allergies were accounted for. I called restaurants to inform about guest requirements like, for example, garlic allergies. Optimistic for my first trip, the wind was knocked quickly out of my sails when I also informed the restaurant staff I was vegan—a statement met with silence on the other end of the phone at the first seafood restaurant. Ergo, I spent my own pocket change and time preparing balanced vegan snacks for myself. Instead of wearing veganism like a badge of commitment to the earth, I sensed animosity from my cohorts. I tried to be subtle, but everyone noticed. The wait staff publicly called out my vegan meals as they laid my plate in front of me. On excursions, I ate GORP while others enjoyed the gourmet cheese and salami picnics I helped prepare.

I plowed forth with sunny grit and integrity, leading the way up island hills and past lavender farms, trying to stay pleasant when asked about my choices. I was surprised at how blatantly people judged me for helping my body while respecting nature; and several guides scoffed at my food choices, as if I were being hurtful or disrespectful to *them* and their choices. Ostracized and alone among my fellow globe-trotters, I grew quietly defensive. In some ways, the loneliness made it easier for me to travel to Portland on my days off.

Then the call came. One of the guides in Switzerland was sent to France and they needed someone in Europe who spoke at least one of the local languages. My boss was clear, "Do *not* decline this time." Instead of settling into the Pacific Northwest routine, I packed my bags and left for Switzerland the next day. Via first class.

With my first sip of champagne (a free amenity, so I indulged), I noticed a pain in my throat. Within the hour, my entire body ached. The cushy, oversized seat offered no comfort, and the fluffy blanket did nothing for the chills. *Do I have the flu? In summer?* I *never* got sick. Except, of course, when....

I was emotionally over-stressed.

I'd never been diagnosed with anxiety because 1. I didn't have panic attacks, 2. I could function relatively well under stress, 3. diagnoses suggested something was *wrong* with me, though mostly I felt fine, and 4. a medical condition meant pharmaceuticals like anti-depressants, which I vehemently opposed. Nope, intense emotions made me feel more alive. I knew how to become aware, come down, calm down: journal and practice yoga and eat high quality dark chocolate coconut-based ice cream.

But the past few months of stress had caught up with me. *Or is it another sign that I've made a mistake?* Somehow, I navigated my way through Zurich and mounted the correct train to Kandersteg, a tiny mountain town in the Berner-Oberland. When I arrived at the house without my bag (lost in transit), the one leader there was (thankfully) my size and had padded biking shorts and a sports bra to lend me. I took a long nap as flu sweats subsided, then geared up to bike for the next three days, alone, and familiarize myself with the seven-day tour route. I spoke no German yet had a map, a kilo of trail mix and dried fruit, my hydro pack, tea bags, and Swiss francs.

Despite feeling like I'd let down the one human I loved most in the world, and despite a killer sore throat, those three days biking in Switzerland healed me from the inside out. It was cold (which didn't help my chills) and rainy (which didn't help my cough), yet the crisp mountain aroma of wet grass and fondue (which I didn't eat), with a side of magical waterfalls, both nourished me and quashed my stress-illness of independence. I was refreshed and alive!

But what would I eat besides trail mix? Would veganism fly in the land of happy cows grazing in luscious green fields and where cheese wheels aged in small huts on alpine mountainsides? Did my environmental and moral reasoning for veganism hold true in the country that housed the World Health Organization, safety shelters in every basement, hundreds of miles of cross-country bike trails, and entire museums dedicated to age-old traditions such as artisan tarts and wheels of *raclette*? The Swiss couldn't possibly feed all the travelers with meat from the idyllic countryside ruminants, could they? Surely, they would not succumb to companies like Sysco, delivering pre-made schnitzel and frozen sausages, would they?

I had no idea. So, I learned how to say "vegan" in German. It went something like this (translated into English): I don't eat flesh, fish, milk, cheese, butter, or eggs. Extra veggies, *bitte*.

The plump ladies who ran the small restaurants regarded me with disdain. Grunting, they wiped their brows with the backs of their hands as I attempted to understand whether there was cream in the soup. These restaurants were quaint and homey, decorated minimally with dusty shelves of teacups and plates painted with dairy cows and castles. It was like sitting in the chef's own dining room—what were they doing in the kitchens anyway? Surely, making their own *rösti* from scratch. I reasoned that it didn't matter what *they* were making or whether it contained cream, butter, or cheese. It was *my* impact on food production that mattered. One less animal-eater meant helping to keep places like Grindewald as beautiful as possible. I felt mollified by that.

Preparing for client trips was smoother than in the San Juans, with fewer leaders to confront about my diet. I requested the task of driving to Interlaken for groceries. I stocked up on tofu, canned lentils, and beans to supplement meals at the leader house, as well as flax meal and vegetable oil (coconut oil wasn't a "thing" yet) to make cookies for the first round of guests. I reserved a few extra cookies for myself for later.

By the end of the first week, I managed to feel a sense of peace when walking by well-orchestrated, 5-star buffet breakfasts brimming with butter croissants, *Alpkäse, jambon*, and yogurt in the castle above the lake. I insisted on organizing the fondue dinner and barn performance, so I didn't have to sit with the guests and decline hot, melted Gruyere and Emmentaler goodness in their presence. I signed up to teach early morning yoga and guide early morning hikes for those wanting more

111

adventure, in part to avoid eating in community. On one trip I volunteered to make a special pasta meal in the middle of the countryside (yep, Gramma Truppi's sauce) so that I could revel in cooking under the trees all day without judgment. I made local beef meatballs for the guests, grateful for the alone time to meditate on the awkwardness of shaping ground meat in my hands for others while it felt morally wrong for myself. There had to be balance between my efforts for others and my personal preferences.

In late summer, after dinner on the last night of my last trip in a centuries-old, idyllic Tudor-style castle, one guest was prodding me about my life's vision—a conversation that has stuck with me ever since. I adored her, the company owner's dear friend. She didn't agree with my veganism, yet politely acknowledged my environmental passion. She sensed I was a go-getter, a seeker of knowledge, an academic, and someone who took the bull by the horns. What she said next caught me off guard. She stated bluntly, "Jamie, if you want to get anywhere in life, you can never date—let alone marry—a waiter. That would be settling for less than your full potential."

Offended, I replied quietly that I honored Chris for being who he was, for pursuing what he did well. "Status and money are not important to either of us," I said. "Plus, he knows I don't want to get married." But my reply remained on my mind during the sobering midnight drive down the winding road. As the Sprinter van curled around the lake through Brienz toward the train station, I ruminated on what she meant. *Is she attuned to something I don't yet understand? Does she see something specific that would help me achieve my "full potential"?*

For now, I knew Chris and I were happy and in love—Chris was on his way to me that very moment. I was picking him up to bring him back to the castle dormitory. After breakfast I'd say goodbye to the guests, help pack the gear, and then Chris and I would be off for our next together adventure—just like in Thailand. The other trip leaders agreed we could borrow bikes to pedal through small towns and spectacular mountains. Having just learned of Chris's surprise visit a few days prior, I scrambled to pack extra snacks into the panniers, harbor unused train passes, and book a night in a quaint hotel in Mürren—high above the valley of Lauterbrunnen, accessible only by gondola.

Recipe for Doing My Own Thing

I'd return to Kandersteg to help pack up the leader house for the season before traveling with Chris to hike under the shadow of the Matterhorn. He remained patient as we traveled between my Francophone friend's apartment in Paris, where we helped prepare truffled eggs and *coq au vin* (neither of which I ate) and he thoroughly enjoyed the sausage-heavy BBQ at my friend's international dinner in Brussels. I struggled to learn whether there was dairy in Belgian waffles. From there, we'd fly home to Portland to begin anew, all over again.

So it was, I went about the world in my own way, relied on my intuition to guide me, remained true to myself, and found that the man I loved still wanted to come along. It meant I could have my vegan chocolate chip cookies and happily eat them, too. But the concept of "settling" was, well, unsettling.

RECIPE for DOING MY OWN THING

Everyone loves a delish homemade cookie. Hopefully health-conscious people (and vegans) will enjoy with the healthier ingredients that make these relatively guilt-free. I do my own thing with recipes—mixing up ingredients every time—and I encourage you do the same.

Vegan Chocolate Chip Cookies
Yield = 12-18 cookies
Time = 30 minutes

Ingredients
- 2 flax eggs (2 tbsp ground flaxseed & ¼ c water)
- ½ c unbleached whole grain flour
- ½ c oat flour
- ½ c buckwheat flour
- 1 tsp baking soda
- ½ tsp sea salt
- ½ c coconut oil, melted
- 2/3 c unrefined coconut sugar
- 1 tbsp blackstrap molasses
- 1 tsp vanilla extract (or ½ tsp vanilla paste)
- ¼ c unsweetened, non-dairy beverage of choice
- ¾ c dark chocolate chips (vegan, if desired)
- ½ c chopped walnuts

Instructions
1. Heat oven to 350 degrees F.
2. Prepare the flax egg: in a small bowl, whisk ground flaxseed and water. Set aside for 5 minutes.
3. Combine flours, baking soda, and salt in a bowl.
4. Melt the oil.
5. In a small bowl, mix the oil, sugar, flax eggs, molasses, vanilla, and non-dairy beverage until creamy.
6. Add the flour mixture into the wet ingredients a little at a time, mixing with a spoon (not a mixer) until everything has been well blended.
7. Fold in chocolate chips and walnuts until just combined.
8. Drop the dough by spoonfuls onto a silicone baking sheet, shape into balls with fingers, then bake for 8-12 minutes, depending on the size of your cookies. When the edges are golden brown, remove cookies from the oven and let them rest on the baking tray for a couple of minutes before removing them—or eat them right away if you like them hot and gooey!

CHAPTER 13

Recipe for Dieting

We were more financially strapped that fall than ever. Quite irresponsibly I'd followed my heart by taking a job that paid little, lured me away from reality, landed us on another expensive voyage, and left me penniless (again) without job prospects (again) or enhancing my résumé (I *know!*). Chris returned to his job at Wildwood where his position had been held for him. Apparently, he'd told his manager, "I'd like to go to Switzerland to propose to my girlfriend." He told me he didn't intend to *do* that and wasn't even sure what prompted him to make that statement. *Phew.*

I did, however, have a renewed sense of finding my footing and I knew what I needed to do (because I'd done so many times before): find a part-time job in the food industry affording me enough time to figure out next steps, while also literally feeding me. It was easy enough to narrow down my choices to where organic vegan food was part of the gig.

Running home one day from Forest Park, I saw a "Help Wanted" sign in a new café next to a wellness spa, both owned by a naturopathic doctor and a massage therapist. Hired immediately, my job was to make plant-based soup from scratch, artisan coffee, smoothies with superfood extras, and simple lunches for the afternoon shift. I adored the owners, their commitment to plant medicine, and the quaint neighborhood a short jaunt from my own. Time creating plant-based food reconnected me to my love of cooking, and time with like-minded people helped me regain confidence in my commitment to eat a vegan diet. After more than six months trying to sustain veganism in California, Utah, and Europe, I found my flow with conscious, well-balanced food. For the first time, my food choices were accepted by others. In the city that celebrated "weird," veganism was perfectly normal. I also discovered how diet didn't mean *dieting;* my diet reflected my lifestyle and values. I found some peace in that notion.

Though I cooked most of my own food at home (it was obviously cheaper), my few city food explorations targeted vegan and vegan-friendly restaurants, vegan food carts, the vegan grocery store. The quest was for real food—not processed seitan or unidentifiable soy—and chefs who knew how to cook, spice, and adapt veggies as if they were sacred. Chris still wasn't on board with "the vegan thing" but he often accompanied me to vegan-friendly restaurants, where we witnessed vegans drinking plenty of alcohol, too. *Just sayin'.*

In full-on vegan joints, I people-watched, wondering who else fixated on this way of life. I was surprised to notice many overweight vegans. Analyzing more, I observed two subcategories: 1. "Conscious vegans" ate primarily plants and lived a more mindful lifestyle, focused on honoring the body and the planet; 2. "Other vegans" chose to eat animal-free versions of processed food, such as sausage, donuts, and muffins, while seemingly overlooking health on any front. Perhaps the latter were conscious animal lovers vs. health nuts. Nonetheless, the distinction was evident.

I often dubbed category one "conscious vegan yogis" because many typically had a dedicated yoga and meditation or other spiritual practice. They were thin, calm, tattooed with feathers, root veggies, Om symbols, and carried that "after-mat glow" in their cheeks and (sometimes) compassion in their eyes (sometimes criticism, too). Mostly they were the Portland metro version of modern hippies. I loved to be around these people— outwardly, I felt very at home with them. Inside, I wondered if I was spiritual enough to commiserate with their kind.

The "other vegans" seemed aligned with my lack of confidence, drinking habits, and cravings for vegan baked goods. I often found myself amongst them while hungover and ordering vegan croissants, scones, cinnamon rolls, or chocolate-banana Bundt cakes as sides to the "morning-after" cardamom soy lattes with coconut sugar. They, however, smoked cigarettes, were dressed in faux leather and chains, dyed their hair, and moved with an air of radicalism.

Waffling between the two, I wondered whether omnivores noticed the differences, and what they truly thought of me. Ultimately, I decided not to care or to categorize myself.

And as I relaxed a tiny bit about money, I decided it was time to find a real job. I kept searching for lucrative environmental work, but instead I took a position at a contemporary art gallery. Don't judge—this place was *different*, exciting, with a refreshing perspective on artistic intelligence, passion, and design in artwork made from kiln-formed glass. Bullseye Glass Company was phenomenal, with a mission extending well beyond art sales and, importantly, pushed education, science, and cutting-edge creativity to the limits. My boss, Lani, allowed me to help create the menus and source local food when planning artist brunches, docent tours, and other such events (of which there were many). Those efforts became a source of joy in my work. I capitulated to earning a living in a field with creative people and in which I was experienced. I converted my earthly endeavors to weekend shenanigans ranging from blackberry picking to mason bee projects. Plus, veganism was, inherently, an environmental pursuit.

Chris completely had moved on from our Little Known Planet café idea, quite enjoying a stable job that made enough money to pay the bills with a little left over to enjoy some down time. Notably, someone had already created a reputable café with a similar concept to our own, with locations scattered all over the city. In the aftermath of the 2008 financial crisis—and fatigued from financial strain—I, too, relented the business plan.

Since I had plenty of free time after gallery hours, it was only natural to focus my social life around food. Namely, the all-affordable Happy Hour. My gallery co-workers and I frequented a Pearl District pub where my "other vegan" self consumed eco-friendly hoppy IPAs (strong enough to give me a buzz on an empty stomach, as I didn't yet have the funds for food, too). When my pocketbook allowed, I went for the only vegan options on the menu: truffle fries served with vegan mayo or Brussels sprouts drowning in garlic and balsamic vinegar.

Other days, I'd bike across town or take the light rail to meet Michelle and Art, our friends form Malaysia, and other new or old friends. I felt selfish dictating location based on my dietary needs, so I let others choose. Soon I actually *preferred* places with a meat-heavy menu because I could easily decline food I would not eat. Not only did I save money, I also made the wise decision to decline another drink so that I could get home safely. Back at my condo, I'd offset my cocktail with homemade leftover lentil loaf (or something similar). As such, frugality and veganism had evolved into awareness of my body's response to food and drink, thereby increasing my cash flow and improving my habits. Apparently, I had plenty of "conscious vegan" in me, after all.

In fact, my favorite vegan café—recommended by the guy I met in Costa Rica—was located inside a yoga studio, a short bike ride from our condo. When I could finally afford to, I committed to 5:30 (that's am!) yoga classes twice a week. Yoga became another a perfect excuse to opt out of Happy Hour events the night before or drinking late at Wildwood with the other boyfriends and girlfriends awaiting partners after the dining room closed.

Yoga became a non-food way of nourishing my body. Vinyasa flow kicked my ass from the inside out, making it imperative to be both hydrated and awake. I sweated—a lot—and often was dizzy amidst the rapid movements in the sun salutation series. I'd always needed to eat every few hours or I'd become nauseous and shaky, losing my vision and balance if I got up too fast. Now I know those symptoms as classic hypoglycemia (probably driven by years of excessive alcohol and caffeine consumption) but, of course, I didn't understand it back then from a biochemical perspective. I've also always had extremely low blood pressure, which explained the shallow breaths, the need to yawn frequently, and the difficulty of pranayama (I was always a breath or two behind). Yoga was another wake-up call to treat my body with ultimate respect: ample sleep, hydration, nourishment. Well-balanced meals became ever more important and intentional.

Recipe for Dieting

I relied on mostly whole foods versus more expensive packaged foods: grains, nuts, seeds, lentils, beans, tofu, vegetables, and fruit. I'd given up all the crap, hard as it was not to indulge or "cheat" sometimes (except a vegan baked good here or there). Feeling strong and energetic, it was evident that unprocessed, nature-derived foods were more than just fuel; they seemed to supply me with plenty of *nutrients* I needed to feel alive. Plants seemed to explain the beneficial changes happening inside my cells and a metabolism that urged me to appreciate my body more and destroy it less.

Grains. I drew the line at seitan, a highly refined fake meat derived from textured wheat gluten—the vegan version of a hot dog. *No thanks.* I wanted my gluten fix to come from artisan bread. Super-food ancient pseudo-grains were just becoming a phenomenon, so my options were expanding. I began exploring the bulk bins—colorful quinoa, forbidden rice, farro, teff.

Nuts and seeds. Already my favorite snack, I found that soaking seeds and pureeing nuts made for tasty desserts, especially with my favorite additives: fresh fruit, coconut, cacao, coffee, dates, spices. And healthy enough to grab for breakfast as I ran out the door in time to order a latte on my walk to the gallery. Still, I struggled morally with the nut industry, as it seemed unsustainable.

Lentils and beans. Simple, economical foods packed with nutrients—that's all I knew about them. I enjoyed a plethora of legumes in my dinner rotation, made plenty of veggie burgers with beans as the base, and often ate organic soy in its simplest form: tofu.

Soy! It was in *everything,* and the negative estrogenic effects of soy were a newly debated hot topic. I dabbled in tofurky and other plant-based meat-like products that tasted too unnatural to enjoy. Lack of vegan food diversity sank in when I took inventory of soy foods: Tofutti "cream cheese", tofu scrambles, tempeh in stir fry and tacos, soy-based ice cream, silken soy-based pie, soy protein powder.... Knowing most soy was genetically modified (fast forward: 94% by 2018), I wondered about the long-term effects of daily intake of multiple GMO soy products modified to withstand glyphosate (which keeps *only* the GMO soybean plant alive). How would veganism with potential soy-dependence change the way my body *functioned*? Importantly, how was GMO soy even *better* for the environment than, say, beef?

That question inspired some research into genetically modified organisms, modern agriculture, and processed foods. I started by assessing the most challenging area of my diet: plant-based milk options. Because, um, lattes. And vegan yogurt, cheese, butter-like spreads.

Dairy. Alternatives were an ever-changing but still constant issue. Rice milk contained exactly no useful nutrients (that I could surmise), and I was hard pressed to find almond milk (none was organic), let alone cashew, coconut, hemp, macadamia, oat, pea, pecan, pistachio, or any other non-dairy beverages back then. I found one coffee shop offering hemp milk, and I became a regular there. At home, I experimented with my VitaMix to make date-flavored nut milk to enlighten my granola. But I wanted something creamy and nourishing in my lattes: soy was the norm. Soy yogurt, soy cheese, and soy-based vegan butter rife with preservatives and chock-full of other highly refined vegetable oils. *Gross.*

During my plant-based food origins and discovery phase, I attended a LiveWire Radio performance featuring the documentary filmmaker of "King Corn" who discussed the shocking prevalence of corn-derived products. Mostly genetically modified and sprayed heavily with chemicals, corn biproducts spanned from toilet paper to the corn oil in fries and fuel (ethanol); cornstarch in buns; high fructose corn syrup in soda; dextrins and maltodextrins in pretty much everything labeled "sugar free" (at the time); sorbitol in toothpaste; and corn derivatives in antibiotics, aspirin, cosmetics, cleaners, and chewing gum. I started reading processed food ingredient labels for corn, which shockingly also permeated my diet.

The two main mass-commodity, plant-based crops of my lifetime—corn, and soy—contributed heavily to soil depletion; the industries were polluters of our air; and the biproducts wreaked havoc inland and flowed to our ocean waters. Our bodies were inundated with them (so said the hair analysis of the King Corn guy). Plant diversity was suffering. Animal and insect species were disappearing. No wonder the world was sick! We humans were not meant to eat like that. Modern agriculture, aided by the government and abetted by lobbyists, was cheating us.

To survive off a plethora of commercially modified soy and corn products seemed quite unnatural. I assumed people of traditionally vegetarian cultures (*were there any?*) could thrive by eating the same whole plant foods I was eating, yet more in tune with the seasons and their geographical location. Could I, a modern vegan, thrive from plant foods grown the modern agriculture way while also sourcing them ethically? Scientifically, was it even possible to obtain all my daily nutrient needs from food? The vegan body builders said they could (almost—with B12 supplementation). But was that nature's way?

I wanted to test it out, so I became a "conscious local foodie vegan yogi" and spent the next 18 months trying to create recipes with protein-dense, nutrient-concentrated plant foods grown on local, sustainable farms. Notably, it was impossible.

How complex it had become to keep meals simple and ethical!

It was pie crust experimentation that finally got the best of me. Homemade pie was my favorite! Not only for the crispy, buttery crust contrasting the sweet, bursting fruit flavors, but because it was soul food. During summers on our childhood backcountry dude ranch, we didn't have access to much foraging at 6,000+ feet, but we had huckleberries! My sisters and cousins and I would pick berries for hours, then return to the lodge to make pie with our moms. On the hottest of days, we hand-churned ice cream to à la mode our pie (using hail we gathered during summer thunderstorms and stored in the freezer). I cherished those girl-days in the woods—they were endless, joyful, adventurous, and free.

Ever since, making pie has transported me from realism to idealism. In Portland and the Pacific Northwest in general, berries and apples are abundant, so the very act of making pie took me back to my roots. U-pick farms dotted the city environs, wild blackberries lined the roads in wine country, and apples dripped onto every sidewalk.

I'd tried making all imaginable versions of a vegan pie crust using whole grains and oil as unprocessed as I could locate. But the crusts were dense, not flaky, too earthy, and quite simply an utter disappointment.

One day, I shuffled around the corner to City Market, the crème de la crème of Portland grocery shops (which, sadly, has since closed) specializing in traditionally crafted foods like handmade pasta, artisan bread and cheese, and local fish, dairy, and eggs. It also was renowned for hand-crafted charcuterie made from local pigs. The friendly butcher with tattoos of meat-cuts of beef on his forearm asked about the frustration I exhibited. "Oh, you know, I'm stumped at my failed attempts at pie crust." Under my breath I added, "*Vegan* pie crust."

He reached into the refrigerated deli case, then handed me a pint of lard. I stared at the heavy plastic container, whitish and slightly greasy even on the outside. After a long, analytical pause and quick moral exploration, I handed it back to him. He insisted, "Take it. It'll be the best pie crust of your life."

I took it home. It sat in my fridge for a few days until I feared it might go "bad" from prolonged decision making. I tossed it into the freezer, where it sat for months, out of sight yet on my mind. Lard, a biproduct of an animal. No waste. The way hunters and gatherers ate for centuries. My own ancestors probably used it to make amazing pie crust.

Then one day I had a hankering for the duck eggs I'd been buying only for Chris. Darting home from City Market like a kid anxious to open a new toy, I made scrambled eggs guiltily (with veggies and shrooms). I struggled with the pleasure of eating not just an animal-derived food, but an *egg*. The most complex organism on the planet, containing all the DNA and nutrients needed to grow a *chicken*. I managed to choke down those eggs, all right.

Weeks later, one stop at a Saturday market booth and one conversation with one goat farmer about raising and milking goats the natural way opened the *aha!* realization door that environmental stewardship and animal welfare were not just a *thing* in Oregon, but an *obsession*.

"Do you name your goats?" I asked.

"Of course! Well…my children do," replied the farmer, who proceeded to explain the entire *way of life* of raising goats alongside his small flock of hens, a veggie garden, and an orchard.

Recipe for Dieting

It seemed so divine, intuitive, like human nature. I thought I'd found all my peeps in the "conscious local foodie vegan yogi" camp, yet these "intentional enviro-locavores" were really on to something.

I bought the goat cheese. And some walnut-raisin sourdough bread from the booth next to the goat cheese farmer.

At home, I ripped off a chunk of still-warm bread and smothered it with the fresh, creamy cheese. I closed my eyes and breathed deeply before devouring it (*Oh. My. God.*). Silently I thanked the farmer and the baker for this perfectly crafted bite of heaven. I was reborn. Again.

The transition from veganism back to vegetarianism was slow and my solo Saturday morning jaunts to the farmers market became ritualistic. I meandered intentionally from goat cheese booth to aged cheese booth, inquiring about hormones and animal husbandry as much as about the cheese-crafting and rennet processes, while also keeping my dairy intake in check (for all those lactose intolerant reasons). Incorporating small amounts of cheese, eggs—and then raw, local honey—back into my diet was blissful, though I very much enjoyed vegan food most of the time. I still used only flax in my zucchini breads. Why waste pasture-eggs at $6.50/dozen when I can use linoleic-rich flax that not only gives me omegas—albeit tough to convert—but also improves my gut and brain? I used banana or beet puree in my dark chocolate cakes. Again, mostly plants, even before Michael Pollan made the same suggestion.

The next time I made pie crust, though, I used butter from pasture-raised cows. The texture of my pie crust was *much improved*, and I was on the path to more diverse baking experiments. It was a step in the right direction, though I couldn't yet bring myself to use *parts* of an animal. *I mean, what residues from the pig's life permeate the lard?*

I was also progressing along a path toward a quality-food fixation synonymous with dieting culture—restricting foods that didn't fit into my definition of healthy (for me or for Earth), and completely eliminating many pleasure foods out of sheer principle. For me, the shift was poignant, opening up a whole new world of eating and honoring nature's way. Chris, on the other hand, was less than pleased when our restaurant patronage morphed from vegan (clearly defined on most menus in Portland) to inquiries about the origins of the eggs and cheese. Even before Portlandia mocked me for it.

The lard remained in my freezer for some time.

RECIPE for DIETING

This chocolate pie full of healthy fats, protein, and natural sources of satisfying sugar. It may not satisfy every dietary restriction, allergy, or environmentally conscious purchase, yet it's delicious, nutrient-dense, and doubles as a yummy leftover for breakfast alongside a hemp-milk-and-honey latte.

The Best Vegan Chocolate Pie (Tofu-free)
Yield = 8-12 slices
Prep time = 30 minutes
Total time = 2 hours 30 mins (ideally 8 hours)

Crust Ingredients
- 2 tsp coconut oil (preferred)
- ½ c each raw pecans and raw walnuts
- ½ tsp ground cinnamon
- ½ tsp sea salt
- 1 c pitted dates

Filling Ingredients
- 1 c raw cashews
- 2 tsp coconut oil1 1/3 c semi-sweet chocolate chips
- 1 tsp real vanilla or ½ teaspoon vanilla paste
- 2 tbsp pure maple syrup
- Pinch of sea salt
- 1 14-oz can full-fat coconut cream (just the fat/cream on top, ideally refrigerated)

Instructions
1. Boil the water. Place cashews in a bowl, then pour hot water over them. Allow to soak for at least 10 minutes while you prepare the crust.
2. Lightly oil an 8-9" glass pie plate with coconut oil.
3. Prepare the crust.
4. Pulse pecans, walnuts, cinnamon, and salt in a food processor until crumbly.
5. Add dates. Pulse again, scraping nuts and dates from the side, and pulse until the mixture forms a ball.
6. Scoop into pie plate. Use your fingers to press evenly into the bottom and sides of the pie plate.
7. Prepare the filling.
8. Melt chocolate chips in a double boiler (on low). Add vanilla, maple syrup and sea salt. Stir together until perfectly smooth. Remove from heat.
9. Strain cashews and add to a high-speed blender along with just the fat from the coconut cream and the chocolate, maple, vanilla mixture.
10. Blend until creamy, scraping down the sides as needed.
11. Pour filling into pie crust and spread out evenly. Cover and refrigerate for at least 2 hours until the filling sets (ideally 8 hours or overnight). You can speed this up by freezing for an hour, then transferring to the fridge for another hour.
12. Remove pie from fridge about 10 minutes before serving. Enjoy!

CHAPTER 14

Recipe for Different Folks

Chris proposed to me on Kauai during a December downpour that deterred all other tourists from the touristy beach. Apparently, he'd been carrying the ring around in his board shorts for 10 days, but I kept ruining potentially sweet moments with complaints about mosquitos, shrimp-contaminated sushi, and other such tropical minutia. After five years together and plenty of travel, I certainly hadn't considered that particular trip would double as a proposal adventure. I was totally shocked, yet more surprised that I said YES without hesitation. I guess I thought we'd proven we were rock solid.

We both agreed to wed in the summer at the crest of our favorite mountain hike in our beloved Idaho mountains with just a few people and a million wildflowers. We'd planned our reception for several weeks later, on the garden rooftop of my favorite historic brick building in Portland with a band and, of course, locally sourced foodie food and craft brews. Neither event happened.

Apparently, our families cared little about Portland beer culture, food carts, or urban experiences. They could drink anywhere, were happy with simple meals, and preferred natural mountain air. So, we canceled the PDX gig and invited everyone to the mountains. I'd never had any wedding fantasies (except not getting married at all), so the changes mattered little to me. What mattered is that I'd been freaking out (internally) about the "'til death do we part" thing.

One day, an acquaintance asked me specifically if I was ready for marriage. "No! I'm not sure I'm meant for marriage!"

She calmed my nerves, "Truppi, do you love him *now*?"

"Yes, I do."

"Then forever doesn't matter. Marriage isn't what it used to be—it can be whatever you want, and it can last as long as it works for both of you."

I never considered marriage as potentially temporary, but as I thought about my family members and a few friends who had been married and then divorced (including my own fiancée), I was consoled by the idea that I didn't need to overthink *forever*. At the same time, I felt committed to Chris *right then*. I'd also determined that marriage didn't have to mean loss of independence. We could carry on as we always had, right?

In early July, on the morning before our wedding day in Sun Valley, Chris woke me at 6:00 am to provide valuable insight about beer and hiking. Groggy-eyed, I dressed and, as we drove in silence, I wondered if I was to find out I wasn't "the one." Thirty minutes later, we arrived at the trailhead of our wedding hike, where I learned about the case of Bud Light. Before dawn, Chris and his dad planned a father-and-son excursion to hike to our wedding destination and to deliver beer and games. Within a mile, Bill was winded (remember, he lived at sea level), and they both reasoned there'd be no possible way my pregnant older sister-bridesmaid could hike four miles with 2800-plus feet of elevation gain to the saddle at 9400 feet. We'd already decided a helicopter flight for my grammas (and a keg) was a luxury far out of our price range. We'd invited my grammas to the reception a few days later.

My mother and stepmother, Chris's mother and stepmother, and my older sister Jessica wouldn't witness our ceremony. My dad was already risking a heart attack (but he made it!). No grandparents. It wasn't right. We'd have to change the location to meet everyone's needs. I was adamant that, at least, we'd still hike early with whomever still wanted to join us, take pictures in my wedding dress and wildflower bouquet, surrounded by 360 degrees of pristine wilderness views.

Now what? From the trailhead, we drove around the backcountry for a frantic couple of hours until we found the perfect meadow: an off-grid group campsite, which was remarkably unoccupied considering it was the week of (ironically) Independence Day. There was plenty of parking under the evergreens, an easy trail with a slight pitch everyone could navigate to the creek, and a place to set up a cooking area to prep an impromptu dinner for everyone after the ceremony.

Back in town, I penned detailed instructions on a half sheet of paper: drive about six miles over the sketchy summit on a 4WD-only road; a mile or two after the National Forest sign, take the first left before the Forest Service campground and drive another couple of miles to the meadow… Don't forget to breathe and bring a spare tire! I added a few notes like "there's no cell range" and "bring a fleece and bug spray." I printed 50 copies and designated people to start delivering them. I called Gramma Day, who lived only a few hours away, but she couldn't find anyone to drive her up until the reception in two days, as planned. *Dang it.* She was the one who'd wanted to be there the most.

At noon the next day, 28 of us trekked up a winding trail through aspens, over creeks, atop the softly padded trail of pine needles, through sagebrush open slopes, and across meadows that should have been bursting with wildflowers—the entire reason we'd planned our wedding in early July. In the musty old skier's cabin, I donned my second-hand cowboy boots, vegan silk wedding dress (yes, there is such a thing), and toxin-free eyeshadow as my girlfriend tucked a few Forget-Me-Nots into my hair. Our super uplifting metaphysical yet grounded friend-turned-officiant conducted a beautiful white sage "clearing ceremony" as we gathered in a circle overlooking the endless expanse of mountains. We felt small and insignificant, yet wholly embraced by the vast oneness of nature connecting us with close friends and family.

By the time we hiked down and I showered and changed, a downpour delayed our drive over the summit. But when the sun came out and we drove over the pass to the ceremony meadow we were greeted with a rainbow. I was surprised to see rows of white chairs set up with a river-rock-lined aisle between them leading to the creek and an arbor built by my soon-to-be father-in-law, constructed out of wood he found around the campsite. Someone had installed our homemade "Gettin' Hitched" party flags between trees, and two of my besties had clipped giant poppies from a blooming garden for my bouquet (since wildflowers were scarce). Everything was perfect.

In front of the trickling creek and meadow-mountain backdrop and everyone we loved, I promised to make smoothies for Chris when he was well and veggie broth when he was sick. He vowed to go to the ends of the earth to find real-butter croissants for me.

In the chaos of changing everything about our wedding day, I don't remember thinking about food or feeding anyone. Thankfully, my family did! An elk taco dinner magically appeared out of nowhere. I can only guess who planned the meal and set up kitchen prep tables, tents to shield the rain, an assembly line of camping stoves, and a hand-washing station that would double for dishwashing. I was asked to ignore the waste of paper plates, napkins, and disposable cutlery (for just that night), and just be grateful for the immense effort that went into both the meal and ceremony set-up.

The entire wedding marathon week was a massive group endeavor. With a small budget, I was fixated on serving everyone the best quality food for days, which meant cooking from scratch. The night before our wedding, we a prepared a huge and hearty family meal of homemade pasta sauce, meatballs, spaghetti, and salad—another group undertaking. The wedding reception menu—two days after we married—was a bit more calculated: a salad bar for 125 people. It was also quite laborious.

Every great wedding requires delish food and free-flowing drinks. Since I'd been forewarned by family not to offer a vegetarian meal—I mean, why make the meal about the bride?—I shifted my ideals just slightly. Goal One: Feed everyone with high-quality, hearty, filling, and plentiful food. Goal Two: Offer a delish array that our favorite people were pumped to eat, and which complied with my vision of healthy eating. Goal Three: keep it affordable and collaborative by asking everyone to pitch in. Nourish everyone…that was my love language. I proudly announced the "build-your-own-salad-and-sandwich bar!" With *meat*. Potluck style.

Bring on the excel spreadsheet! My favorite organizational tool for mapping, complete with grids, categories, and splashes of color. On one spreadsheet, the grandiose food list. First, a few appetizers and simple side dishes. Then, salad ingredients: greens of course, plus every possible fresh topping I wanted (no to those mini corn things, but yes to cornichons, grated carrots and beets, cooked quinoa, candied nuts, hard-boiled eggs, sheep feta, olives, and artichoke hearts). For the meat eaters, elk steak I pre-ordered from a local ranch and free-range chicken from an organic farmer ("pasture-raised" wasn't a clarifying term yet), which Chris and I would supply for the omnivores. Next, the sandwich bar: Italian cured meats (prosciutto, Genoa salami), different breads (locally sourced), cheeses (several varieties), toppings (sliced tomatoes, arugula), and condiments (Dijon, Vegenaise, etc.). Finally, beverages: alcohol and good mixers (no Coke or Margarita Mix, thank you very much), sparkling water with actual juice (no "natural flavors"), organic juice drinks for the kids, iced "swamp water" (homemade). Someone convinced me to supply bottled water, despite my fear of toxins in the eternal pollutants of plastic bottles and the waste of money on what I viewed as a commercialized tap water industry. I cringed yet conceded.

On another spreadsheet, following every guest's name were columns for their food preferences, the number of adults and kids in their party, and their food assignment. In lieu of gifts, we asked everyone to bring a potluck item or two. I carefully considered their budget, their understanding of my vision for the item, their love or loathe of cooking, and whether they'd be traveling a long distance or had access to a local kitchen. For a large family on a tight budget traveling from hours away, and without regard for GMOs or toxins: "four cans of large black olives." For my Francophile friend who had no kids and wrote her own cookbook: "a side of prosciutto-wrapped and grilled asparagus." For my busy former gallery boss who appreciated good food: "a spread of nitrate-free Italian salami, a wedge of semi-hard sheep cheese, and figs or dates." Other locals were assigned simple to prep items like sandwich rolls from the local artisan bakery while those flying in had simple items like organic lettuce.

Everyone seemed game to pitch in, but we didn't really offer a choice. I was so caught up in socializing and infinite other details that I admit I didn't notice the incredible amount of effort it took for everyone to lay out the food. Did we have enough serving bowls, plates, utensils? Who was conducting the food table placement? What to do when people showed up late with an important item? I had implicit faith in my new hubs, who had managed many-a-catering-event in his work. Whether he did, in fact, oversee our potluck banquet, I still have no idea.

And the dang cake. My dad was adamant that every wedding must have a wedding cake—I wanted pie. I probably should have *ordered* a cake but, again, we didn't realize we'd have 100-and-something people coming to Idaho. I asked one of my old roomies, Louise, an amazing baker, to create our wedding cake. Vegan not required. I gave her carte blanche, with some suggestions. Wow! She crafted a three-tiered, 18-layer cake with alternating mini-layers of cinnamon, coffee, vanilla (or something equally delightful) encased in a slick white icing and adorned with beautiful, orange poppies from one of her client's gardens. She knew the flowers would complement my makeshift bouquet two days prior and the flavors would complement bourbon, per her esteemed palate and my drink of choice.

Louise's masterpiece also paired well with a liberal scoop of Vanilla Island, a delectable and creamy coconut-based, vegan ice cream. At the time, Coconut Bliss (now called Cosmic Bliss) was still a small company based in Eugene, Oregon, and a friend living there knew the owners. Sally encouraged me to reach out to them about bulk ice cream, which she would bring to our wedding. The ice cream gurus generously gifted us *five gallons* of Bliss in exchange for several professional photos of the wedding couple serving the tasty treat, to post on their blog. Done!

So, ya see? The groom, my father, and my new in-laws had their steak and cake, and the bride got her vegetarian salad and ethically sourced, vegan ice cream.

RECIPE for DIFFERENT FOLKS

Keys to a successful salad meal: balanced nutrients, complimentary flavors, options, and consideration for everyone's dietary differences. This recipe template offers a virtually endless options, so consider numbers, cultural theme, and type of celebration as you build your ingredient list and prepare. Add sides, breads, desserts, and beverages to complement your meal—or, ask your guests to bring them!

Salad for Everyone
Yield = 2-125
Prep time = variable

Ingredients
VEGGIES
- Mixed greens of choice
- Something purple, like radicchio or cabbage
- Colorful bell peppers or tomatoes
- Colorful carrots and/or beets (raw or cooked)
- Cruciferous, cooked or raw (Romanesco, Brussels sprouts, etc.)
- Green beans (blanched) or peas of choice (fresh)
- Mixed potatoes or root veggies (roasted)
- Fresh herbs like dill, parsley, or mint

GRAINS (cooked)
- Quinoa
- Farro, wheat berries, or another whole grain

PROTEIN
- Hard-boiled eggs
- Beans, like garbanzo or white/cannellini
- Steak, fish, or chicken (for omnivores)
- Nuts & seeds

FRUITS
- Avocado
- Green, black, and purple olives
- Dried cherries, currants, apricots, and/or figs

DAIRY
- Goat cheese or sheep feta
- Parmesan or pecorino
- Mozzarella di bufala, or other genre-related cheese

PICKLED VEGGIES
- Sauerkraut
- Asparagus, radishes, red onions, etc.
- Capers

DRESSINGS
- Caesar
- Herb, garlic & shallot
- Simple lemon, Dijon, olive oil & honey
- Oil & vinegar

CHAPTER 15

Recipe for Distinguishing Values

Whenever I ventured from a metropolis, I prepared myself mentally for the difficulty in locating food that satisfied me. Sure, I could find a vegetarian breakfast of eggs and spinach almost anywhere, but my aversion to conventionally raised products caused a moral dilemma in my heart and my vocal cords resisted ordering inhumane and potentially toxic menu items that were also uninspiring. After much inner turmoil, I reasoned there must be enough nutrients in plant-based foods to offset the chemicals used to grow them, so eating as vegan as possible seemed the best route while on the road.

Unfortunately, rural towns were the worst places to experiment with such pragmatism. Why, with agricultural land as far as the eyes could see, were small town restaurants relying on cheap, mass-produced monocultural foods from major supply corporations, delivered frozen in semi-trucks from lord knows where, versus serving up a diversity of fresh, locally grown food?

Because…modern agriculture was a far cry from family farming.

In small touristy towns touting a wine culture, the food was surprisingly sub-par in terms of quality, offered nothing of the terroir, or tried to mimic wine culture from somewhere else rather than celebrating its own. Recreational, outdoorsy towns were ripe with joints touting the locals' gut-wrenching "greasy spoon," with few to no choices exhibiting local harvest or history. Restaurants everywhere served similar iterations of rich, saucy, meaty foods and giant plates of melty cheese, cured pig, and bland bread. The same scenario was commonplace all over the country, relying on Agribusiness and wreaking havoc on our precious, expansive land.

There were anomalies, of course, but no small-town restaurant compared to the food sanctuary my little sister has cultivated over the years. Visiting Jaclyn's property in the middle of nowhere along a Central Idaho river canyon was like entering a portal to a food fantasy. To this day she cultivates a huge garden supplying all her own veggies, tubers, herbs, and berries. She sources most of her fruit from heirloom orchards and forages from the backcountry. She eats and barters with eggs from chickens she raises and harvests most roosters for the winter. She hunts game, procures pork from farmers she knows, and buys salmon from the Native tribes. There, we eat like royalty.

At her house, food is at the root of every activity—a hike to scout elderberries, wild morels, or a fall herd. A river float to fish for trout. Full-day excursions planned around huckleberry picking. A drive up the canyon to load up bushels of apples or peaches for homemade crisp.

Though it had become our family's norm, this kind of food was no longer the cultural norm even in Idaho. We'd been raised by a mother who cooked most meals and baked most desserts from scratch. In our teen years, our father had taken to gardening and transformed our backyard into a mini organic farm. We'd been raised to grow and harvest food, and we knew it tasted better than anything we could buy at the grocery store or eat in a restaurant.

In Jaclyn's kitchen, though, I had little to contribute. I focused on bringing specialty items like fresh bread from my favorite Portland bakery; pinot noir from Willamette Valley; "fresh hop" beers from Deschutes, Rogue, and Ontario brewing

Recipe for Distinguishing Values

companies; and a joint rolled with weed grown in NE Portland. But it wasn't the wine or weed that made me forget my food principles. It was while visiting Jaclyn's house that I'd grown curious to taste meat again.

It was a relief not to fixate on what I "could" or "couldn't" eat, because we shared the same values for quality and harmony with nature. Tucking vegetarianism aside, I ate the grilled steelhead (caught two days prior) my sissy prepared with fresh-harvested garden herbs, barbecued beets, and her version of Gramma Truppi's *meneste* (beans & greens), 90% of which was grown on her land. It was the first fish I'd eaten in almost two years, since our fateful marine excursion in Costa Rica. I don't know why, but somehow it seemed different to consume food that was harvested from inland freshwater versus on a recreational tour.

Jaclyn's hens' eggs lured me in, too. To this day, I've still never seen yolks as orange as those from her coop, nor shells as perfectly robust. Naturally, I also wanted to sample breakfast in its entirety: potatoes, tomatoes, and peppers from her garden; morels from the woods; eggs from her feathered friends; rosemary-lemon no-knead bread that we made the night before; grape juice Jaclyn made from the neighbor's fall harvest; and fair-trade coffee roasted in Portland (my single contribution). A sumptuous breakfast. Perfect in every way. *What will I do upon leaving her food haven?*

I'd eliminated conventional animal bi-products and mass-produced vegetables and was physically stronger (and looked and felt) better than ever before. And yet, I was morally fatigued—from taking on too much, lack of life purpose, and perhaps actual depletion at the cellular from the stress of living up to my ideals. I'd cherry-picked my food because I was privileged enough to do so—in my life, in a city, and even on a small budget. Tofu from overseas, nutritional yeast from who-knows-where, organic beans and lentils from Fred Meyer, cheese and eggs thanks to local farmers—but was it sustainable (and wholly ethical) long-term? It clearly wasn't sustainable everywhere. I had to get to the bottom of these conflicting sentiments.

Our dinner experience in North Idaho that very night was helpful in doing so. Jaclyn and I drove to another small, Idaho agriculture town on a wide prairie to meet our dad for dinner.

Town was nestled between miles of fields irrigated by endless links of metal sprinklers on giant wheels stretching out all around, herds of black cows against golden, autumn hillsides that flanked the freshly cut fields. From the steep grade descending into town, the highway seemed to run right into a looming, silver grain silo, the hub around which the John Deere outlet and Angus beef restaurant sprawled out like cogs in a well-oiled wheel. We met our dad there for dinner—at the *steak* house.

A typical small-town joint, a 1960s-era flat-roofed building, the restaurant reeked of everything I loved and hated about rural farming. There were stuffed animal heads mounted salon-style on every wall—a 7-point buck, a 7-point bull elk, a moose, a mountain lion…. As we waited for a table, I read the framed newspaper review on the lobby wall. It boasted local meat: beef, fattened in a town four hours away and processed in a plant even further from there. Then, what? Shipped back to town? What's the definition of "local"? No mention of "grass-fed," though the fields appeared to grow grain and alfalfa.

It was clear I knew little about commercial farming and the beef industry, but it must have meant something to the locals to have "local beef" because the place was packed and the menu replete with a variety of beef options I'd never heard of—flat iron, ribeye, short ribs. (Also, coconut shrimp—in the middle of Idaho!).

When I asked if there were any non-meat options, the 12-year-old hostess chirped, "Salad."

Right. Salad. Every salad included meat: BBQ chicken, strip steak (what's that?), shrimp, ham. There wasn't even a choice of salad *without* meat, although the "Choice Caesar" came with a choice of chicken, salmon, or shrimp. Lovely.

Did the Caesar dressing have dairy? Eggs? Anchovies? I was afraid to ask. I ordered the Choice Caesar with dressing on the side, no meat, a side of steamed broccoli, and bread. With olive oil. Basically, I ate dry romaine, broccoli, and bread for dinner. I critiqued the nutritionally imbalanced meal I'd created, while others critiqued me for my choices. Nothing new. As usual, I'd rebalance with the next snack, or meal, or the next dinner back at my own home in Portland.

Recipe for Distinguishing Values

On the long drive back to the city, the scattered clusters of wind turbines on I-84 seemed peaceful, beautiful in some manmade way that instilled hope for a more harmonious future. They commanded my attention, somehow compatible with the dams and factories, and yet less intrusive than other jarring, man-made structural feats. Cattle grazed peacefully under the turbines and powerlines. At first, I thought, "How sad for the cows to live next to the noisy, polluted highway! I wonder if the electricity affects the quality of the meat?" And then, "How lucky they are!" They had no idea how great their lives were compared with their unfortunate relatives who were corn fed and crammed into barracks somewhere in rural America and, likely, also nearby.

I was starting to view all open areas with a renewed sense of beauty, longing to have a meadow and a hill of my own, an expansive landscape to farm and maybe even raise a couple of kids (eek! I mean, goats).

That night I made spaghetti squash (from my dad's garden), roasted with tomatoes and garlic (both from my sissy's garden), and potatoes (from the Portland farmers market); canned lentils (from the co-op); sauteed greens (from Trader Joe's); fresh basil and oregano (from the herb pot on my porch); ricotta forte (from City Market, but actually imported from Italy); and apples (from a neighbor's tree).

It was the perfect seasonal meal to nourish me, and to get me excited for our upcoming second-annual Harvest Party. The event was the single gathering I wanted to be known for, an excuse for Chris and I to gather with friends in costumes to celebrate the seasonal abundance. The requirement was that at least one part of every potluck dish was thoughtfully purchased from a local farmer or harvested from a garden. It was also a way for me to start a tradition around food since I didn't have a garden or seasonal café of my own.

Portland—such a mecca for people like me. I felt at home with others' food values ranging from quality carnivorous to global vegan; where food eccentricities were celebrated, not scorned; where artists, writers, athletes, and business-y people were proud to be on the waitlist to sample Vietnamese fish-sauce wings, bone marrow chowder, or bacon-and-bourbon-infused donuts. Or vegan *bibimbap*. In a city demanding to keep things weird, I felt oddly normal and at home. I now had some idea how privileged we were that our food cravings could so easily be satiated. Food that met my standards was accessible all around me.

RECIPE for DISTINGUISHING VALUES

I love this recipe because it's easy and hearty. One of my grandmother's hidden gems, it originally calls for pancetta and spicy pepper flakes. I tend to make mine with elk sausage or locally raised fresh pork sausage. Caution: this recipe might convert a vegetarian into an omnivore.

Swiss Chard with Cannellini Beans & Pancetta (Meneste)
Yield = 4 as a side dish
Prep time = 10 minutes
Total time = 40 minutes

Ingredients
- ¼ c pine nuts
- ½ c onion
- 6 cloves garlic
- 2 large tomatoes
- 2 bunches Swiss chard (or kale, spinach, or other leafy greens)
- 1 tsp dried oregano (or 1 tbsp fresh)
- 1 can (15-oz) cannellini beans (or another white beans)
- ¼ lb pancetta
- 3 tbsp extra virgin olive oil
- ¼ c pecorino

Instructions
1. Toast the pine nuts in a dry cast iron skillet on medium heat, stirring every few minutes. When the nuts begin to turn golden and slightly aromatic, reduce heat to medium-low and toast for another minute or so. Turn off heat and remove from heat.
2. Prep veggies.
3. Peel and dice the onion and peel and mince the garlic.
4. Chop tomatoes.
5. Wash Swiss chard, remove the ribs and chop ribs into small pieces. Separately, stack the greens, roll them into a "jelly roll" and slice into "ribbons".
6. Pluck oregano leaves from the stems, if using fresh herb.
7. Rinse and strain liquid from beans.
8. Slice pancetta into strips.
9. Grate cheese.
10. Heat olive oil in a large cast iron or stainless-steel skillet (with lid) on medium. Add the onions and cook covered, stirring occasionally, until they become translucent.
11. Add garlic and oregano and sauté with onions for about 1 minute.
12. Add Swiss chard ribs and pancetta and sauté for 1-2 minutes, covered.
13. Add tomatoes and beans and cook, covered, 1-2 minutes more.
14. Stir chard ribbons into mixture. Cover. When they turn bright green, stir one last time, then turn off heat. Toss with toasted pine nuts and top with pecorino.

CHAPTER 16

Recipe for Dietetic Advice

Don't even get me started on hospital food. I've always hated hospitals, but not *because of* the crappy, nutrient-poor fare. It's the sterile smell of hand sanitizer, bleach, plastic tubes, and rubber gloves. The boxy waiting rooms with stock images of mountainscapes, Formica counters and floors with alternating shades of pukey beige and not-quite-sage. Heart-rate monitors beeping and employees typing on keyboards in the otherwise silent hallways. Uniformed staff reminding me of sci-fi movies with people placement by caste, unable to evolve or escape. Maybe that was how I viewed Western medicine in general—our society blindly caught in an illness trap.

As I entered the oncology wing, I avoided the solemn faces and apathetic movements of hospital staff and other patients while searching for my older sister's room-with-a-view. The air was ominous, confusing, overwhelming and I was desperate for a glimpse of hope.

Jessica was recovering from a stem cell transplant. I'd driven 350 miles to keep her company while she was attached to IVs. A steady stream of family had been cycling in and out of her home over the past nine months, cooking, cleaning, and playing with her young son on days when Jessica was too toxic from chemo to be in the same room with him, other days too weak to get out of bed at all. That day, our mom was grandmothering at her house, so I could be at the hospital. From an outsider's perspective, Jess was handling this whole shitty cancer diagnosis and treatment with grace—connecting with her version of God, trusting her medical team, taking advice from others who'd had the bandwidth to research the benefits of functional mushrooms and grass-fed bison.

From my perspective, she was fearful and uncertain (as was I).

I watched in silence from across the room—far enough not to infect her with whatever I might have brought with me from the city, silently witnessing the flow of technicians, nurses, oncologists, and others whose roles were unclear to me. Subconsciously, I kept holding my breath while tracing the tangled mess of interconnected wires between contraptions measuring her body's levels of platelets, neutrophils, leukocytes.

My head pulsed after repeated, failed attempts to decipher the foreign words she spoke: dolasetron for nausea, fluconazole the antifungal, some kind of antibiotic, another med to prevent some disease I'd never heard of. It was the language of allopathic medicine, to which I was grossly unfamiliar. I only wanted to know whether she was recovering well or not.

Trying to understand a stem cell transplant inside my sister's bones—and how that would help heal ovarian cancer, which had seeped throughout her body—I pictured the only related process: our permaculture project in Thailand. First, remove unwanted life (extract the cancerous marrow); then spray herbicides, insecticides, and fungicides on whatever remains (obliterate the "bad" stuff with highly toxic chemicals); after decimation of even the healthy plants, follow with restorative layers of compost and microorganisms (transfusions of new blood, infusions of nutrients); eventually, recover (a regenerated, thriving ecosystem).

Evidently, the IV was the hospital's mechanism of restoration, artificially supplying life-giving fluids with vitamins and minerals for recovery when a weakened body has lost appetite, vomits, expels. Unlike nature—which heals naturally—the chemo, radiation, and stem cell treatments appeared to make my sister's body hover on life's tipping point. Does the body see this kind of rapid marrow destruction—meant to extinguish imminent death itself—as an opportunity to begin anew? And do medical humans really understand how to oversee that process? Or is it a crapshoot every time?

My mind was ablaze with analyzing and ineffectual attempts to comprehend the semi-synchronistic activities going on around me, around her, inside her. As if she could read my skepticism, Jessica cautioned me to "withhold dietary commentary in approximately fifteen minutes." I presumed she was warning me against saying anything explosive that might offend her caregivers.

When the Registered Dietitian entered the room, Jessica shot me a look that meant, "Listen to *this*." Then she asked the dietitian about foods to help her recovery. The RD shook her head, looked down at her clipboard and replied, "I'm sorry, but food is not going to help you heal. Just eat whatever you want."

Wait, what!? Wasn't food like the compost for depleted soil, rich and chock-full of nourishment? I didn't understand. What could the RD possibly mean?

My sissy's eyes met mine, *"I know, right? Can you believe that?"*

Truly, it was unbelievable. I looked down at my six-pound bio-chem book I'd brought to keep up on my studies, but which was simply burdensome on my lap. The open pages displaying shapes and acronyms and compounds all formulaically functioning, designed as if by some miraculous mathematical formula to sustain life against infinite odds. How could healthy, nature-derived food—with concentrated nutrients that literally formed the essence of everything on earth—not matter in healing the very life form it created? How could humans, who studied chemical reactions, cell function and disease, misunderstand what seemed so fundamental to the wellness or illness of all organic matter? But maybe dietitians didn't study science. At the time, I honestly didn't know. Maybe they were trained to simply to adjust the electrolytes in the IV per doctor's orders. No idea. I'd assumed their role was to monitor a patient's *diet*; but then, the hospital food, so processed and unappetizing, could hardly be called food.

I shook my head and glanced down at my textbook. I'd been studying for months and was in my second course which, through my tears, now looked like a jumble of positives and negatives and letters, a foreign language, a human's attempt at interpreting the natural world. Food. Soil. Cells. Energy. Life. Though uncertain where my studies would lead, the urge to understand the effects of food on the human body had guided me to entertain graduate programs in nutrition, which required a science background. Science *and* nutrition. They were one and the same. Why, then, did the medical field view food and it's biochemical activity in the body as ineffectual for healing?

Even before studying the role of food on our interconnected matrix of functioning, I knew Jessica's body was chemically active. Yes, it had been depleted first by a tumor, then by cancer, followed by chemicals. She trusted that her medical team understood the potential of chemical interactions to result in renewal. And like me, she also had faith in food.

When the RD left the room, I asked my sissy what she wanted to eat, since she was given the go-ahead to choose literally *anything*. She was fragile and pale. Malnourished, although I didn't yet understand the gravity of malnourishment. I had only a basic understanding of nutrition and the human body. I had experienced how cleaning up my own diet reduced both weight and inflammation. Energy from certain foods created energy in my body, and lack of energy from other foods sucked energy out of my body. I believed the right foods could help Jessica recover.

Unfortunately, the anti-nausea meds also eradicated her appetite and, ironically, everything made her sick to her stomach. So, she was afraid to eat—especially her favorite comfort foods—for fear that she'd throw them up and be unable to eat those foods again.

Tears ensued. Hers, and then mine.

It was the first time I'd seen Jessica cry since her cancer was identified. Unlike me, she cradled her emotions, kept them reserved. A while back, she clearly stated she didn't want to talk about her cancer—no discussion of the diagnosis (rare), the prognosis (dire), the data (or lack thereof), the treatment (a headache *and* a stomachache), or the fact that her insurance dropped her (something about fine print). She shared details

Recipe for Dietetic Advice

with her husband and our parents about her panic, the pain in her body and in her heart, and her desire to "make peace her spirituality" (per her oncologist's advice). When she wasn't actively in treatment, she wanted to feel normal, live an ordinary day, simply be a mom, a wife, a friend, a teacher.

But she couldn't eat, and nothing was normal.

Her insinuation on privacy meant I was off the hook for not completely understanding, though it also fueled my naivete: I was certain Jessica would be in the less-than-one percent who survived this rare, fucking cancer. She was a Truppi, after all.

When she mustered up exactly zero suggestions for food she might be able to swallow, I decided to make the decision for her. Otherwise, what the heck was I doing there besides feeling frustrated, confused, and helpless? I was sitting around in an oncology room *not* talking about cancer and doing a half-assed job of finishing my homework. She needed me, and I felt totally useless. I started hyperventilating (hospitals trigger that in me), and I was desperate for fresh air.

I zipped up my raincoat, marched right out of the room, and trekked to the health food store, which was, surprisingly, only a mile or so away. Despite the bitter rain, I marched up the hill in my waterproof boots, reusable grocery bag in tow, and cacophony mushrooming in my mind. My task: buy food. Something nourishing. Simple. Not too spicy. A smattering of foods, perhaps, in case one item was a bust. I wandered around, buying a bit of everything I considered both comfort food and healthy food. A perfectly ripe banana. A small box of butternut squash soup. A protein bar with some dark chocolate. Green juice. All organic.

When I returned, our dad had arrived and was keeping her company. He'd been with her a lot, witnessing infinitely more of the crazy ovarian cancer shit, intimately entangled in her treatment. He watched as I displayed the options on top of the mostly empty mini-fridge near the window. She thought she felt well enough—and was hungry enough—to try the banana. She ate it, slowly, reluctantly. She threw it up. She cried. I cried. Dad sighed. I apologized. She just lay there, in her hospital gown and sheets, defeated. So was I. So was Dad.

Years later, I'm still plagued by the dietitian's inept advice, poignant as it was. Witnessing a dietitian shrug off the potential of healing foods was the fuel that propelled me to finish my science coursework and pursue an advanced degree in integrative health. I slowly unpacked her meaning of "food doesn't matter." Perhaps she was saying, "It doesn't matter *what* you eat, just eat *anything* you can keep down." Is that what underlies serving the worst hospital food imaginable—that at least it's *something* sick patients could swallow and, if they were lucky, also digest? Perhaps the rationale was that the IV supplied anything else needed? While I judged the RD's advice and, generally, the entire Western medical model (because no part of me understood), I sensed an insatiable hunger to comprehend what I didn't know then.

Over the course of the next year, when Jessica was home, caught between trying to heal and trying not to die, we discussed simple recipes for grass-fed buffalo meat, avocado smoothies with ginger, turmeric atop sweet potatoes. She couldn't swallow pills (they made her puke), so medicinal mushrooms were out. So were anti-inflammatories. Organic chemistry provided no viable solutions—I hadn't yet learned the connection between cell function, the immune system, nourishment, and disease.

When Jess was well, she made her childhood favorite comfort food—boxed macaroni and cheese. Each time, she prayed she wouldn't throw it up. While I wanted her to eat something more nutrient-dense, I knew the dietitian would approve because that high-carb, deliciously creamy and salty meal brought her courage and maybe a momentary spark of what it felt like to live without worry. Like when we were young kids and our parents worked around the clock. Once Jessica was old enough to turn on the stove without supervision and strong enough to carry a hot pot of noodles and water to the colander in the sink, mac & cheese was the first meal she prepared for her two little sisters. It was her growing-up moment of confidence, capability, nurturing. In her adult illness, it was still the meal she provided for the child inside who needed to be taken care of.

I bought organic mac & cheese for her. It was the only thing I could do to feel slightly helpful.

RECIPE for DIETETIC ADVICE

When given the green light to eat anything, why not a homemade, super healthy version of our favorite comfort food? My kids love it because Auntie Jessica loved it, and that's comfort enough for me. Consider breaking the steps into 2 days and ask someone else to wash the many dishes.

Homemade Healthy Mac & Cheese
Yield = 6-8
Prep time = 40 minutes
Total time = 1 hour 30 minutes

Ingredients (all organic, if possible)
- 1 small butternut squash, cut into cubes
- 2 tbsp olive oil, divided
- 2 tsp sea salt, divided
- 1 head cauliflower, cut into florets
- 12 oz noodles of choice (I prefer shells)
- 1 head broccoli, cut into florets, or 1 c green peas
- 1 tsp garlic powder or 2-3 garlic cloves, peeled
- 2 tbsp butter, ghee, or olive oil
- 8 oz gruyere, grated
- 1 Costco-sized log of goat cheese or two normal logs of soft chèvre
- 1 c veggie stock, ideally low-sodium and homemade
- Optional: 1 can wild-caught salmon

Instructions (the short version)
1. Heat the oven to 375 degrees F.
2. Prep all ingredients.
3. Toss butternut squash cubes into half the olive oil and sea salt. Bake until soft, 20-25 minutes, turning once.
4. In another casserole dish, toss cauliflower florets with the remaining olive oil, sea salt, and garlic. Bake alongside squash for 20 minutes or until soft.
5. Cook the pasta according to the package instructions.
6. Prepare the cheesy sauce. In another medium pot add butter and melt on medium heat. Add the gruyere and goat cheese. Stir until melted and well combined. If too thick, add stock.
7. Add 1 c squash and 2 c cauliflower to a high-speed blender with 1/2 c stock. Blend until creamy, then pour slowly into the cheese sauce. Stir to combine. Stop when you've reached desired consistency. Taste and adjust flavors. Freeze leftover cauliflower/squash/stock for a future meal.
8. When the noodles are almost al dente (done), add the broccoli or peas to the same pot. Simmer with noodles until veggies brighten, about 2 minutes. Strain.
9. Add the noodles and broccoli back into the large pot. Scoop cheesy mixture over the top. Stir until well-coated.
10. If you'd like to increase protein and healthy fats, fold in strained, canned salmon.
11. Serve warm. Grate extra cheese on top if you (or your kids) need more salty goodness.

CHAPTER 17
Recipe for Decision Making

I'm not sure what it is about the expectation of baby-making after marriage, but it didn't take long for Chris to remind me about my public wedding vow for bearing fruit. I was perfectly content using our life challenges as excuses for "waiting." Money was one of them, but we'd already recovered from some of the hardest times and were out of the recession depths without foreclosure or bankruptcy. We'd sold a couple of properties—including our beloved historical Portland condo. We moved into a LEED-Certified high-rise that aligned with Chris's vision for a swanky pad yet opposite my desire for a humble, affordable apartment that would free up some monthly funds (shockingly, not to travel).

I was budgeting to have flexibility to visit Jessica when she needed help, and to continue my education, which Chris didn't exactly support. Besides the permaculture course (the knowledge of which I wasn't using), I'd also invested in a yoga teacher training course (yet lacked the self-confidence to teach). With my shift toward nutrition, naturally Chris was skeptical that more education would mean anything more than occupying time and absorbing money. I simply loved learning. Wasn't that enough?

And I had the independence to take classes, thanks to Chris's night schedule and my boss's flexibility. Plus, I loved so much about my work, which often trickled into weekends, nights and traveling—artist events, educational tours, gallery openings, art fairs. I felt purposeful in gallery efforts that helped push the envelope of science and creativity. Studying chemistry would complement all that; having kids would botch it up.

Internally, I also argued I was finally content with my body—why mess that up with pregnancy too? I was as fit as ever: still overly long-limbed and short-waisted but strong, toned, and muscular. To enjoy wearing different kinds of clothes was surprisingly freeing, as was the newfound feeling that I could conquer anything physically, even with tendonitis in both forearms and a persistently sore piriformis resulting from my yoga practice itself.

Plus, having finally reached peace and balance with my food choices, I wasn't keen to distort my meals, either, with morning sickness or random cravings for foods that didn't fit into my value box. In fact, eating out had become fun again (and we could afford it) because my diet was more flexible. Socializing included gathering at trendy new restaurants all over the city advertising collaboration with Oregon farms. Family gatherings and travel became easier, too, because quality and sustainable food replaced veganism as the root of my meal planning. I felt at ease with alcohol—drinking less while enjoying it more from craft distillers and brewers, many of whom I knew personally.

I loved my freedom! Unbound by mortgages, finances, inflexible food restrictions, I wanted to deepen my experiences with people and places—and reexamine my dreams, of course! Surely, children would halt my evolution. In the shadows of that plentiful life, I selfishly ignored the elephant in the bedroom. And time was ticking. Chris wanted a family; I had an aversion to everything motherhood.

To my core, I was a Bohemian not cut out to be a mama. I'd never been drawn to kids. I was repulsed by their snotty noses, whiny voices, dirty faces, soiled clothes. As a teenager, I babysat only to earn money to travel to Europe with my French class and acquired only one useful tool: plopping kids in front of a movie. I preferred mowing lawns, selling berries, and harvesting

Recipe for Decision Making

the garden. As a young traveler, I was the person on planes and trains who cringed and cleared my throat when babies cried.

As an adult, when my friends began having children, I jumped at planning baby shower menus and bringing a hearty postpartum meal, but it never occurred to me to *hold* their infants. They smelled like spoiled milk and dried poop. They were sticky, messy, and required constant attention. Their cooings were the anti-music to my nervous system; surplus cheap-plastic toys were stifling; overflowing diaper bags seemed excessive and burdensome; food-strewn dining rooms and filthy car seats and cutsie onesies made me grimace. The very thought of babies caused my chest to tighten, restricting the free flow of my breath. *Of my life.*

To me, all moms looked suffocated, drained—in airports with kids crawling all over them, pushing strollers in the rain, and navigating the grocery aisles with kicking babies in car seats conveniently attached to shopping carts so you couldn't make the mistake of leaving them in the car in exchange for a few minutes of food solitude. You could never get away from them. Moms were bound by some invisible umbilical cord that sucked the life out of once vibrant, pheromone-rich, voluptuous young women. Moms were disheveled, lonely, and there was always a vacuousness behind their tired eyes, half-hidden by graying hair they stopped maintaining. And dads seemed equally unhappy. It was easy to discern the apparent friction in marriages when young kids stole the limelight and altered their mama's sex hormones.

Why would I want *that* when my life finally seemed smooth and perfect?

As I envisioned my life as a married woman, and with the distant memories of permaculture or an eco-café and a yogic awareness of my mind-body as the epicenter of internal and external life, I kept coming back to what I loved: nature, food, traveling, and wellbeing. Perhaps I was meant to follow in the footsteps of Julia Child with a life of cooking and traveling. There was a reason people were *inspired* by her (yes, *Ms. Child* was in fact childless and openly admitted that children would have hindered her life's dreams). There are dozens of amazing career women who also had children, of course, but I wasn't ready to submit to a similar path.

Secretly and with trepidation, I started paying attention to my cycles—not for conception, but for contraception. To ensure I would *not* be ovulating during intimacy. As much as I'd been tuning into my body and how it was affected by food and movement, I knew relatively little about female reproduction. Until then, I had given little thought to my own fertility. Even the miscarriage was a forgotten episode.

One of my besties (who conceived her first child in our guest room) taught me about sticky discharge and other such signs of ovulation, though I never went so far as to monitor temperature (too complicated). Turned out, I'd become pretty dang regular after recovering from some disastrous side effects of birth control pills, the NuvaRing, and the miscarriage. Since I was committed to being *au natural*, simply knowing my cycle was my favored step toward getting a grip on this whole "making a miracle" business.

It seemed pathetic that I was a woman in my early 30s lacking a deep understanding of my own fertility. My *body*. What the hell are we teaching women when we *don't* teach about reproduction, cycles, and hormones? Why are 21st century values still under the veil of a patriarchal, Puritan society, when women are not taught about their bodies yet are held responsible for them? Total bullshit.

My own intellect could be lured by the history of craft-cocktail culture; I was resourceful enough to easily investigate the most beneficial B12 vitamin for vegans; and I'd gained insight into my body's physical capabilities. Yet I never considered how food affected my reproductive cycle (or how my cycle affected my food), let alone dive into the depths of culturally suppressed baby-growing information. Not knowing, of course, meant circumventing my fear of having one or more of those wiggly wah-wahs.

Anyway, my friends, mother, and mothers-in-law had long since abandoned the topic of babies because my response was always the same—diverting eye-contact, shallow-breathing, rapid change of subject. Avoidance itself had landed me on the cold, uncomfortable situation of ultimatum.

Even Chris tiptoed around the topic. We'd stopped discussing it, though he was extra loving and sensual while feeding me

RECIPE FOR DECISION MAKING

longing looks that I knew held his desire to become a father. He wanted *my*—*our*—children. What could be more loving that that? I trusted him with my heart, yes, but I certainly didn't trust myself with the task of rearing a snotty-nosed kid.

My apprehension stemmed as much from loss of freedom as from fear of failed marriage. I loved much about my childhood, but my parents were unhappily married, and it was deeply distressing to be raised by people who seemingly hated each other. I wanted to love people, myself—and Mother Earth—and never wanted to be pigeonholed into a decision about staying together "for the kids" nor splitting up "for one's own happiness." It seemed both inevitable and unfair. To me, motherhood meant the end of a happy marriage, and the end of hope for a happy life.

I was afraid, and wanted to run from motherhood, just like I'd repeatedly run from prospects of love and settling. Instead, I started discovering baby making in my own way—through books, inquiry, and awareness. I needed to understand what the hell I'd be getting myself into, physiologically. What I completely failed to do was circle up with my hubs and talk about what *we* were getting into. Unless you're Mormon or Catholic or some other designated religion with high priests or "fathers" (ironically, many who've never been married, let alone been fathers) who mandate pre-marital sessions to discuss what life might look like once kids come into the picture, American culture all but ignores the marital challenges that ensue when babies arrive and, seemingly, complicate everything. In addition to hushing useful info about reproduction, the impending result of procreation—parenthood—is not readily discussed.

We also don't talk about the role of food in baby making. There is little that warns us to stop drinking alcohol and soda; to replace fast (non-)food with whole (real) foods; to eliminate toxic chemicals in our living environments and circulating throughout our bodies after 18–42-ish years of living on this polluted Earth (before fertilizing eggs); that birth control depletes many of the nutrients required for normal biochemical and neurological functioning (and fetus-developing); or other useful information about nourishing a body with nutritious whole foods in preparation to *grow a human.*

To be fair, there was (and still is), a clear recommendation to take a prenatal supplement. Instead of "eat beans and other foods high in folate—which also contain fiber, healthy, fats, and plenty of other nutrients—so that your baby's spine grows well and so that you have the necessary nutrients to fuel yourself and your baby's development," the implicit message was, "just take the dang supplement made in a lab from synthetic materials so you don't fuck up your baby." Loud and clear.

But how could I (negligently) oppose a supplement containing 400 mcg/day of folic acid when avoidance tapped into fear of producing an unhealthy baby? Because, of course, women—even conscientious, healthy women who paid attention to their food intake—couldn't possibly be held responsible for obtaining all the nutrients they need from food, right?

That concept plagued me, and I was surprised by the lack of recommendation for a micronutrient test or dietary record to assess nutrient status. Doctors couldn't possibly add to the burden of conversations with women of child-bearing age further discussions about food habits or evaluate nutritive intake. Turns out, most docs don't study nutrition in med school unless they take a one-semester elective. Plus, ya can't talk diet in a 15-minute patient visit.

To boot, many healthy women didn't *go* to the doctor to find out if they were *actually healthy enough* to conceive. That's called "preventative" medicine, though it should be called "proactive health" or something similar. However you perceive it, supplements are like a first aid kit for relinquishing worry—you feel better psychologically when you've got them, so you're less likely to get emotionally banged up.

I located *one*—and only one—food-based prenatal supplement that contained a couple of organic ingredients. And I bought it. Just in case. The bottle sat unopened in my cupboard like the pregnancy test of yore.

Nutrient assessment aside, I felt certain my body was more prepared for baby-growing in my early 30s than it was in my early 20s, when I'd completely abused myself. Without a scope inside my organs, I felt sure my liver had overcome stress at least from excessive alcohol and other substances—an array of environmental toxins, personal care and home chemicals, pesticides

RECIPE FOR DECISION MAKING

approved for growing the majority of the nation's food, surely a small dose of high fructose corn syrup, innumerable corn derivatives, inescapable preservatives in food and beauty products, perhaps a few recreational drugs that also may have been grown with pesticides or developed with chemicals.... Though I still drank wine (a highly toxic industry) and heavily inhaled city life on my daily walks/bikes/runs, my toxic overload certainly had been eased somewhat. I'd rerouted myself onto a wholesome path instead of a malnourished one.

But my mind was a freakin' mess.

In August, after tracking my cycle for several months, Chris and I attended my friend's wedding on the coast just north of Seattle. I was on fire—cocktail in hand, happily socializing with my college drinking friends. Chris seemed distant, which I attributed to my having dragged him into a social setting where he didn't know anyone except the bride and groom. We were in that familiar "this dinner party ain't for me" scene, so I exited the dance floor to walk with my husband on the pier and enjoy the salty evening sunset. Just us. I breathed in the familiar sea breeze of my past. Embracing me, Chris exhaled a phrase about our future, "So...are we going to *DO* this or not?"

What a buzzkill. And a wakeup call to the present moment, putting a halt to many months of my evading the inevitable.

He wanted us to make a baby. It sounded like an ultimatum. We'd been together nine years. "How much more time do you need?" he asked.

Shit. I needed to be on board *right then* or risk losing the man I loved. The decision was mine, and it wasn't even a decision I'd be making in that moment. I'd already told him that I understood marrying him meant having children together.

And I was ovulating. Intuitively (see, I *did* possess some intuition), I knew we'd conceive that very night if I'd let it happen. But still...*I wasn't ready*. I needed help. A boost. A confidence builder. I needed something to quell the fear, to *relax*. Shut off my overly analytical mind. Chill the fuck out.

Perhaps not so coincidentally, two of my guy friends invited me into the parking lot across the street from the reception. I knew what they meant because they'd always generously offered to introduce me to recreational substances. That night, they were snorting lines. I hesitated. I'd done very few drugs in the past several years, starting with my conscious-vegan-foodie phase. But I remembered all too well how cocaine made me feel—beautiful, sensual, present. Would I screw up my baby *this* way, with one incident of one drug made in a lab? How hypocritical was that decision? Quickly, I reasoned it was no different from poor-quality, lab-derived prenatal supplementation or anti-anxiety meds that something like 78% of women were taking. I needed that intervention.

It was an immaculate (as in flawless) conception, even within the confines of Chris's Toyota Tacoma. As I predicted it would be. I had to trust the baby would be perfectly healthy. That I would be okay. That family life would be right for me. I had to trust that motherhood (and marriage) would work out swimmingly.

RECIPE for DECISION MAKING

Many birth control products deplete B-vitamins, including folate, hence the need to replete nutrients with a prenatal supplement. Or, with food. Lentils, for example, are full of folate and more, incredibly versatile, affordable, and easy to make. This delicious meal offers tons of key nutrients to support pregnant mamas.

Indian-Spiced Lentils & Asparagus
Yield = 1-2 servings
Prep time = 10 minutes
Total time = 40 minutes

Ingredients
- ½ white onion or whole shallot, finely diced
- 1-2 cloves garlic, minced
- ½ tsp ginger, freshly grated
- 1 14.5-oz can crushed or diced tomatoes
- 2 c raw spinach
- 8 spears fresh asparagus
- 1 tbsp coconut oil
- 1 tsp garam masala
- ½ c dry red lentils
- Grass-fed ghee or butter
- Squeeze of lemon or lime
- Salt & pepper to taste
- Optional garnishes: avocado, dollop of whole, plain yogurt, fresh cilantro

Instructions
1. Prep onion, garlic, ginger, tomatoes, spinach. Snap the ends off the asparagus spears.
2. Add coconut oil to a cast iron pan (which provides iron) on medium heat.
3. Add onions. Cover with lid and stir off and on until onions start to become translucent, 3-5 minutes.
4. Reduce heat slightly. Add garlic, ginger, and garam masala. Stir for 30 seconds, until spices become aromatic.
5. Add lentils to onions/spice mix and stir until well coated with the spices.
6. Add tomatoes and stir together. Bring back to a low boil, cover, and cook for 15 minutes or until lentils are soft, stirring every 5 minutes.
7. Meanwhile, in another cast iron skillet, heat ghee on medium heat. Add salt and pepper. When butter bubbles, add asparagus. Stir in skillet to coat asparagus. Sautee for 6-8 minutes—don't overcook! Asparagus should be crunchy and bright green.
8. When lentils are soft and chewy, adjust spices and texture (add a bit of water or broth for a soupier meal). Gently fold spinach into lentils and turn off heat.
9. Just before serving, add a squeeze of lime or lemon (which also helps absorb iron from plant-based foods). Scoop lentils into bowl. Place asparagus alongside. Add slices of avocado, a dollop of whole yogurt, and/or fresh cilantro to garnish.
10. Enjoy warm!

CHAPTER 18

Recipe for Dark Days & Dishes

Even before bearing fruit in my womb, life had boiled down to rushing. Rush to work, to school, to yoga, to the store, to sleep. I even rushed to go running and wondered why it always took me a mile or more before finding my stride and rhythmic breath. The rush of discontent, worry, and wasted time caught up with me.

We moved again, across town, to a tiny, old one-bedroom rental with ample character but poor design. It felt like moving to the burbs until I bought a hybrid bike, warm biking gloves and panniers, and embraced the five-plus-mile commute to work and back (rain or shine). In addition to rushing for 5 miles (instead of 12 blocks), I was also sleeping less and hitting the snooze button more. I rushed to buy or make coffee.

Fatigue set in, likely also from melancholia, the diurnal drizzle that chilled me to the bone, and going-along-with-the-norm boredom. My period was two weeks overdue. *Are these signs to give up caffeine, or drink more of it?*

I sank into uncertainty again. What life path was I treading? My husband was literally glowing at the idea of starting a family while I was dreaming about all the other things I aspired to do, could become, should be. I wanted to attend more art openings; read more books; write books; master asana inversions; grasp meditation; make more money; plant more trees; run more trails; prepare pasta from scratch; take more trips to eat pasta and run more trails in the trees.

It seemed each time I drifted into the loss-of-independence worry in my brain, something along the morning commute would jolt me back to the present—the pungent smell of wet sewer or cigarette smoke, a waft of freshly baked bread juxtaposed with the burnt aroma of roasted coffee beans, a car horn followed by a sideways glance from another ruby-cheeked bike-commuter. Caught in the pulse of city life around me, I'd think of Jessica—one year into her cancer battle—and how thankful I was to be alive if only to be her sister. I was grateful to be healthy enough to move my body anywhere I wanted it to go. And as she chose not to talk about her pain, I could *choose* to enjoy little things that made life worth living, even the rain slapping at my cheeks and frizzing my hair. I could eat my favorite foods without queasiness. And I could approach family life with curiosity and an experimental outlook.

A few weeks later, even before I took a pregnancy test, I knew. Sore, swollen boobs. Churning discomfort in my abdomen as if I'd eaten too much. Nausea (uh, oh). I craved macaroni and cheese, potatoes, bread with butter, and (strangely) peaches. *But I should eat lentils, kale, and plenty of veggies.* Instead, I'd just stare at my tomato and basil salad, unable to bring the fork to my mouth. I could hardly choke down a pesto, squash, and cucumber sandwich. The tofu chèvre I'd made was revolting so I threw it out, cursing the wastefulness.

While on a (painfully slow) jog, my friend Beth said to me, "I have this feeling becoming a mother somehow will transform your career." That seemed like a stretch, but I needed some positive sentiments to counter the chronically unsettled feeling in my body, the dominating mental frustration, and the doubts that kept bubbling up in my soul. If this was real—and I kept pretending it wasn't—my first task would be to come to my senses about motherhood.

I couldn't quite *embrace* it yet. I lamented the loss of my adventurousness when I was unstoppable and full of life. Gone were the moments when I could just *be*. Everything already revolved around the baby growing in my uterus. Life's little gifts were replaced by stressors looming on every horizon.

Yet nothing beckoned to me. My freedom had been replaced by lists—I had lists of lists! A priorities list at the gallery for the art visionary tours I was guiding; a grocery list of the healthiest comfort foods (but mostly crackers and aged, salty sheep cheese); a list of medical numbers to call (both hospital and alternative) attached to a four-page list of questions to ask a midwife if I ever called one; a list of people to whom I wanted to write a letter (but when?); a list of all the events, shows, visitors, and travel in the subsequent weeks. I kept adding to the lists and staring at them. I'd become a listless wife leading a life of lists.

It was too much. I needed space—head space and nature space. I needed the mountains.

I drove to The Ranch. Not the dude ranch where I grew up—my parents had sold their share 20 years prior. Another Idaho ranch connected with my family—a working backcountry ranch two-hours by car from the nearest town with a grocery store, and an hour from the crooked old mining community that faux-hosted an annual "Spotted Owl Shoot." The final 11 miles to this wilderness country (where occasional rednecks ventured beyond the Private Property signs or nature lovers turned up claiming to be lost) descended thousands of feet on a one-lane dirt road with hairpin turns into a remote river canyon.

My aunt and uncle had lived there for almost 30 years, caretaking full time and raising their three daughters through summer and fall, while hosting all who came to work, frolic, and stay a few days off the grid. Gramma Truppi came out for a month every September, after the high heat of summer lifted and when the garden exploded beyond maintenance, when black bears sneaked into the orchard at night, and fire season likely had passed. It was the time of year to enjoy afternoon dips in the river without being stifled by wildfire smoke or frigid water.

It was also the time of year when most meals centered around ranch-grown veggies, foraged fruits, and hunted meat (to free up space in the freezer for the upcoming season). Naturally, it was my favorite time to visit.

Because it was impossible to "run to the store" for a missing ingredient, the ranch's huge freezer was filled with wild game, plan B Costco foods, and ice cream. A sizeable pantry inside the house was lined with canned tomatoes, grape juice, salsa, and pickles. Every visitor arrived with a bundle of items that had been requested of them, typically a fresh supply of what couldn't be grown or made there—avocados, mushrooms, cheese, milk, flour, sugar, and oats.

The ranch was a place where you didn't live *off* the land but *in tune* with it. Bears invading the orchard became bratwurst; the cougar eating the chickens became breakfast steak alongside emu-egg omelets. It was where we learned to kill rattlesnakes in the yard with a random brick (then skin and sauté the meat with morels to accompany lunch because nothing was wasted). Where elk and venison were crafted into every imaginable form, including summer sausage for sandwiches with store-bought cheese and ripe tomatoes. Where your fingertips were black with berry stains in the summer and calloused from pushing wheelbarrows piled with squash in the fall.

As hard as it was for me at that time to chew and swallow animals shot for foraging too close to humans, I loved almost every moment I spent on the ranch. Not so much cleaning the chicken coop solo, or the mosquitoes eating me while asleep on the porch at night, but I loved the ease and merriment. Work never felt like work because it was shared, changed daily with the seasonal tasks, was physically satisfying, and included plenty of outside time.

I felt at peace upon setting foot on the creaky front porch, glancing at the onslaught of stuff that foretold what I might do that day. A line of rubber boots of all sizes for the "day help"; a boot scraper and a bunch of muddy shoes; patched-up chairs with cushions and springs so well-utilized it was hard to get up once you sat down; rain coats or puffy coats for the inclement weather; coolers full of beer and a garbage can full of empty beer cans; fishing poles; WD-40; bug spray; binoculars; hummingbird feeders; hanging plants; an old guitar. The card table covered in bright blue weatherproof vinyl housed the food-harvesting project of the moment, sometimes the bread bag with PB&Js, tools that needed to be toted back to the barn, and other such items shuffled from the house to various locations on the 1800s wilderness homestead.

With no cell service and spotty internet (recently installed), time stood still. During my childhood, I didn't realize timelessness was the draw—I'd have said riding horses to the petroglyphs and jumping off the cliff into the swimming hole with my sisters and cousins. With nowhere to go, we came up with infinite ways to spend the days.

As an adult, I realized the ranch was where we'd disconnect to reconnect.

Though I missed out on planting the garden in spring and haying in summer, I preferred the quieter autumn when more time was spent on food projects. After moving irrigation pipe in the fields, we'd swap boots for flip flops to press apple cider in front of the laundry shed, or bare feet to can salsa or homemade V-18 juice (my uncle's term because, yeah, 18 veggies) inside the house.

The kitchen was both a main thoroughfare and the room I liked best in the house. Someone was always coming in from the porch or going back outside, closing the door quickly to keep out pesky flies. The faded Formica counter housed bowls of scraps for the chickens, peppers just picked from the garden or plums from trees plucked on the way back up from the barn. A ubiquitous pile of dishes. A century-old, wood-fired stove with oven was the focal point. I believe the old house was built around it, because I couldn't imagine how it would fit through any of the doorways. It functioned now as a countertop and storage table for blackberry crumble, plastic bins of my aunt's granola or somebody's cookies, baskets of bread, squash, and tomatoes that needed to be eaten or processed immediately.

There seemed always to be someone at the newer (but decades old) electric stove too. With all the mouths to feed, meal prep was constant, especially big batches of soup, sauce, or sourdough pancakes. I remember Gramma Truppi holding up a huge aluminum pot, all banged up and clearly well-used. "This was my mutha's pot," she said in her New York accent. "It was made in the USA."

I imagined my great-grandmother on the boat from Naples, arriving on Ellis Island with three or four of her kids and a trunk. As her family grew toward 13, likely she bought the pot in Queens to make sauce that would last for several meals. I pictured my grandmother, the fifth eldest, grown up and making sauce for the babies she took in by day and, years later, boiling homemade ravioli for a neighborhood of 20 or 30 (including her own family) in the Jersey burbs. By the time she and Grampa relocated to northwestern Pennsylvania and all four of their kids had moved away, I'm sure she was pleased to pass on the pot to her only daughter, who cooked feast-sized meals at the ranch.

Generations. Traditions. Heirlooms. Timelessness. Simple food. The sweet life.

And I, possibly six weeks preggo and freaking out about starting my own family, focused on picking bucketfuls of Italian plums, the last of the zucchini, and the first of the winter squash. We wouldn't be there long enough to make and can pasta sauce, but I helped pluck the rest of the basil and harvest bushels of tomatoes. Aunt Judy insisted I take home something like five pounds of basil to make my all-time favorite food: pesto.

On my final night at the ranch, we feasted outside early enough to catch the last rays of sunlight sinking behind the mountain and before it became too dark and chilly. We sat under the honeysuckle at the picnic table made crooked by years of activity and the sloping yard. Hollyhocks leaned over to see what we were eating: daily bread stacked on both sides of moose burgers with grilled zucchini strips, a side of grilled sweet corn, and a green salad made entirely from veggies we'd harvested that day. We topped the mixed greens, tomatoes, cucumbers, carrots, and peppers with shaved parmesan and seeds (from town) and dressed it with homemade balsamic vinaigrette (a family staple).

Though on the slow boat away from pure veganism, I was surprised at my readiness to eat the wild game on my plate, as with the salmon at my sister's house a year or so prior. Something felt different, but it wasn't the moose burger itself. I was thankful for nourishment from pure, untainted meat procured by my family and just as lovingly prepared as the abundance of veggies and fruit. To some, ground moose burger may have seemed a rare delicacy, to others, an abhorrent meal. In that moment, to me it was sacred. The fruits of my family's labors to nourish the fruit of mine.

We toasted to the abundance spread out before us, raising thick, etched crystal thrift store wine glasses half-full of two-buck-Chuck. I pretended to sip, hoping no one would notice otherwise. As I set down my glass and inhaled the feast, I caught a whiff of the pesto I'd made that afternoon and gagged. My uncle noticed and asked if I was pregnant or something. I shrugged it off, joking that his homebrew was easier to swallow than cheap table wine.

Woah. Please, not pesto! I heard pregnancy could ruin a mama's favorite food, but I cannot stomach the idea of never eating pesto again. My reaction to pesto was my "positive" pregnancy test. There really was something growing inside me. What other daily pleasures would change?

That night, I offered to do the dishes on my own, even though I was breaking the ranch dish rule. There was no dishwasher, so during the day, everyone just pitched in. At night, though, we kids (even as adults) picked cards—the highest card washed, the next highest rinsed and racked, and the third highest swooped in after tea to put away dishes so we'd start the next morning with a clean slate. It was the only place I loved nightly dish duty. It was an opportunity to connect with my sisters and cousins or another kid-guest I'd met just that day. Shoulder-to-shoulder, dish-to-dish we'd swap stories—at the ranch, there was always a story.

But that night I needed alone time to consider the trajectory of my own story, to contemplate while the water flowed effortlessly from the faucet and disappeared in the darkness of the drain, to ponder birth and death. I recalled the day Grampa Truppi died. I'd received the call at work—an art college in downtown Seattle. My boss sent me home to mourn, but not knowing how to soothe myself, I cleaned the kitchen. As I began washing dishes, I noticed a spider trapped in the sink. Instead of rescuing him (my normal inclination), I killed him by washing him down the drain. Immediately, I felt remorse for taking its life, yet wondered if its spirit would meet my grandfather's spirit.

Then I thought about how badly my sister, Jessica, had wanted a child, how the very organ for childbearing also birthed a tumor inside her, and what a gift my own child would be to

Jessica and her son as she faced the fragility of life and the likelihood of death.

As three generations of family played cribbage in the other room, I washed the last of the wine glasses while considering the prevalence of seasons at the ranch compared with one distinct gray season in Portland. In modern life, seasonal food was celebrated at farmers markets, and we complemented fresh food with the same offerings at grocery stores year-round. I wondered how my ancestors nourished their pregnant bodies and growing fetuses with ripe, seasonal food in the summer and fall, dried or canned winter foods through winter, and with whatever was left come spring. Like most people, I'd strayed from eating with natural life cycles, yet I felt grateful to have the choice.

I stared past my reflection in the window and watched the dark sky blanket the mountains. I felt the same darkness entombing my dreams. Everything was changing. I was in my own autumn, laying to rest one life and preparing to birth a new one come spring. Despite the beauty of the life cycles, I was sure motherhood would become exactly what I'd imagined, and, simultaneously, what I'd feared.

RECIPE for DARK DAYS & DISHES

One of the things I love about pesto is its versatility—both in the ingredients it takes to make it, and in the myriad ways to consume it. To this day, I make a variation of pesto almost weekly, focusing first on the greens in season, then modifying the oil, nuts or seeds, and sometimes cheese (or no cheese) to complement the other ingredients.

Easy Peasy Pesto
Yield = varies
Prep time = 10 minutes

Ingredients
- 2-ish c seasonal leafy greens, herbs, or a combination
- 1/3-ish c nuts and/or seeds (traditionally pine nuts)
- ½-ish c extra virgin olive oil
- ½-ish c parmesan or pecorino Romano cheese (try ¼ c nutritional yeast if dairy-free)
- 3-4 cloves of garlic (3 if home grown, which are more potent)
- A dash of pepper (optional)
- A squeeze of lemon or lime (optional—may help preserve the "green" color in some herbs like basil)

Instructions
1. Add all ingredients to a food processor.
2. Pulse. Scrap sides. Pulse again.
3. Taste.
4. Modify (add more greens, nuts, oil, cheese, etc.)
5. Blend again until you've reached desired consistency and flavor.
6. Use immediately or store in a sealed glass jar in the fridge.
7. Label the jar because, if you're like me, you'll pair the different pesto variations with complementary meals or you'll invite a guest who is allergic to almonds or walnuts, and you'll just need to know.

CHAPTER 19

Recipe for Depletion

The concept of "morning" sickness turned out to be a bad joke. I endured "all-day-every-day" sickness. For five months.

At the gallery, my smoothie waited idly aside my computer on my two-inch-thick glass desk. As the minutes and hours passed, I watched the fiber separate from the liquid, the fruit separate from the greens, the vibrant colors disintegrate into muddiness. Each day, I'd make a different version of nutrient-rich goodness, but neither the kale-mango, nor the avocado-chocolate, and definitely not the spinach-cherry combination was appetizing. How was a pregnant woman supposed to eat for two when she could no longer eat at all?

Or drink. One morning I tried stomaching a small glass of Jaclyn's homemade grape and plum juice. The tartness gave me a dreamy brain freeze, stopping me mid-thought at this pleasureful beverage. Thirty seconds later, Chris had to veer off the narrow neighborhood road so I could puke into the gutter.

Oh, boy. Reliance on a multivitamin, I guess.

Before I knew it, I was held hostage by cravings for burgers and pepperoni pizza. I caved. Chris was pumped! He took me out to eat "the best burger in town" at a trendy restaurant in a boutique hotel where I used to frequent thanks to their bourbon selection. The grass-fed-meat burgers hailed from cows raised in the neighboring county, homemade tomato paste from local tomatoes, and caramelized onions grown up the road. All for a whopping $16 (not including a side of garlic fries).

Nervous to eat beef again after so many years, but grateful for food consciousness, I took a moment to thank everything when the picture-perfect burger arrived at our table. But the experience digressed at the first, unsatisfying bite. The grease coated the inside of my mouth like sticky pollen. My tongue and teeth moved the mushy meat and oily gristle around, in search of any spark of exciting flavor or texture that would prove its worth. Bite number two yielded the same results. I scooted the plate over to my husband, who was eager to assist, while I ate the acceptable fries.

The next experiment produced a better outcome. A local pizza chain boasted the most locally sourced ingredients in P-town and delivered their pies in solar-powered cars. One location was two blocks from our house. So, one day, after walking home from a movie at the brew-and-view with Jaclyn and her boyfriend Jeremy, I was overtaken by the smell of pizza suppressing diesel fumes and wet leaves. Without thinking, I announced, "I'd love some pepperoni pizza!"

Jaclyn stopped dead in her tracks, looked at Jeremy in bewildered excitement, then glanced at my shrugging husband, before responding, "Let's go!" It was probably the first time we'd eaten *normal* food together since before Costa Rica. I vowed not to overthink the dairy or meat, and simply enjoy. That time, the cheese fats were perfectly salty, the dead pig perfectly spicy, the crust perfectly chewy. I was sated in a way I had forgotten was possible, perhaps by the letting go of my rigidity (but more likely, I just needed salt, protein, and carbs).

Soon, the dark chocolate peanut butter cups from Trader Joe's replaced my afternoon apple-and-nut-butter snack and, somehow, I managed to consume an entire Costco bag of cheddar Pirate's Booty (it took me months but, still, adding up the calories from the nutrition label subsequently made me sick to my stomach—again). How could I grow a baby on pepperoni pizza, PB cups, and puffed corn? I knew better. What compelled

Recipe for Depletion

me to abandon my convictions? *Argh! What am I doing to my unborn child?*

Still, no one—not my midwives, if I recall, nor Dr. Google—questioned whether I was nutrient sufficient. I vaguely remember one conversation about conscious vegetarianism, black beans, and lentils. Regardless, my cravings were "perfectly normal" during pregnancy. "We're not worried about you—just eat whatever you want," my midwives said.

I'd heard that before.

A visit to the doctor yielded three interesting results: 1. we were not having twins (both of our grandparents had been twins); 2. my baby was due on Mother's Day (ironic for someone who was unsure she wanted to be a mom); and 3. I was too stressed out and too busy to bring a child peacefully into this world.

Well, that's just great. To be a mom, I have to change myself. I knew it would come down to this. Hmm.

I decided to make a list of potential stressors within just that month: a trip to a wild island party in California; hosting friends from Seattle to see a series of concerts; a road-trip to Bend with friends; hosting my friend from LA (also preggo) for a week; hosting Chris's brother and friend, too. All that, and I was studying for midterms while planning our annual Harvest Party, anticipating the Broadway show "Oklahoma!" the following day, and organizing to leave the day after that for a week-long work trip to Chicago (plus all the work lists associated with the art fair).

Too busy, huh? I loved all that stuff—the shows, the traveling, the education, the gallery, the *experiences*. That's what filled my bucket. If I slowed down, what would I do? I thought it was the baby business freaking me out. My sleep was compromised. I wasn't performing as well at work. I was tired and not taking care of myself. With much consternation, I realized there was one rational thing to do—and I *detested* rational.

"I should probably quit school," I declared.

"I agree that's the smartest choice," Chris wholeheartedly replied. Then again, he'd never really been on board for that, anyway.

Though a lightness came over me, I paused filling out the paperwork—couldn't I just finish the last six weeks? It seemed counter-intuitive to put off pursuing my dream of studying nutrition in graduate school. Plus, school was self-care. I was studying *cellular function* because I wanted to expand my mind in the physical sciences, to help guide people with food choices that suited their unique needs and, mostly, to be myself until that baby came out.

I resigned, anyway. During my final chemistry lab, I was struck by the unsettling aroma of chemicals, and had to leave the room once for fresh air and twice to visit the bathroom. My biochem professor was bummed to hear of my decision to withdraw, yet complimented my work ethic, stating I was one of his best students. I tucked that away. My dream was not lost, just postponed, a pause between the in- and outbreaths. Sitting around doing nothing might bring me some clarity about grad school and a subsequent career. In the present, maybe focusing on my gallery work would help me circle back to the many things I enjoyed about it.

But my ease and flow had changed. The commute was less enjoyable in the rainy months and with my growing abdomen. Hot lemon water was a depressing replacement for my favorite sweet-and-creamy caffeinated beverage that used to warm me up. And after work, I couldn't unwind with a fermented drink with my gallery friends. Sitting with (yet another) hot lemon water was not exactly partaking of the scene. The truffle sauce was no longer appetizing, and the Brussels sprouts drowned helplessly in their balsamic bath.

Everything was a drag. I was a drag!

But some clarity did ensue: I needed to take care of my mental health. My super-inconsistent meditation practice was fruitless, my friends had no idea how to respond to my turmoil, and the tobacco-smoke-and-exhaust-ingesting jaunts on the riverside greenbelt had lost its mind-clearing allure. I needed help grasping the idea of becoming a mother while eliminating seemingly everything I loved about my life.

After my first therapy session, the counselor suggested that meeting weekly would be a good idea. Week after week, I yearned for *something* that would save me from my despair. I needed just one thing to supplant my doubt with hope. It turned out to be this: women are physiologically designed to love their children.

Physiologically designed. For some, it happens before conception. For others, love comes while growing a baby in the womb. For others, it strikes when the baby is born. We cannot always determine *when* it will happen. But loving my baby was inherent, and I needed to trust that it would happen. That resonated. So, I just needed a plan to get my mind-body ready for this baby-rearing life that *could* be full of love.

I noticed sunny skies peeking through the drizzle. I started attending prenatal yoga and also a sound-healing class where we chanted in gratitude for the trees, the earth, and our bodies. With nothing to keep me up at night (no shows, no events, no caffeine), my sleep improved. I practiced breathwork. I focused on being present at work, at home, with myself. Even my morning sickness subsided by dinnertime, and I could stomach cooked root vegetables and cheesy kale chips (but not pesto). I replaced my anxious journal entries with a food diary (just staying atop my nutrients, y'all). I nourished my baby-body. I had no idea if my efforts were truly helpful.

One night, after a burrito bar dinner at a friend's house, and a live music session with first children I'd ever adored, my friend's husband hugged me goodnight and said, "There's a change in your voice, Jamie. You seem to be speaking from your throat and not from your gut. It's like your words are softer and more intentional. I haven't seen you since learning of your good news, but I hear the change, the calm."

His young daughter piped in, "I noticed, too!"

Proof! There I was, on the intentional path between chaos and calm. Maybe change wouldn't be so bad after all.

Around Christmastime, work ramped up for art fair season with innumerable events, several weeks of travel, artists to entertain, exhibitions to plan. One major commission was almost lost, and I scrambled to save it. Despite my efforts to multitask, I was failing to keep it all together. I was dropping balls at work and flailing to pick them up again. I was drained. That was the new me: brain and body no longer able to keep up.

I read everything I could get my hands on about stress and pregnancy. The literature about stress and its potential lifelong impact on the fetus—positioning my unborn child for a lifetime of existing at an elevated sympathetic state—echoed in my head. My mother said I was born into emotional distress. But while I could mentally understand the need to freakin' relax, stress was in my DNA. It was a key personality trait, often functional and funny, but equally destructive and draining. Also, when in a state of stress, many physiologic functions shift—like digestion. So even ample nutrients I was consuming might not have been enough for a healthy mama and baby.

Hence, I looked forward to the post-Christmas week Chris and I had been planning in the snowy Idaho mountains. I looked forward to quality time with my girlfriends, snowshoeing on quiet trails, ringing in the New Year in a winter wonderland.

But the day before we left, my boss dropped the bomb: she passively invited me to *extend my trip*. She said maybe I wasn't too good at multi-tasking after all.

What did that mean? I was putting out fires everywhere, but she meant I was fired. Looking back, she'd laid off about 20% of the staff in the company's main location, and none of the gallery staff. I was the most obvious—I was pregnant, pursuing other fields of interest, and about to take maternity leave. I'd always been open with her about my interests outside work, but still, I loved my job and had planned to be there for years to come. I felt cheated. I'd taken so many steps to simplify life *outside* of work so that I could be more effective and focused while *at* work. I was proud of my efforts and dedicated to my team, clients, artists. Evidently, that wasn't enough. Because, she reminded me, it wasn't my *passion*.

The connection between the environment, food, and the human body had become my passion.

Our mountain getaway turned out to be a necessity for emotional recalibration rather than a peaceful respite from my crazy city life. Sleepless nights ensued along with failed attempts to find deep breaths while my growing baby pushed my uterus into my diaphragm. Gentle yoga, falling snow, and sunshine. Chris went back to Portland, but I stayed and was supported with absolute generosity, attentive ears, and open hearts. Over mushroom-and-sun-dried-tomato polenta, my girlfriends shared stories of mom and marriage struggles. They gave advice on the shifting tides of motherhood—the most rewarding yet difficult effort imaginable. With conviction, they described how they loved their children more than they imagined possible. They knew I would, too—I had so much love to give.

In my New Year reflections, I considered how my idealistically nourished body had been usurped by cravings for a Standard American Diet (albeit slightly higher quality than most). I'd quit school to focus on my mental health and my work, only to lose my job and spin into a mental frenzy. Everything had turned upside down. I cried a lot. I was angry. Even trying *not* to stress was stressful. I needed to start and end each day in tranquility, but I had a hard time staying calm through the turmoil. Trying to grow this child peacefully, I kept looking for a silver lining in it all.

Either by erratic intervention or divine force, I was shedding one life and emerging into another. Against my will, everything I'd put effort into, it seemed, was being taken away or morphing into a life I didn't think I wanted.

With a bit of emotional detoxing and the help of astute, loyal friends, I clarified my needs and my baby's needs, and I made a case for them. Through acceptance and determination for a positive outcome, and with the guidance of an attorney, I got what I wanted. My gallery exit turned out to be a blessing. In the quiet aftermath of being unemployed and five months pregnant, the morning sickness subsided, and I found myself cooking again. With pesto. A bit of gusto. And I lumbered into my third trimester with a desire to just *be*.

RECIPE for DEPLETION

This seemingly fancy meal is simple, comforting, and surprisingly full of nutrients. And it's a perfect meal to enjoy with girlfriends and a glass of wine (unless you're growing a baby and, even then...)

Polenta with Arugula, Beans, Shrooms & Sun-Dried Tomatoes
Yield = 4 (as a main dish)
Total time = 30 minutes

Ingredients
- ¼ c pine nuts
- 1 lb shrooms (cremini, portabella, or both)
- 1 c sun dried tomatoes
- 1 large or 2 small shallots
- 4 cloves garlic
- 1 tbsp each fresh sage and thyme (or 1 tsp each dried)
- 1 15-oz can cannellini beans (or another white bean)
- 1 tbsp olive oil
- ¼ c white wine vinegar or champagne vinegar
- 4 c arugula
- 1 ¾ c veggie broth (or milk)
- 1 ½ c water
- 1 ½ c quick-cooking polenta
- 1 c grated pecorino or parmesan
- 2 tbsp butter (ideally unsalted)
- ½ tsp black pepper

Instructions
1. Add pine nuts to a dry cast iron pan on medium heat. Stir every few minutes until they become golden brown and fragrant. Remove from heat (they will keep toasting).
2. Clean, dry, and chop mushrooms.
3. Slice sun dried tomatoes into thin "julienned" slices.
4. Peel shallots and garlic. Chop shallots; mince garlic.
5. Chop sage and thyme.
6. Strain cannellini beans.
7. Add mushrooms to a skillet and heat to high. Cook for a few minutes, until the water starts to release from the shrooms into the pan. Reduce to medium, then add shallots and garlic. Sauté for another 1-2 minutes. Add oil, vinegar, herbs, sun-dried tomatoes, and cannellini beans, stirring to combine. Turn off heat while you cook the polenta.
8. Bring broth plus water to a boil in a medium saucepan. Slowly start adding polenta, stirring constantly. In a few minutes it will start to thicken. Bring back to a boil, then add butter, cheese, and pepper, stirring to combine. Remove from heat and cover. Let sit a couple of minutes to thicken more.
9. Meanwhile, fold arugula into the warm mushroom mixture. It will wilt slightly.
10. Spoon polenta into bowls. Add shroom/bean/sun-dried tomato/arugula mixture. Top with pine nuts and, if you'd like, extra pecorino.

CHAPTER 20

Recipe for Deliverance

Mother's Day was surprisingly sunny and warm, so we partook in a Portland bike-and-foodie festival, pedaling from park to park and food cart to food cart. For the first nine miles, my full-term pregnant self felt quite energetic. I indulged in organic soy ice cream. I soaked up the moment, one of the last before a baby would occupy all moments.

No labor pains. I believed a baby would come when a baby was gosh-dang ready, but of course I was guided to fear that overly simplistic, nature-knows-best belief. Western medical messaging makes mothers-to-be believe 40 weeks' gestation must be *exactly* 280 days. If baby comes before that, the baby is "early," after that, "late."

Another week passed, and we edged into the possibility of a hospital birth, though our homebirth midwives were not worried quite yet. On Monday morning, my acupuncturist noticed the baby had turned again—into prime position (*phew!*). That afternoon, my hospital midwife, Mary, informed me, "You have *no signs* of having a baby this week—you're eight days past due and not dilated *at all.*" She firmly suggested we schedule an induction for Friday.

Chris and I looked at each other, slightly panicked. "We'll think about it."

In a last-ditch plea, Mary asked, "May I at least strip your membranes to move things along?"

Yikes! Whatever that meant, it sounded awful and invasive. "No, thanks."

We couldn't get out of there fast enough, except, of course, I was HUGE (and, therefore, slow) and hyperventilating while picturing a hospital induction: IVs, drugs, sterility, stress. Fluorescent lights and hideous hospital gowns. Processed hospital food. Synthetic nutrients. *Hell freakin' no.*

I'd already cured myself of group B strep (with food and herbs)—something Mary had never seen anyone else accomplish in her 25 years of experience with pregnant mamas. It had never occurred to her it was possible test *positive* for GBS, then change one's inner bacterial landscape to evade IVs during birth, which was supposed to be the most divinely natural process on Earth.

I would do whatever else it took to (naturally) avoid the hospital. My big-picture home birth was all about the tiny details—the smell of cinnamon to permeate the house and the sound of soft piano music or kirtan chanting. I wanted to be in my yoga pants, in our cozy little house alight with candles, our cat padding around.

I had to get that baby out.

So, we hiked—fast. Uphill. Back down. In the rain. We ate spicy Thai food and pineapple. I took a double dose of Evening Primrose Oil. I steeped three bags of raspberry leaf tea in my favorite mug. We had sex. I took a hot bath. We put pressure on the pressure points. *What else did Dr. Google and the birthing class say we could do to stimulate natural progression? Black cohosh? Wait, no. Castor oil?*

Apparently, I didn't need anything else. At nearly 3:00 am I woke up to pee. Something was different. I paused. Then a contraction. *Oh, shit!* It hit me like a ton of bricks. Then another… and another. A minute and a half apart.

It was 5:00 am before we called Kate, my friend from the biochem class I'd dropped and who had just finished her doula training. She needed to attend a couple of births—we were her first. She lived a few blocks away and arrived with her basket of goods. I'd already taken two baths. Puked my brains out. Put in a load of laundry. Shat my guts out. The back labor pains were *so intense. Why hadn't anyone told me to expect back pains?* Another load of laundry. I whimpered in the fleeting moments between contractions.

When Kate took over massaging my back, Chris asked what else he could do. I looked him in the eye and said, "Bake muffins."

He repeated my words slowly. "You want me to… *bake muffins?*"

Yes, I wanted muffins. I wanted the house to smell like muffins (cinnamon, remember?) and I wanted warm muffins for the midwives whenever they showed up. I thought he and Kate might want a muffin because it was almost breakfast time. And I thought I might want a muffin later. Right then, I could only drink coconut water through a straw, between retching and puking.

I thought I'd be the one making muffins—we'd expected the early phase of labor to "last for hours or even days." But pre-labor was not part of my DNA, apparently (my mom's experiences were similar). I'd moved straight into "active labor," where I'd been now for five hours.

Between episodes of intense pain, I guided Chris to locate the vegan cookbook and the recipe I wanted him to make—with carrots, raisins, walnuts, and cinnamon. By then, my contractions were less than 30 seconds apart, and going strong. I writhed and shifted my Thai triangle pillow between the kitchen and the bathroom while explaining the notes I'd scribbled in the cookbook margins. The substitutions—quinoa flour for half the regular flour, coconut sugar instead of cane sugar. I explained how to make flax "eggs" first and why it was important to soak the raisins in hot water for at least five minutes, then strain. Step by step.

Every time I opened my eyes, I observed Chris reading the recipe, measuring awkwardly, checking every instruction. He fumbled around the kitchen as the sun came up and brought gray, morning light onto the scene from the east-facing sliding door, dappled with raindrops. With my eyes closed, I heard the opening and closing of cupboards as he searched for the stash of baking ingredients and equipment, not unlike how I might search for tools in the garage. There was a frenetic clanking of a muffin pan dropped accidentally atop the granite counter; the quick scraping of the batter; the *shhhh-ing* of avocado oil spray as he greased the pan; the heavy clank of the ceramic bowl landing in the ceramic sink. I was soothed by the Morse code of the oven—first the punching of numbers, the alert of inner temperature readiness, followed an eternity later by the long, steady beep of the timer.

I believe that was the first time (perhaps the only time?) Chris had baked anything, and I am forever grateful for his efforts. As he set the muffin pan on the wine-cork trivet to cool, the aromas of (yep!) cinnamon and vanilla welcomed the midwife-in-training, Kelsey, up the stairs from the basement with the birthing tub. In sync, just as I'd hoped.

I was happy in those moments of physical pain.

While the tub inflated in our kitchen and the muffins cooled, Kelsey helped me walk into the dining room. She asked if I could stand at the dining table. Nope. It felt like the baby would drop right out. We moved to the living room couch so she could check "down there." Her eyes widened, but I was in too much pain and way too focused on the contractions to wonder what she witnessed between my legs.

She left to check on the progress of the tub. I heard her speaking on the phone with one of the other midwives: "Oh, you're at Trader Joe's? I think you need to come here. Like *now*."

It was then Kelsey realized she'd brought the wrong tub liner. She left us, drove to the midwifery center, and returned 40 minutes later with the correct liner. The two seasoned midwives still hadn't arrived, and I was starting to wonder how much longer I could withstand the muscle aching and throbbing that no birthing class had prepared me for. This "natural" childbirth phenomenon was *insane*. Primal.

I listened as Chris, Kate, and Kelsey fumbled with the tub liner, hooked up the hose to the sink, and turned on the hot water. *Crap.* No hot water. With my baths, two loads of laundry, and the washing of muffin dishes, we'd run out. Kate and my hubs started heating water on the stove in pots. I climbed into the cushy tub, anyway—into barely a foot of lukewarm water that soothed my hot, clammy skin. It was surprisingly relaxing,

Recipe for Deliverance

like a welcoming pillow compared to the unforgiving cast-iron tub and the faux-wood kitchen floor where I'd spent the past several hours.

Soon, hot water was poured in from one pot after the other, warming the bath and raising the water level. I felt calm. I couldn't have been in there more than 15 minutes before I sensed the end—or the beginning—was near...the climax, for sure. At some point during the four pushes, the other midwives arrived just in time to witness our baby boy coming into the world.

Unfortunately for me, I wasn't wearing my glasses or my contacts (*why didn't I think about that?!*), so I would never have a clear picture of him slipping out of my body and into the water. But I felt it, and I'll never forget the immense orgasmic relief and elation. When I held my baby in my arms, I marveled at his purple-colored flesh and how tiny he was—6 pounds 10 ounces. I felt the sticky film over his body, rolled up in some parts like he'd just come out of a sausage casing. The midwives told us he was born "in the caul"—in his amniotic sac—which is why my water hadn't broken (not that I'd noticed). After my baby slipped out, Kelsey punctured the amniotic sac so he could take his first breath of air.

"Welcome to the world, Avery," Chris said, holding me from behind.

Having delivered over 250 babies, the elder midwife said she could count on one hand the number of babies she'd witnessed born in the caul. It was very special and, in fact, was one criterion for selecting a new Dalai Lama. In hospitals, they break the mother's water, so it's even more rare in Western societies.

From the shallow tub of bloody, now-chilly water in the middle of the kitchen, I looked from the tiny, precious gift in my arms, to his beaming father and the earthy women helping us transition into our new life as parents.

As I was helped out of the tub, wrapped in warm towels, and moved to the couch, Kate busied herself preparing my first post-partum meal: a fresh muffin (bravo, hubs!) and a milkshake with coconut bliss chocolate ice cream, coconut water, peanut butter, and molasses.

I held our own wriggling Dalai Lama in my arms. And I was perfectly in love.

RECIPE for DELIVERANCE

Muffin recipes may seem complicated to a new baker, yet it's the small details and step-by-step progress of creating something truly delicious that underlies a baker's passion. It's like having a baby—labor intensive and worth every ounce of effort. Recipe adapted from Isa Chandra Moskowitz's recipe in her "Vegan with a Vengeance" cookbook. Isa says this is her favorite morning muffin.

Carrot Raisin Spice Muffins
Yield = 12 muffins
Prep time = 15 minutes
Total time = 40 minutes

Ingredients
- ¼ c coconut oil, melted (plus more for greasing muffin pan)
- ¾ c raisins
- 1 flax egg (1 tsp flaxseed meal + 3 tbsp water)
- 1 tbsp freshly grated ginger
- 2 c grated carrots (about 3 medium or 2 large carrots)
- ½ c chopped walnuts
- ¼ c coconut oil
- ¾ c coconut, soy, or oat milk
- 3 tbsp blackstrap molasses
- 1 tsp pure vanilla extract (or ½ teaspoon vanilla paste)
- 1 c whole wheat flour
- ½ c quinoa or oat flour (or freshly ground oats)
- ¼ c coconut sugar
- ½ tsp each baking powder, baking soda, sea salt, ground cinnamon
- ¼ tsp freshly grated nutmeg

Instructions
1. Preheat oven to 400 degrees F.
2. Grease a stoneware muffin tray with coconut oil or use muffin liners.
3. Place raisins in a small bowl. Pour hot water over them and soak for 5 mins. Strain (drink the water or add to a milkshake, smoothie, or ginger tea).
4. Prepare flax egg by mixing flaxseed meal with water in a small bowl. Set aside.
5. Prep ginger, carrots, walnuts.
6. Add coconut oil, milk, molasses, and vanilla to a small pot. Heat on low just long enough for the coconut oil to melt. Stir to combine. Remove from heat.
7. Combine flours, sugar, baking powder, soda, salt, and dry spices into a medium bowl. Make a well in the middle.
8. Stir flax egg into the wet mixture, then pour into dry mixture. Stir until just combined, then fold in raisins, ginger, carrots, and walnuts.
9. Spoon batter evenly into the individual muffin spaces and bake 18-22 minutes.
10. Let cool slightly before eating and sharing. Enjoy with pasture-raised butter.

CHAPTER 21

Recipe for Death

Birth and death don't have to co-exist, but sometimes they just do.

In the wake of my son's birth, Jessica ventured to Portland to meet my son, her new nephew. My sis was thinner than ever in her life, clearly bald under her fuzzy, pink beanie, yet her cheeks were rosy, and light shone from her gray-blue eyes. Her smile was so big. I thought she was going to share some lottery-like news that she was in remission.

But no, her joy was purely because she was now an auntie, elated to meet Avery for the first time. Though she was a teacher and had struggled for years to have her own child, I didn't realize before then how much she loved kids. I knew her joy ran deeper than that—she knew her own son James would have at least one cousin to grow up with. I was giving her a gift of life as her body was dying. Jessica held my son while her own chubby toddler quietly explored our home. I felt a spark of wonder witnessing new life so revered in the arms of fleeting life—it took my breath away.

And I hadn't given my sister enough of my attention while she was alive.

I may have been verbally and emotionally helpful, but I'd been the least supportive as a caregiver. I'd visited a few times: when my cousins, little sister and I shaved our heads in solidarity; during Christmas; and post stem-cell transplant. It wasn't enough. I was selfishly living my own life, thankful (of course) that others were readily available, but also not prioritizing time with her. I guess I didn't believe she'd *actually* die. I heard the dire statistics, but I didn't believe the poor prognosis. She'd been fighting a rare and aggressive ovarian cancer for almost two years already. Anyone who lasted one year was considered a "survivor." So, I naively buried the worst-case scenario and assumed she was on the road to recovery.

She was a Truppi, and Truppis don't die from cancer. Heart attacks, yes, but we're too tenacious for malignant cell proliferation. I'd overlooked the fact that my mother's father died of lymphoma and, strangely, so had my mother's aunt—Gramma Day's identical twin. Grandma Day claimed everyone in town eventually "got the cancer," so I blamed deaths from her generation on the water or nuclear toxins from the not-so-secret underground missile base or decades of DDT in the soil of nearby potato farms. There were plenty of environmental concerns to blame. But not genetics. And certainly not "bad luck."

A few weeks after Jessica's visit to my house, I felt strong enough post-partum to visit her. I boarded the train to Spokane with my 11-week-old baby. En route, my sissy called to tell me she'd just left an appointment with her counselor, who urged her to see the oncologist immediately. Something was off. By the time we arrived in Spokane, she'd been admitted back into the cancer ward. Her husband, Jason picked us up and delivered us to the hospital—he went to run errands.

My sister was alone, propped up in bed, awaiting results of a blood draw. Her cheekbones were emaciated, eyes sunken, neck thinner, and her arms devoid of muscle. Her breathing was shallow, and her teeth looked unusually white against her pale skin.

In contrast, her tumor was massive despite four liters of fluid having just been drained. It bulged from under the blankets, the size of a thriving full-term fetus in the womb. My sissy lacked the strength to sit up, so I placed Avery in her bony arms, and watched her struggle to shift him so the weight of his body didn't tumble onto her swollen abdomen.

Soon, the doctors came in with news we all silently feared and expected: the tumor had returned with a vengeance; she might have two weeks to two months to live.

Our eyes met. She'd already known. Unlike me, she'd been thinking of this day since her diagnosis. So, she knew exactly what she wanted in her short time left: to feel no pain, have enough strength to be mobile, and to experience happy moments with her friends and family. She wanted to prepare for a trip, too, either to Glacier National Park or to Alaska.

She gave me instructions. First, go shopping for empire-waist dresses—the only thing she could wear comfortably over her "bump." Then, clean out the downstairs closet to ensure all the children's books she had collected and labeled by grade would be evenly distributed amongst me, our younger sister, and her own son. *Dresses and books. Got it.*

"What about food?" I asked her. Surely, there must be *something* she'd been waiting to eat until she "got better."

"I can't think about food. The hospital will take care of it. I know—it's crappy." The look on her face revealed that food was not a priority. It's not that she didn't care, but the chemo had changed her relationship with food and her palate. I could see her thoughts were elsewhere, perhaps considering all the details of planning the last days of her human life.

As I picked up Avery to leave, our mom arrived, followed by Jason with baby James and a bag of hamburgers, fries, and chocolate milkshakes. Jessica might not have been able to eat it but clearly, Jason had thoughtfully brought this comfort meal from his wife's favorite joint. Who could have predicted the burger gathering would be one of her last happy moments?

I was hungry but not for burgers from who-knew-where. I left immediately to avoid 5:00 traffic—something I've regretted ever since. I found Jessica's car in the parking lot and set out to find the big box store my practical sister suggested for ease of location, wider selection, and affordable prices. Like hospitals, those places sent my blood pressure through the freakin' roof. But it was her dying request so, obviously, I had to talk my brain out of claustrophobia and my body out of hyperventilation. I strapped my son onto my chest and focused on the task: buy dresses. I struggled to figure out which size and shape would fit her, and settled on several in different shades of blue to bring out the color of Jessica's eyes. I paid, left, took a deep breath of parking lot air, buckled my son into the car seat, turned on the ignition, then paused to eat a piece of dark chocolate, which turned out to be my dinner. Then, I cried.

Eventually, I drove to Jessica's house, parked her car in her driveway. And cried again.

It was late by then, after dark, and everyone but my sister was back home. When I put Avery to bed, I asked Jason where they decided to go and how else I could help prepare for their trip. "I can pack gear, food, stay home with James, book flights or a hotel…" He hesitated.

I asked, slowly, "Is she…strong enough to go?" The devastating look on his face was answer enough. I cried again.

Downstairs in the guest room, I started hitting inanimate things and yelling—sometimes out loud and sometimes silent inner screams—*DAMN IT! DAMN IT! DAMN IT!* And, yes, the F-bomb. Plenty of them. Tears gushed and sobs subsided into whimpers. It wasn't fair! Where was God in all this mess? If he existed, where was mercy? How could my sister find faith in God when there was so much pain?

Was there really no way to save her? Was it really time to give up? She was still alive, alone in her hospital room, and we were already grieving her death. She was just 35—I wanted more time with her. Would her son remember his gentle, graceful mama?

Damn it. Fuckity-fuuuuuck!

I wrote down 26 questions I wanted to ask my sis the next day about her pregnancy, James' birth, her favorite places to hike and camp, things to do, to eat. Of course, I knew many things about her, but what would she want her son to know?

The next morning, we received news Jessica had fallen into a coma during the night. *And our last conversation was about beating traffic to buy goddamn dresses at a strip mall in suburbia.* I should have stayed and asked her all those questions. I should have known.

Recipe for Death

Jason, until recently an Emergency Medical Technician, called his buddies to bring his wife home by ambulance so she could die at home, per her request. Newly-hired as a firefighter, Jason's fire chief—a man Jason hadn't even met—personally escorted the procession in his firetruck. The chief had also lost his wife to fucking cancer.

That procession kickstarted a string of phone calls and visitors. Friends, co-workers, Chris and, of course, Jaclyn, our dad, and family from several states. The front room became the waiting and grieving room and portal to the stairs leading to my older sister's room, where she lay unconscious and pumped with morphine.

James smiled at the stream of people who came to see him as well. What a gift to see his chubby smile amidst the overwhelming grief.

I was sure Avery, whom I carried on my chest day and night, could feel my emotional pain through my attempts to find deep, steady breaths. I had to find some peace, for his sake.

I found myself in the kitchen, staring mindlessly at the coffee pot. It had been almost a year since I'd consumed caffeine. Jason had been fixating on coffee-making and other such distractions to focus on something other than his dying wife. For me, it felt like time to welcome a mineral-rich, high-vibe beverage back into my blood and psyche. I'd slept like shit the previous night, and I contemplated staying up all that night, just in case she came out of her coma. I was naively hopeful.

But Jessica took her last breath early the next morning. *So much for two fucking weeks.*

Jason woke up Jaclyn and me. We went upstairs where our parents sat weeping over their eldest daughter. Her body was already stiff and cold. Her mouth agape, nose like a skeleton, a few wispy hairs remained on her scalp, half-painted fingernails and lifeless fingers that reminded me of Gramma Day's before arthritis. Jessica held a rosary in her right hand and a bright scarf in her left hand, placed there by Jason and Jessica's best friend since college. Tubes were still connected to her arm, her port, a catheter. I was struck by the incredulity that the sacred temple that was her body, having carried her soul through decades of mostly good health, had succumbed to this unspeakable plight.

Untimely, senseless death—was that the dark side of nature?

I sat on the bed next to my sister's body, witnessing the scene, the sobbing. My eyes were drawn to a single ray of morning light slipping through the closed curtains. A golden line extended to her profile, illuminating a few dust particles floating around the room. *If that's God, he's too late. Or is that her spirit lifting?* Was she at peace? I could only believe she must be. My dad begged for her to give him a sign that she was okay. We all felt a cool breeze despite the closed window and no fan.

I stayed in Spokane to co-organize details of the subsequent week, help feed everyone, and oversee the tent city that was popping up in the backyard. Hard as I knew it was for my dad to leave, he drove home to gather photographs. Jaclyn went home, too, for a few days. My mom, Jason and I dragged ourselves around, making funeral plans, feeling like wilted flowers bogged down by heavy rain and rooted in deep, impenetrable mud. I needed to stay strong, to make sound decisions grounded in love for life, despite the shroud of death.

Now more than ever, I knew good food was the most beneficial means to sustain us all. Some wanted hugs, others preferred space, and we all needed to eat.

Death used to bring mourners carrying casseroles in ceramic dishware and canned fruit stirred into whipped cream. Instead, the kitchen was filling up with aluminum containers of store-bought food covered with plastic lids that, each time they were opened and closed, grated on my ears and wrenched my thoughts out of my sadness. I recognized the offerings of kindness and generosity, but it was sad food.

All variations of SAD food arrived. SAD—not code for comfort food in the wake of death. Standard American Diet food: chalky hoagie-bun sandwiches with imitation cheese and processed meat, wilted lettuce, and yellow mustard with a sidekick of conventionally grown potato chips fried in highly refined vegetable oil and delivered in toxic plastic grocery bags. Those hoagies would neither soothe nor sustain me. I couldn't eat them. And in the stress of organizing people, property, and plans for a celebration of life, even the salty, crunchy chips were displeasing.

When Chris's mother drove down from her small mining town near the Canadian border, she took us out to dinner at

Red Robin. Chris and I joked about that restaurant chain and an unfortunate gut experience with a California Chicken Burger in high school (when I'd given up chicken). I ordered the only thing on the menu that didn't overly oppose my food values—a veggie burger.

Sure enough, mid-meal I quickly excused myself to rush to the toilet. I'm not sure if the bowel disaster was from the food itself, my overarching analytical aversion to the quality of the food causing distress, or my mother-in-law's remark that I was "clearly lost in my personal life." *DUDE! My sister died four days ago. I am planning her funeral, nursing a newborn, and living in a house full of mourning people—and shitty food!* Of course, my personal life was a mess.

I spent the next 24 hours shitting my guts out, rehydrating with coconut water and becoming irritated with other little kitchen things—wasteful paper plates (so that dishes didn't need to be washed); people who dirtied dishes (yet didn't clean them); guests who loitered and ate (yet never lifted a finger to help with the innumerable details).

I realize most grieving people don't have the capacity to consider nourishment. If they eat at all, it's for comfort. That's one reason traumatic events are a trigger for illness. Body in shock. Brain hyper focused on survival. Immune system depleted. Chronic stress.

With budding knowledge of how food from the earth heals, I'd scratched the surface of understanding the power of food—it can make you well, or ill. We get to choose. In the wake of my sister's death, I refused to bring *dis*-ease to my own body with lifeless, hollow foods. My mentality, however, wasn't helping me remain. I judged others' behaviors while I was also grieving, nursing, and not sleeping. I was at a breaking point.

It was breastfeeding that ultimately helped me keep my head on straight—besides nourishing food, Avery needed me to stay as energetically calm as possible. He was my true north in the hellish storm. I knew I'd only get through the week by committing to activities that centered me. I stole away to the basement room to breastfeed in silence and breathe deeply while tears streamed down my face. I relied on my yoga mat, resting often in child's pose when too fatigued to move, while my baby napped. Other times, I forced gentle twisting postures to uncurl my taut insides.

In that room, I ate my own meals separately while others perused through the coolers and cupboards upstairs. I scorned myself for criticizing the food I would not eat, and I didn't want people to see me *not* eating it. This only provoked guilt that my food issues were heavy enough to overshadow the guilt that my sister had died instead of me—the reckless, irresponsible one.

When I emerged to be helpful to others, I prepared food that was both comforting and actually good for us. Zucchini bread with walnuts and dark chocolate chips, half the sugar, real butter, ancient grain flours, oats, and flax. I increased nutrients in smoothies with nut butters, greens, avocadoes, whole yogurt, organic berries, cinnamon, fresh ginger. Those small bites and sips were quickly devoured.

You can imagine my relief when Jessica's childhood bestie, also a foodie, took over the kitchen upon her arrival from Brooklyn. Jenny had missed saying goodbye to my sissy, but she came to say her hellos to my family. Confident in herself and knowing that Jason cherished her as my sister had, Jenny was quick to take up residence in the kitchen, assessing ingredients in the fridge and cupboards as I always did. She was a breath of fresh air, and no one had uncomfortable ties to her "whole foods fixation" as they had with mine. I was ecstatic when she announced she'd use Jessica's garden tomatoes and peppers to make Panzanella for dinner! No one else had ever heard of that classic Italian meal (shocking!) and the frenzy of pleasure from others was matched with a marked appreciation from me. That night, we even mustered up a few laughs in the kitchen, which cut through the mournful air like a cleaver (and was just as quickly replaced by the splitting reminder of death).

From that point on, the food improved (for me, at least). Michelle had sent a dozen eggs from her backyard hens with Mackenzy, who drove from Portland toting my favorite vegan pizza with cashew cheese and cornmeal crust. Melss flew over from Seattle to scoop me up and treat me to the most pleasureful medicine: a farm-to-table dinner of roasted beets and burrata with citrus followed by a house-made linguini in a garlic sauce with local, farm-raised sausage and foraged morels.

Yes, I needed calories and dense nutrients, not to mention something to talk about other than tumors and tombstones. Those food gestures reminded me I also needed to bring the essence of life into the somber air. Cooking with confidence, soul-nourishing take-out, and farm-fresh food brought a vigor that carried me through the tedious details of funeral days.

I returned all but one of the blue dresses, the last of which Jessica wore to her cremation. I helped with flowers and the photo boards. The memorial service came and went. Someone—but not me—organized a luncheon for the masses. They set up plastic picnic tables and chairs in the yard. Jaclyn and our cousins prepared dishes with garden greens, squash, and other August abundance. Maybe there was supermarket Jell-O and potato salad. I can't remember—it was a blur. Images from that day show only empty paper bowls and plates, lots of turquoise ribbons signifying ovarian cancer, and many a mournful attempt at smiling.

Back in Portland as I harvested vegetables in my own garden, I thought about how Jessica would never again taste an in-season tomato. My sister was gone. Her son James, whom she adored more than life itself, was her miracle and her legacy. And Avery was mine. Her cancer aggressively overtook her will to live. My own will to remain strong to raise my son became my new purpose in life. My son's wellbeing helped me through my sister's death, and now he was the life I vowed to live for. My forever job would be to cultivate ideal health in my mind-body so I could overcome any "bad luck" bullshit disease. Because my sister could not, I would thrive on this Earth while doing everything in my power to help my son—and others—to grow up healthy and strong.

RECIPE for DEATH

In August with the onset of basil, cucumbers, garlic, peppers, and tomatoes, this underappreciated Italian recipe is one of my faves and a surprisingly comforting meal. Use artisan bread to complement the fresh veggies. For a complete meal, serve with a protein like white fish or cannellini beans.

Panzanella
Yield = 8-10 side dish servings
Prep time = 15 minutes + 30 minutes to rest
Total time = 1 hour 15 minutes

Ingredients for the Salad
- 3 tbsp extra virgin olive oil
- 1 small-medium loaf of sourdough bread, cut into 1-inch cubes (~6 c)
- 1 tsp sea salt
- 25 large basil leaves, coarsely chopped
- 2 medium cucumbers, unpeeled, seeded, and cut into 1" cubes
- 1 each red and yellow bell peppers, seeded and cut into 1" cubes
- 1 shallot, thinly sliced
- 8 Roma tomatoes, cut into 1-inch cubes
- 3 tbsp capers, drained
- 3 tbsp pine nuts, toasted

Ingredients for the Vinaigrette
- 1-2 garlic cloves, minced
- ½ tsp Dijon mustard
- 3 tbsp Champagne vinegar
- ½ c extra virgin olive oil
- ½ tsp sea salt
- ¼ tsp freshly ground black pepper

Instructions
1. Prepare toasty bread.
2. Cut bread into cubes.
3. Heat olive oil in a large sauté pan or cast-iron skillet with sides.
4. Add the bread cubes and salt. Cook over low to low-medium heat, tossing frequently, for ~10 minutes until nicely browned. Add more oil as needed.
5. Remove from heat before bread cubes become too hard (you want bread that is slightly toasty on the outside and chewy on the inside). Add to a large bowl.
6. Prep basil, cucumber, peppers, shallot, tomatoes. Then add to the bowl with bread.
7. Toast pine nuts. Add to the bowl.
8. Make vinaigrette. In a separate, small bowl whisk together all ingredients.
9. Pour vinaigrette over bread cubes and veggies. With a large spoon, gently fold everything together. Season with salt and pepper to taste. Allow the panzanella to sit for ~30 minutes for the flavors to blend, then serve.

CHAPTER 22

Recipe for Depression

I typically enjoyed fall in the Pacific Northwest knowing the next rainy day could be the first of eight or nine months of drizzle. On clear days Chris and I would pack in one more forest hike, neighborhood bike ride, movie in the park, camping trip. I rallied for one more garden tour, gallery walk, city circuit with out-of-town guests, cocktail on the patio at a trendy bar. Like other Portlanders, I relied on the innumerable odd events to get out and about before the soggy fall-winter-spring. I was equally comforted by the long rainy season with extra indoor time and an excuse for another cup of craft coffee or loose-leaf tea. Now a mother, I tried to embrace the blanket of rain as our family hunkered down into a slow, methodical shift to indoor life.

With so-called maternity leave (unemployment benefits) coming to an end, and holding a new life in my arms, I meditated on the depth of my brother-in-law's recent words (at least, my interpretation of them) when my sister died, "Don't waste this precious life by whittling away the days. Most importantly, show love."

I *was* in love. I loved my son, just as my mental health therapist predicted. I loved my husband and his enduring patience with my upending life circumstances and the way I processed them. But "wasting the days" bothered me. After months of turning my attention outward—pregnancy and birth, being quasi-fired and meeting with lawyers, unemployment, losing my sister and the grievous aftermath—I'd lost my way inside.

Five years prior, we'd moved to Portland for a fresh start, but my aspirations had not materialized. I'd studied permaculture, yoga, science. I'd fallen back on a previous career that ended abruptly. My social life was still mostly separate from my husband's. My nights were spent alone. Raising my son gave me a reason to find direction and, precisely for his sake and our family's, I felt compelled to decide on a career that would both expand my knowledge and be impactful to the wellbeing of this earth. Once again, I was without internal compass or map. My creativity was zapped.

So, I did…nothing. At least, it felt that way. Once an overdo-it-and-enjoy-it socialite with a zest for human connection and meaningful experiences, I'd become a milk machine with the sole purpose of nourishing a fragile, innocent little human. I sat for hours nursing and musing about the world that continued to spin slowly all around me, but without me. Despite unending support from friends who came to visit and play with my baby while I attended yoga classes or to get me outside, an internal rift was widening between motherhood and its inevitable separation from the busy work life I'd once known. No more vintage skirts and funky stockings; après-work local gin cocktails; artsy cities and their funky culture; whiskey parties and brunch events; sprints in the rain with lattes; jogs along the greenbelt between work and chemistry classes.

As I sat at home in neighborhood silence while my son nursed, my mind wandered to all the events I was potentially missing out on. On the periphery of the action, across the bridges from downtown, there were no more spontaneous invitations to anywhere. I deeply craved the freedom simply to sit in a coffee shop for several uninterrupted hours.

Baby chronically strapped to my breast, I took to wandering around the streets under an umbrella—window-shopping, searching for used cloth diapers and unpainted wooden toys.

Recipe for Depression

I wanted to ease into this new life with positive perspective. Instead, I was frigid with financial fear, frozen with indecision because of my loss of independence, crippled by the overriding question of whether I could truly enjoy the baby phase of motherhood.

My son was wrapped in his mama's turmoil, physically on tour of crazy town, emotionally everywhere. He slept cradled to my chest while I cooked, while I walked to the grocery store in the drizzle, while I cleaned house. He slept between his father and me at night.

By day, he hung wide-eyed from my hip, observing the world from my dimension, in rhythm with my breathing, guided by my pulse. Already, I couldn't imagine life without him. I relied on him to ground me, but he was not yet my companion or my teacher. He was years from being a sounding board for finding my path, though his wellbeing would become the key to my future.

And so passed the first few months of Avery's life on Earth. I'd inadvertently become a stay-at-home mom, a label I never wanted, a homemaker who resorted to routine. Deprived of adventure.

Motherhood was largely a pain in the ass.

The anxiety of "settling down" rushed in on the coattails of motherhood, and I wondered how a career would fit into the equation now. Would I find satisfaction in a steady job with a reliable income? Would there be time to explore? Was grad school ever going to happen?

I was unsure what to do next. The ideas flowed, but the sitting made me restless. I started researching graduate programs again and traced the path toward a nutrition career—it would be many years in the making. The inaugural nutrition program at the natural medicine university still hadn't been announced. Next term, the registrar assured. Or maybe the next.

In the meantime? I could not commit to a 40-hour per week job while nursing, plus I didn't want to get stuck in the grind or lose my vision, like I had with permaculture. So, I re-enrolled at Portland Community College to continue with the science pre-requisites. *Check.*

Now an income. I needed flexible hours and something impactful. Yoga. It was the only other thing besides food keeping me centered and sane. I'd practiced through pregnancy, through postpartum, through my sister's death. Through yoga, I maintained connection with my body and its needs—movement, nourishment, stillness.

I enrolled in a 500-hour Hatha yoga teacher-training course (not exactly an income). My first training—two years prior—was amazing, but hot, power yoga was unsustainable for my choleric personality and lanky tendons. A gentler, more traditional style suited me more. I agreed to a work-study trade at the yoga studio, only a short bike ride away.

Alongside yoga, I searched for a way to reinvent myself. I wrote entries for a blog called "milk and meditation" while I ate, drank, and thought about my stoic life. I sewed party flags and a quilt for Avery. I started reading "The Happiness Project," which captured the author's neurotically organized method for *creating* happiness. Each month, prompted by the book, I integrated one thing that brought me joy, then assessed how it worked. Small steps to overcome the monotony.

Around Christmas, Chris couldn't take it anymore—the drone of the rain as well as the monotony. The fog of my grief and stupor of exhaustion parted for a moment, to reveal that he, too, was in a funk. No longer attached to this city of gray skies, stagnation, and chill, we both longed for a change. We decided to spend the following summer back in Idaho (assuming, of course, we could endure six more months of torrential blah).

In the meantime, I continued to find ways to uplift myself and lighten the mood around the house. By the fourth or fifth Happiness Project month, I realized *all* of the activities I reinstated were food-related. I carved out time weekly to shop natural food stores (my soul incarnate) with their bulk bins, sunlit produce sections, artisan chocolate sections. I was magnetized to farmers markets, artisan bakeries, restaurants with menus boasting local everything. I dehydrated apples and preserved plums. I started hosting themed dinner parties again. I tested Asian recipes by myself at home.

Preparing food was also the only endeavor I could work on continuously without self-judgment, with child, and with a useful outcome. I released perfectionism in cooking. Starting with the best possible quality ingredients, it was easy to make delicious food. A meal that didn't knock my socks off was perfectly edible (except for one, memorable "savory tofu pie"—the only meal I've ever dumped into the compost bin).

In tandem with my renewed kitchen experimentation, I was feeding solid foods to my chunky, curious baby. Strapped to my chest, Avery watched my face as I tore lettuce. He peeked into the fridge when I rummaged behind jars of nut butter. He moved rhythmically with my body as I buttered bread and smashed goat cheese with fresh berries on toast. When on my back, he peeked over my shoulder as I chopped carrots or minced herbs, his feet often tapping the cabinets or counter on either side of me.

I was surprised at the lack of guidance for feeding real food to babies. I had one very dense book articulating every excruciating detail about how to cook and puree a very few, specific foods to introduce to babies and exactly how to store them and for how long. The author and mother had seemingly no educational qualifications or nutritional background. Her whole-foods approach made sense on some level, though the book did not explain why these efforts mattered. Beyond formulaic, her methods reassured my sense that serving bland rice or wheat cereal wasn't a very appealing—or natural—way of introducing flavors or sustenance to new eaters.

Shouldn't my baby eat the same, nourishing foods I was eating?

Blessed to be proficient at nursing Avery with "liquid gold" mama milk for six months already, it was disheartening to think about serving him commercial food from boxes and jars. Or letting him suck on plastic squeezy packs. Or masticating puffed air imperceptibly flavored with beets, kale, or mango housed in non-recyclable containers.

Quite simply, I didn't understand why there were professionals aplenty in the field of lactation, loads of books about sleep training, and oodles of advice about potty training, yet next to nil about "how to" introduce babies to the wonderful, wide world of solid foods beyond purees! And the internet was all over the place.

I looked to friends who were raising vegan babies (slightly sallow skin, but full of energy and curiosity) and omnivorous babies (often with rosier skin, but equally thriving). Some of them fed babies with the food straight off their own plates. Others exclusively nursed their babies well beyond a year. Still others offered French fries and MSG as soon as baby could sit in a highchair at the neighborhood brewpub or Vietnamese restaurant.

Making it up as I went along, I procured some ice-cube trays with fitted lids and was gifted a smattering of silicone bowls and utensils. A friend gave me her baby-food mill; I assumed I could just grind up whatever I was eating—quinoa, sweet potatoes, beets—and thin almond butter or avocados with coconut cream or breast milk.

I knew nothing about iron-deficiency in breastfed babies, or how pureed food led to picky behaviors (which other moms tolerated and, perhaps inadvertently, propagated). I'd lost a ton of weight thanks to my son's nursing proficiency, so I knew I, personally, needed to eat lots of protein and healthy fats. Avery was perhaps the chubbiest baby in my circle of mom friends, yet I never restricted his food intake—I let him explore, be curious, eat what he wanted of the foods I offered, and stop when he was satiated. This approach seemed intuitive, and I felt immense pride in witnessing my little boy enjoy peanut-sauce-soaked tofu, lick hummus off steamed cauliflower, and dip quinoa-lentil-kale fritters in yogurt. Outfitted with a bib directing onlookers to "Give Peas a Chance" my son and I were well on our way to baby-foodie experimentation.

Little did I realize I was sowing seeds to sprout forth later as both a baby food and mama food expert.

Raising my child with natural foods and intuitive methods took my mind off my sister's death, lack of career focus, boredom, and impatience as I reclaimed my dream to pursue a graduate degree in nutrition. My efforts to nourish myself and my tiny human (and Chris, when he wasn't working) afforded me a viable excuse to fixate on this specific outlet of imminent joy in my budding motherhood journey.

Swaddled in kitchen bliss, I counted down the days until our summer departure.

RECIPE for DEPRESSION

The mere suggestion of a dragon in this meal insinuates the powerful healing energy of food—tangible and supernatural, intuitive, and traditional. Mothers, with our miraculous ability to bear children, easily become nutritionally depleted. This meal provides nutrients for energy, hormone balance, and mind-body nourishment. It's my go-to recipe when I bring a meal to families with a new baby.

Dragon Bowls
Yield = 3-4 servings
Prep time = 10 minutes
Total time = 55 minutes

Ingredients
- Quinoa, cooked in unsalted veggie broth
- Beans, beans, the musical fruit (ideally, soaked from dried, then boiled)
- A bunch or two of kale
- Wakame (rehydrated)
- ¼ c extra virgin olive oil
- 3 tbsp tahini (ideally raw)
- 2 tbsp lemon juice
- 1 tbsp coconut aminos or tamari
- 2 cloves garlic, minced
- 1 tsp ground coriander
- Avocado slices
- Sprinkle of sesame seeds

Instructions
1. Prepare quinoa. Rinse in a fine colander. Add broth (2 parts water: 1 part quinoa) to a pot with lid. Add quinoa and bring to boil. Reduce heat to simmer, covered, for about 20 minutes.
2. Meanwhile, open and rinse a can of beans of choice or, ideally, use beans you've already presoaked and cooked. Any variety will do. Heat beans if you'd like.
3. Prepare kale. Remove ribs and chop leaves into large pieces. Prepare another pot of water with a steamer basket. Add kale but don't cook it until 5 minutes before you're ready to eat.
4. Rehydrate wakame. Add pinch of wakame to a small bowl of water. Set aside.
5. Prepare sauce. Whisk together olive oil, tahini, lemon juice, aminos, garlic, and coriander until creamy. Taste and adjust for flavor and texture.
6. Check the quinoa—when it's done, add a few pinches of salt. Fluff with a fork. Remove from heat.
7. Turn on pot for steaming kale. Steam 3-4 minutes, until the leaves are bright green.
8. While the kale is steaming, assemble bowls. Add quinoa, beans, then steamed kale. Top with sauce, avocado, wakame, and sesame seeds. Or, add to containers to bring to a new mom.
9. Adjust flavors as needed, keeping in mind that a. canned beans likely contain sodium; b. tamari in sauce may have plenty of sodium; and c. wakame contains lots of sodium.

CHAPTER 23

Recipe for Disillusionment

That spring, our son turned one and we turned to the Idaho mountains for a reprieve. Of course, it couldn't just be a getaway—Chris decided to remodel his Sun Valley condo which he'd been renting out and into which we'd be moving for the summer. That was a jarring start toward my vision of finding peace.

In one frenzied week, we moved out of our Portland house, welcomed in our subletters, drove to Idaho with a small U-Haul, moved in with friends, remodeled a condo, found jobs and, finally, transplanted ourselves into a 492-square-foot one-room studio for the summer. Yeah, it was a frenetic mess of juggling demolition, presenting to job interviews, working around toddler naps, painting walls (twice), scheduling carpet installation (more than twice), being hospitable house guests (with our furniture stacked up in their garage and diapers stacked in the spare room), and driving up and down the valley in one vehicle. One of us was always stranded. Both of us were hurried. And I was super stressed living out of the back of a truck, stretching our budget to the limit, eating less-than-high-quality store-bought lunches, feeling obligated to eat dinner at our friends' house (30 minutes south of the condo), while craving kitchen space to cook even the simplest meals.

Yet every time I looked around me at the mountains and trees, I returned to deep gratitude for our life. We had a place to live in a small town, close to nature, where we could inhale the clean air and slow down. We settled into a new routine, each of us I working only three days per week to ensure we cultivated plenty of family time. I worked the morning shift at a health club (free yoga, wellness-minded people, smoothie bar) and Chris easily found work in a high-end restaurant in Ketchum. Early afternoon, we'd meet somewhere in town, high-five each other, talk poop, milk, feedings, naps, and hand off the kid. Chris would leave for his dinner shift; I'd bike back to the condo with babe in tow.

On nights when Chris worked, Avery and I would ride the bus in circles around town, explore bugs in the groomed landscaping, or trek up the backside of the bunny hill. On the hottest days, we'd stay inside listening to French music to circumvent toy cacophony in the tiny play space while I made berry-and-banana popsicles for my teething son. Naturally, I also reconnected with my local friends for hikes, playdates with our kids, and dinners that no longer resembled our parties from life before motherhood yet were equally comforting (and customarily without my man). On our days together as a family, we enjoyed Ketchum and Sun Valley as if we were tourists, picnicking in parks, drinking coffee in the town square, hiking, and camping.

It was small town Idaho life as we knew it before. Déjà-vu. Plus one.

Some days, I'd take Avery on drives, stopping alongside scenic backcountry roads, where I nursed, changed poopy diapers, or calmed a hysterical baby. Under the shade of pine trees, I'd feed him the grapes I'd painstakingly quartered with sliced cheddar and homemade monster cookies. I carved out time to just be present, though my mind often wandered to childhood memories with my older sissy, or images of her in those final days. Sometimes when the tears flowed, obstructing my ability to drive safely, I'd pull over at historical monument, which became markers of grief and presence.

Recipe for Disillusionment

Other times, I thought about the future, which complicated our simple life. Not just the next campout and the many trips back and forth from condo to truck, to pack and unpack camping gear, beer, books, yoga mat, camera, headlamps, extra water, bag balm, mosquito spray, energy bars, first aid kit, camelbacks, baby wipes, and bikes. But the tough life shit layered beneath mothering, moving, mourning—my application to grad school. Finally, National University of Natural Medicine in Portland was initiating their inaugural nutrition master's program!

On our wedding anniversary we camped in the same place where we were married only four years prior. I was preoccupied with the gift I wanted to give Chris—not an item, but intimacy. We'd lost our sensual connection thanks to chronic breastfeeding, conflicting schedules, and (I realized much later) stress, anxiety, and depression that stripped me of my urges. Relationship unrest had been escalating and Chris became unresponsive to rekindling the sweet, spontaneous affection we'd had before; he neglected to buy fruit or pick wildflowers (anniversary gifts we'd discussed); and then he dropped a bomb. "I don't want to go back to Portland in a couple of months. Or ever. I feel like I need to stay in Idaho."

Woah. In many ways, I totally understood. The city had been fun for both of us, but it was busy all the time, dreary, and harder to retreat into nature. When we did, trailheads were packed, making it impossible to truly get away from it all. Importantly, it had nothing left to offer Chris because, once again, the restaurant he called home had suddenly closed after decades on the forefront of the farm-to-table circuit. But me, I'd been accepted to graduate school. I had goals to fulfill there. Dreams.

"My program is only 15 months. I know we can do that," I asserted.

After a pause, he replied, "You can go back, if you want, with or without Avery. You can finish your yoga program and grad school. We could travel back and forth until you finish, or…."

Wait, what? "You'd rather stay here without me—or Avery—than be in Portland …together? As a family…?" He nodded.

What is happening?

For the rest of the summer, our peaceful and beautiful escapes to the woods became quieter as we kept our thoughts mostly to ourselves. We started hiking and trail running without each other, and I sought solace in my friends and the trees.

By fall, Chris agreed to go back to Portland together. We'd decided I would finish the yoga teacher training along with grad school—it was *my dream!* I'd been building toward it for *years*, a happy progression from permaculture to nutrition; between nature's complementary treatments and Western medicine's science. *My dream* had been partly responsible for my being fired, and heightened after being unable to help my sister through chemical treatment and death. *My dream* for a fulfilling career included a flexible schedule to give more time to our family; to gain the knowledge for our bodies to be healthy and vibrant in the face of an objectionable food system.

In early October, we packed up our mountain gear and found new renters for our Sun Valley condo. The day the couple signed the lease, we both hesitated. We signed because that was the *plan*. But even I felt like we were leaving our true home.

Thirty minutes south, driving through the bedroom community of Bellevue, Chris pulled his truck off the road. He looked at me and said, "I'm not going back to Portland." *No!* My heart jumped through my chest and my mind raced in circles. I had no words or questions, just fear and worry for what was to come. I teared up, panicked.

Chris drove us to his friend's house only a few minutes away. We sat on the porch—I, in a stupor—until Sean came home from work. A childless bachelor, Sean made it clear Chris was welcome to stay anytime, but he did *not* mean his wife and baby. Chris assured his buddy we wouldn't be there long—a few weeks at best—while we figured out our next move. *Our next move? Um, hello? We're going back to Portland, and I want to leave immediately! Remember, I have an ambition there to fulfill?*

We stayed. And, as we did five months prior, we piled our life into yet another garage and spare room. I cried.

The only thing I could do besides brood was help cook, clean dishes, pick raspberries, and weed the garden. Sean was a legit foodie, mixologist, and budding fermentation expert. Though I loved watching him move about his kitchen, passionately focused on every detail of a recipe, I adamantly believed the quality of the food needed improvement. Sean cooked from scratch simply because he loved to. Each meal easily took three hours to prepare and was well worth the wait (for most people). However, while he was interested in the right cut of meat or the perfect combination of flavors and textures, he didn't give a hoot about sourcing ingredients. Artisan and handcrafted, yes; but grass-fed, pesticide-free, or local, not so much. Hence, I declined to sample the dead pig he'd painstakingly smoked during one entire day, and once again I felt immense guilt about my choices in someone else's home.

The tension shifted when I became mesmerized by Sean's sourdough bread. He baked it after work, and I stayed up late to sample it and ask him to teach me how to make it. He was a man of few words, and I could tell my very presence in his home had more than tested his patience. He handed me "Tartine Bread," a book outlining the precise methodology for artisan breadmaking.

I thumbed through the thick, chemistry-like bread bible as Sean worked the enriched semolina dough with freshly toasted and smashed fennel and coriander seeds for one batch, golden raisins and citrus zest for another. I was hooked—sourdough making was the perfect combination of a chemistry experiment, geeky foodie sensory awareness, and Mother Nature's brilliance. I was inspired to do anything—including move out—to absorb this wisdom.

And we needed to make a move sooner than later. The pressure was on. As if Chris's dreams were heard, while running from Sean's house up the canyon one day with Avery in a stroller (he slept only in moving objects) and arguing again about our future, Chris and I passed a house for sale. Without seeing the inside, Chris was smitten, enthusiastic to do anything—even borrow money (something he swore he'd never do)—to purchase the house of *his* dreams.

Now I drew a line: I would move out of Sean's house in exchange for sourdough lessons, but I would *not* buy a home on the outskirts of a characterless, sleepy town. Bellevue was supposedly "The Gateway to the Sawtooth Mountains" but it didn't feel like a portal to me. It felt dry, empty, barren. Devoid of trees. Devoid of society. And it certainly was not Portland, where I felt I still needed to be.

The house itself was solid and a wonderfully blank slate—everything we could want, more than we needed, and with plenty of room to grow and redesign spaces to our tastes. Chris loved the fireplace, the views, the man-cave. I admired the Pella windows with blind inserts, the custom hardware and, of course, the five-burner gas stove.

Chris begged me to make an offer. On the hillside overlooking town, I screamed out, "Nooo! I cannot live in Bellevue! It doesn't feel right to me!" I sobbed. Chris consoled me, then reminded me of the pangs of his childhood, moving every year—often twice—and never planting roots. He described all the ways this town—this Valley—would be the ideal place to raise our son.

I couldn't disagree. I knew he was right. But I gave in only when he reminded me, "Truppi, I've always let you do whatever you wanted. I've never stopped you. Now I'm asking you to help me with *my* dream." *His dream.* A house. A mortgage. Roots. Fuck.

It wasn't the house itself I didn't like—it was the *location*. Although the site was lovely, perched on the hillside with sweeping views, government land to the north and nice enough houses to the east and west, I just didn't want to live so far south of, well, everything we loved about Ketchum and Sun Valley. Like the trails and trees. And my community of people.

Where would our son go to school? Where would we all hang out during the day and with whom? What would Avery and I do at night, while Chris worked 30 minutes north? What about the commute? Chris assured me the drive would be no big deal. That house was the perfect place to raise our family. But my sister Jaclyn, a real estate agent, reminded me, "You can always change your house, but you can rarely change its location."

Most importantly, Chris convinced me he'd do anything to make it happen. "I'll work seven nights a week for as long as it takes for us to be comfortable," he promised. But in my heart, I knew better. This rural township was situated at the north end of pastured land flanked by barren hillsides and a state highway acting as a five-lane main street. It lacked a town center, local shops, or anything interesting to explore other than

Recipe for Disillusionment

the sagebrush canyon itself. The quiet, empty park possessed an ominous Hitchcock movie vibe.

I clearly understood the concept of "bedroom community": empty by day. We'd be displaced from everything I cherished about the magical mountain resort town where we'd both lived, worked, and played before kids and all that summer. We'd be without our peeps, not to mention a decent coffee shop where I could commiserate with other stay-at-home moms, if I could find them at all. Something deep inside me knew instinctively that living in that house would not mean "moving back"—it would be moving backwards. What would I do seven nights a week while Chris worked and didn't come home until well after midnight? What would my life look like each day, in a quiet desolation?

I asked him to humor me and look at a few houses in Hailey, only ten minutes north with five times the population and an actual community where people walked around during the day—to the bank, the yoga studio, the ice cream shop, the grocery store (which was not inhibited by a busy highway). Unfortunately, little inventory offered only houses Chris called "projects" or "too cookie-cutter." I found myself not caring about those things.

"Babe, we can make *any* place feel like home," I pleaded. I just wanted to be where human life thrived.

Chris persisted on the Bellevue house. I saw the passion in his eyes, and I took the leap to trust him. I let him take the reins, urging him not to gamble beyond an amount already stretching our price range. We made an offer; I held my breath. Then a counteroffer; now I cringed. As we awaited a reply and the reality unfolded, I feared my own dreams were about to vanish. I sensed a gloomy future in that house. Nothing felt right.

Eventually Chris agreed that we couldn't counter-offer again. We'd hit our max. I prayed it just wasn't meant to be. We wrote an authentic letter to the sellers, apologizing if our bottom-line offer seemed offensively low, and that we simply couldn't do more.

Offer accepted.

Shit.

We made the very mistake we had cautioned our friends *not* to make: we bought a house requiring two incomes. We made little on the Sun Valley rental condo, and I rightfully feared what we'd endure to "make it work." Worse, the many thousands of dollars I'd saved for grad school went into the down payment. But my biggest miscalculation was giving into the pressure no one could have cautioned me about: supporting the dreams of my partner while sacrificing my own.

In between our accepted offer and the closing, we gave Sean a break from us and visited Jaclyn on her river property on the other side of the Sawtooth mountains. We inadvertently arrived just in time to cut up an elk. *Oh, joy*. Weeks prior, Jaclyn and Jeremy skinned and gutted the cow they lovingly honored in the field before bringing the carcass home to hang in their shop. The elk was ready to process, and I was already processing so much in my mind and heart, I figured slicing up a dead animal would offer the numbing effect I thought I needed. Having never been a part of cutting up game—and often feeling guilty for accepting Jaclyn's gifts of wild-harvested meat—I rolled up my sleeves, was handed a very sharp knife, and declared I was *all in*.

The smell of dead flesh was too much for Chris to bear, so he spent much of our visit outside with Avery doing anything possible to remain in the crisp, cool air. Somewhat relieved to have some space from him, I carefully carved the meat while giving thanks. Inside my heart, however, pulsed an aching not for the elk, but for my own urge to stab something. Not an animal—no, my past vegan life very much resisted what I was doing in that moment. But in my own anger, frustration, and fear of what lay ahead for me, I wanted to lash out. With blood up to my elbows and tears rolling down my cheeks, I felt like I was stripping away some of myself along with cutting strips of loin. Like this cow elk, some of me felt ground-up, other parts left in larger chunks to be severed after grilling. I wondered how I could be wholly me after slicing off pieces of myself for my husband and my son.

I'd have to get creative to find a way.

In our new home, one night in late December I was awake nursing Avery when Chris returned in the wee hours. He was exhausted after working every night for weeks during the holiday rush, but I was wide awake and pumped up! I'd been researching online graduate schools and couldn't wait to tell him about three schools, each offering a master's degree in Science and Nutrition. "Babe, there is a way for me to change careers and fulfill my calling! We can both have what we want!"

His weary expression transformed into contemplation and his eyes shifted from my face to the floor. My heart sank and my shoulders fell when Chris said, "I thought you'd given up that dream when we bought the house, when you said you wouldn't travel back to Portland on your own." He foretold his own vision for me. "You have so many passions—why fixate on that *one*? I thought you could be happy doing something here, contributing to *our* life here…our life at home. Does it really matter if you're a functional nutritionist?"

Once again, I was utterly speechless. I could not fathom how we could agree about the paint color for the kitchen cabinets yet be light years apart about our life vision. It was this resort valley that had transformed us—each separately and then together—from young adults looking for new experiences, to a young family raising our son in a tight-knit, mountain community. But our interpretation of *how* to be there was worlds apart.

RECIPE for DISILLUSIONMENT

No single food, recipe, or meal can soothe the utter disappointment of watching your dreams falling apart before your eyes. For me, nature therapy and movement forge a path through emotional pain.

Nature Nutrition
Yield = 1 refreshing hike
Prep time = However long it takes to gather food, water, layers, and a map
Total time = At least a few hours

Ingredients
- Trail mix with dried fruit and dark chocolate
- Fresh fruit for quick energy
- Sandwich or other small lunch-like item with carbs, fats, and protein
- Hard-boiled egg, jerky, small nut butter packet, or other form of extra protein
- Extra food such as energy bars or nutrient-dense cookies in case you get lost
- A cold beer, coconut water, or kombucha in a cooler in your car (or chill in the creek)

Gear List
- Backpack with hydro pack filled with water
- LifeStraw or another water purifier
- Map and compass (the latter if your sense of direction sucks)
- Mini first aid kit (band aids, duct tape, healing balm, tiger balm, lip balm, etc.)
- Pocket knife
- Waterproof matches or lighter
- Bear whistle & bear spray
- Insect repellant
- Sunglasses, hat, bandana, sunscreen
- TP and a plastic bag (for those who hate drip drying)
- Layers (windbreaker, raincoat, puffy coat, long sleeve, short sleeve, beanie, gloves)
- Wool socks and sturdy shoes
- Journal and pen
- Flip flops for the car ride home

Instructions
1. Decide, in advance, where you'll hike based on your capability. Then, be prepared.
2. If hiking solo, tell someone where you're going. It's surprising how many hikers go missing.
3. Pack all the essentials. ALL of them.
4. Check the weather. Mother Nature is our friend, yet conditions change often.
5. Prep food. Bring more than you think you need.
6. Hydrate. Don't drink alcohol the night before and limit caffeine the morning of your hike. Tune into your surroundings by being physically clean and mentally clear.
7. Fill your gas tank with plenty of gas.
8. Give yourself extra time at the trailhead to organize, and extra time after to rehydrate (or drink a beer), soak your feet in the creek, change shoes.
9. Go. Be. Enjoy. Breathe. Pause. Sit. Listen. See. Touch. Smell. Taste, if you'd like and if you know your local vegetation. Sing, if you're worried about bears or mountain lions. Soak it in. Find peace. Find gratitude. Love the adventure. Love yourself.

CHAPTER 24

Recipe for Disconnect

I'd never felt more alone. There was love—my heart ached with joy when I was with our son, and my love for my husband was rooted, but not blooming as it once was. I sincerely wanted to support him by shifting my perspective about our new life. Our home gave him a sense of pride, hope, and an anchor for raising our son *near enough* to the mountains. But, for me, living in that house meant giving up other sources of deep nourishment, like a sense of belonging to my community, the pulse of life, and my dreams.

Chris worked almost every night. He was tired, true. But from my perspective, he wasn't just "bringing home the bacon," he was *living*—engaging in interesting conversations with guests, socializing with co-workers, enjoying mouthwatering food prepared by someone else (without having to wash dishes), tasting wine from around the world, and (often) going out after work for drinks and to enjoy music. And simply *because* he worked nights, I had none of those opportunities. Our families lived in other states, we couldn't afford a babysitter, and we'd resided in what felt like a ghost town. My friends lived north of us with their own kids and established friend groups.

Had there been other mothers in Bellevue who were home during the day, I would have found them—I walked or jogged daily, not only for peace of mind and exercise but also in search of people. Horses neighed, goats bleated, a rooster crowed. Artists holed up in their homes and second-home owners locked up for half the year. I scooted along the chalky, sagebrush-lined roads with Avery (often asleep). I struggled to find beauty in a town named for its beautiful view. My lonely days shrouded my ability to see splendor—instead, I saw flowers neglected and choked by weeds.

Eventually, I found a Saturday morning ritual that brought the promise of something good. Avery and biked or walked to Main Street to visit a local handmade-furniture shop/bake shop owned by a talented husband-and-wife team. They sold real meat (locally raised rabbit and pork brats), plant starts, homemade pickles, and jam. But it was the cinnamon rolls and hospitality that drew us back every weekend as we let Chris sleep in. There I met a French mama and her two young boys—who also came for the cinnamon rolls. I was over the moon! I liked her immediately—and I could practice my French! *J'etais tres hord de pratique.* She worked at Sun Valley Resort during the weekdays, so I looked forward to our weekend rendezvous.

But during the week, at home alone, I took to the kitchen, preparing gourmet meals nightly for myself and our toddler. Avery was game for much of it. He became my taste-tester. He scoffed at anything brothy yet ate raw mushrooms with pleasure. He was enamored by the salad spinner, though only for 17 seconds. He was content making music with jars of beans and banging on mixing bowls with a wooden spoon. After exploring every cupboard, he'd ditch me to stack blocks, scoot trains, and whack pucks with the hockey stick his Grumpa made him.

After a while, I questioned why the hell I was bothering with labor-intensive meals. Avery would be perfectly content eating straightforward elk burgers and home fries, beans and rice, tofu tacos. Chris didn't care much about leftover chana masala or pad Thai—he ate Asian food at work, though rarely brought home leftovers. I'd supposed I could simplify our meals, especially with grad school on the horizon—I'd been accepted into Maryland University of Integrative Health's online master's program in Science and Nutrition. Spring term couldn't come fast enough!

In the meantime, I tried to enjoy the humble habits of homemaking. I woke daily with Avery while we let Daddy sleep in until after 9:00 or 10:00; then we spent several hours together—as a family. I baked bread and washed diapers while Chris played guitar. Or we'd venture to the mountain to teach our son to ski. At home, we worked side-by-side on the interior makeover. Chris did the grueling, tedious work—tearing out paneling, removing hardware, sanding down cabinets, spackling holes—while I hung with our little man and ensured we were well fed. When it came time to paint, we switched roles so I could meditate over the perfect lines between color tones. It was mostly lovely during those few hours of togetherness each day.

Come late winter, though, my eagerness to complete projects grew as I anticipated the start of grad school. We didn't talk about it, but the angst hung in the air as my energy picked up and we began stepping out of tune with one another. Chris and I bumped into each other awkwardly and huffed about little things. Sure, there was peace in little moments, yet quickly replaced by the impending start of the trimester, fear of the further disconnect that could arise. I also felt some guilt in the enjoyment of home improvement projects, which I envisioned would increase the value of our house. Like the other places we'd bought and sold, I hoped we'd sell that house, too, in the not-too-distant future (so we could move to Hailey). I didn't believe Chris intended to stay there *forever*.

In fact, everything about being in that house—including our present challenges—felt temporary. I was certain we'd find our ease and flow again soon. I envisioned Chris would come around to more than just accepting my endeavor—that he'd be pumped for me (for us!) and that we'd soon see eye to eye. In the past, when one of us had an idea and the other wasn't on board yet, we'd patiently persevere. Eventually, we'd come around. That's how we worked.

But when my daily study regimen started, Chris didn't just drift further, he seemed to jump ship. He became downright crabby, morose, withdrawn. Simultaneously, our few hours of daily family time whittled down to minutes. As soon as Chris woke up, I'd pull his breakfast out of the toaster oven, pour his coffee, and bounce upstairs to my computer, which I'd set up in "the fun room." I'd created a study space in a crammed corner opposite the drums and popcorn machine, where I'd remain for hours. Once or twice daily, he'd bring in Avery to nurse. Often, yet rarely with a smile or eye contact, he brought beautiful salads for my lunch.

It was a strange and dichotomous situation to feel deep, inner joy with my lessons balanced by rising guilt each time I put down my books for motherhood and family life. The problem was, my studies were always on the back burner in my mind, stacking up, penetrating our home as I pined over recipes from my cooking labs while memorizing the properties and characteristics on my organic chemistry flashcards.

I was alive again! Inside myself, at least. Grad school, like a pharmaceutical drug, ignited my brain's pleasure center. It was the antidote to my post-partum depression that I hadn't realized had overtaken me.

But Chris stopped meeting my gaze. I stopped smiling at his jokes. We stopped being affectionate. It felt like we'd stopped being friends altogether, but I loved him and I believed this phase, like others before, would pass. I believed we had a deep understanding of each other, a true appreciation for our differences, which brought us together and kept our life interesting. Didn't we?

Between studying and mothering, I tried to make every moment count. With Chris, it was near impossible—my words of thanks were shrugged off, and he gave short, nondescript replies when I asked him open-ended questions about how he was doing. So, I focused on the things I *could* control and which brought me joy, like meals.

Ironically, while in school for nutrition, I found myself cooking less to study more. I still cooked every meal from scratch (due to our small budget, lack of food choices in Bellevue, and because even my basic meals were tasty). I just pared down. Simplified. I don't think Chris really noticed, but I, personally, accepted the tradeoff with gusto because the lectures, deadlines, and quizzes more than nourished my brain and heart. I felt lighter and more energetic despite lack of sleep and extra effort.

I also found myself enjoying being a mother, discovering newfound pleasure in shifting from studying to doting on Avery. I was a mama with a purpose! Before grad school, I'd sit listlessly in the living room, dreadfully bored by reading the Tow Mater book for the 459th time, uninterested in filling up recycled plastic dump trucks with matchbox cars, only to witness them being dumped on the floor again. But now, I was tuned into this play time and became fascinated by these activities—not the actual games, but watching Avery's expressions, his curiosity, his brain figuring out how to place something square atop something round. Little miracles unfolded in his development as we learned the alphabet and numbers through card games and play. I felt a deep sense of pride in every tiny effort I'd already made to nourish my healthy, thriving son and was equally nourished by him.

Still, it felt like I was child-rearing all alone. My husband felt the same way—daddy daycare by day, worker bee by night; on the flip side, I was grad student by day, single mama by night. We'd become two ships passing at 3:30 in the afternoon, but not like the summer before when we had several days off together. It became an excruciatingly lonely routine, leaving us virtually no time to connect, let alone share magical moments.

And since no one I knew lived nearby, each afternoon when Chris left for work, Avery and I spent time in our yard (alone) or exploring the canyon (alone), against the breezes saturated with Roundup from the neighbor and D-24 from roadside weed control. I would have been infinitely happier in a small yard in a small town with more people and plenty of organically grown weeds.

In my search for a mom community, I fell into a rhythm with a couple of friends—one new, and one from my past life in Ketchum. Both lived in Hailey, close enough to each other that they biked to each other's houses. Nevertheless, one evening each week, when all our husbands worked in restaurants, we gathered for dinner. Our babies played and made messes while we drank wine and relied on each other for sanity. We connected about breastfeeding, crappy sleep, and wife life. We often invited other mamas into our extended family. Those women became my social outlet and gave me hope that, someday, I might cultivate a semblance of the same, simple, easy ways that accompanied life in town.

At first, we rotated hosting dinners. But when their kids started falling asleep during the 10-minute drive from my home to theirs, dinners ceased in my neck of the woodless woods. I lived *too far away* (no shit). My son went to sleep late, so it was easy enough for me to drive five miles to meet them.

Then came baby number two.

In that first crazy semester of school, Chris and I discussed having another baby, *including* how much harder everything would be. We still felt love for one another and respected each other as parents, at the very least. We strongly felt the best gift we could give our son was a sibling.

In my mid 30's, my body and mind were strong. That time, I hesitated not about having another baby, but about the intimacy. With our opposing schedules and a two-year-old sleeping in our bed, it was hard to find time for undisturbed togetherness. I tried to schedule "it" into our week. Nope. Too regimented for Chris. I would prepare mentally for potential impromptu love sessions, but at 1:00 in the morning when Chris returned home from work I was tired, and my hormones said no (I mean, did any breast-feeding mother crave sex after an 18-hour day?). Mostly, it was emotional disconnect.

Even so, we both agreed waiting would be harder than going for it. Might as well have two young children at home. See? Eye to eye on something—*that* was encouraging.

As I predicted, we became pregnant remarkably easily, for which I am eternally grateful—not because I dreaded "trying," but because we'd had enough worry and discontent. Instead, the ease of fertility reminded me we were meant to make babies together, and we both hoped baby #2 would help us rekindle even a spark of what we'd lost.

Nope, not yet. That summer was our busiest ever with a toddler, grad school, and Chris's work schedule. We both needed a break from the chaos, but we hardly had time to eat together let alone carve out one night to chill, relax, or camp. And definitely no time for lovemaking. We felt bound by our routine, and I knew it would become more intense when our second child was born mid-winter. Plus, I was still nursing Avery at night, and when he finally weaned himself from the boob the week of finals, I slipped away for my first overnighter sans kiddo—a backpacking trip in the Sawtooth Mountains with girlfriends.

Recipe for Disconnect

Upon my return, Avery and I flew into the ranch where my aunt and uncle lived, for a few days of calm and family time while river lounging, blackberry picking, and stargazing from the sleeping porch. We rushed home to see Daddy, timing our arrival for early afternoon, before he'd leave for work. But something was off. He'd thrown a party the day we left (I thought he hated parties?) and didn't tell me. People I didn't know had spent the night in our home. Our house had been rearranged—the furniture in the fun room, my desk, my books. The fridge was still full of food I'd bought, and the leftovers I'd set aside for him were untouched.

We were truly living separate lives. I was pregnant with our second child. Lonely. And my husband was doing things with other people in our home—and elsewhere—without my knowledge.

Somehow, we endured the fall. I kept my nose in my books. Despite unwavering support from my mom, Jaclyn, my friends, professors, and peers, I couldn't help but feel *my* choices were ruining everything.

By January, at 35 weeks pregnant, I started the year by seeking help for my emotional issues. I vowed to overcome my cynicism, criticism, control, short temper, and to work daily to cultivate more peace, appreciation, and gratitude for the simple things. I no longer wanted us to exist as a husband and a wife; I wanted us to coexist as a loving couple. We could do better.

I planned a coffee date for Chris and me to rewrite our life goals—dreams, practical finances, career, family, personal and relationship goals. He hesitated to attend, but we found that many of our visions still aligned. Importantly, he confessed his own fears about losing *us*, and not knowing what to do about it. So, we promised to spend every Friday morning together and commit to a date night monthly after our new baby was born. We vowed to find a babysitter to help once a week and start a kiddo trade with other families. I decided to lighten course load come summer.

Before we knew it, there was a tub set up again in our home—this time in the dining room. In another quick labor—entirely different from the first and several days "early." I wasn't ready!

In fact, in the middle of the night in early February I picked up my maternity book to read about what was happening—was it pre-labor? Again, my water hadn't broke, and that time I sensed a dull aching in my cervix, which I hadn't remembered from my son's birth. No vomiting. No diarrhea.

A few hours later, Avery awoke and I managed to get him ready for daycare. As I sat on the stool while he ate breakfast, I was hit with a sharp abdominal pain that made me stagger and cry out. He looked at me in fear and confusion. I assured him mama was okay, and that his baby brother or sister was telling me it was time to enter this crazy, wonderful world.

The contractions intensified, so I woke Chris and told him it was time. He asked if I could make it to Ketchum for our appointment to sign closing papers on his condo. I looked up at him with disbelief. "Babe, remember how *quickly* Avery came out? Please just take him to school and come right back."

By the time Chris returned, my contractions lasted two-and-a-half minutes each (no exaggeration) and I was gushing profanities thanks to the intense back pain—ten times worse than round one. I managed to go upstairs to install my contact lenses—I wasn't going to miss my second baby being born (perhaps in the caul)—and by the time I clocked contractions at 30 seconds apart, I called our midwife, Erin.

Soon, there was a knock on the door, but it was not Erin. It was the woman from the title company who exclaimed, "This is the most exciting closing I've ever experienced!" Chris delivered papers to me and, while crouched on our bathroom floor, I signed 20 or so dotted lines between contractions.

Erin came in next, and I heard her give Chris instructions to inflate the birthing tub. When she came to check on me, she gently scolded me for not calling sooner—whether I was ready or not, that baby was about to come out. She helped me downstairs to the dining room, to undress and climb into the tub. Like the last time, it was only partially filled with water. This time, the water was warm—I hadn't done laundry or bathed. There was no music, no cinnamon smell coming from the oven. In fact, I hadn't prepared any food at all—not for myself, my family, or my midwife and her assistant.

I cannot remember whether Chris climbed into the tub with me that time, but I do remember that in a few pushes, I watched my water break into the tub as our baby slipped out, perfect and healthy. My heart overflowed as we welcomed the dreamiest baby girl into our lives.

A few hours later, when Avery was back home, he resisted sharing Mom and Dad with that baby. Unlike round one, we didn't have a name for her. Avery dubbed her "Pizza," a typical toddler response, grabbing onto the first word that came to mind. For me, it was a blatant reminder of my unpreparedness. I had no smoothie, muffin, or other nutrient-dense food planned. Chris wryly suggested ordering "pizza," a meal that was horrifying to both Erin and me, since we knew I needed an iron-rich meal after significant blood loss, not a meal with excessive salt, cured meat, grease, and simple carbs. Chris was trying to make it easy for everyone.

Analytically, I felt immense guilt for prioritizing grad school over preparedness for the birth of our second child. What a stark difference from Avery's birth, which had consumed my life.

Nevertheless, I had deadlines. The next morning, while our baby girl slept, I took a pathophysiology exam—and passed with flying colors—while a friend worked quietly in the kitchen encapsulating my placenta.

When Chris went back to work, Avery was at preschool, and I resumed coursework, the heaviness and loneliness grew. Thankfully, my love grew, too. Our daughter's bright eyes—the grey-blue color of her auntie Jessica's—lit up my life. Aylee (EYE-lee) Jessica, to whom we'd given two family names, was my beacon in the fog. Whereas Avery anchored me through trauma, mourning, and grief, now Aylee was guiding me through thick, emotional turmoil.

Still, I felt ever more isolated with a second child alongside pangs of guilt when I placed my daughter aside to sleep so I could play with her brother. Though I wanted her to be with me every moment, like Avery had been, there was so much to juggle. How does one evenly distribute the love?

As if my question had been heard, when Aylee was two weeks old she contracted respiratory syncytial virus (RSV), which is untreatable and in babies her age can cause life-long bronchial diseases like asthma. I took this as my sign to dote on her—there wasn't much I could do except attend to her fever spikes, rapid heart rate, and blocked airways. With her inability to breathe normally, keeping her hydrated with breastmilk was a challenge and my primary focus. As advised, I packed a bag in case we had to rush her to the emergency room, but only once did we head there before deciding (with the help of a doctor on call) against the potential trauma.

Knowing my breastmilk was her only source of sustenance, I ate clean food unadulterated by sugar, caffeine, alcohol, or toxins. I drank plenty of water, homemade kombucha, and herbal tea. Perhaps not coincidentally, both my pathophysiology professor and midwife also were herbalists, so I trusted their guidance about teas and a few, safe herbs and tinctures known to cross over into breastmilk and support Aylee's immunity. As she slept and her chest heaved, the sunlight coming through the window swathed her in light energy and vitamin D. Mostly, though, I ate copious amounts of leafy greens, citrus, frozen berries, low-mercury fish, and probiotic-rich foods. Maintaining my diet was the only other thing I could do (besides stay calm). Eventually, Aylee improved, though for years she was prone to upper respiratory infections and even gut issues, which I believe were related though was unsure how.

Determined to equalize time between two kids and grad school, it seemed impossible to also prioritize Friday morning dates and monthly outings with Chris. Always conflicted about my schedule, I took it one day at a time, crossing off "to dos", but mostly just surviving while trying to stay strong mentally and physically. It would go on like that for years.

Meanwhile, Chris and I saw each other less, experienced family life less, and we both withdrew. I stopped hanging out with friends—no weekly dinners or Saturday cinnamon roll gatherings. I'd become burdensome company, even to myself. My efforts to find joy in well-balanced breakfasts or spreads for picnic outings felt fruitless. For one thing, it was a slim chance all four of us would be together to share meals, let alone excursions. Mostly, homemade food had turned into a point of contention between Chris and me, making it hard for me to enjoy making it, and seemingly impossible for him to appreciate it.

RECIPE for DISCONNECT

It's inevitable for new moms and their partners to disconnect on at least some levels when babies are born. The changes women endure upon bearing children are impossible to explain and being in the company of other mothers makes explanations unnecessary. Mama solidarity is vital both for our sanity and for the welfare of our families.

Cinnamon Rolls & Coffee
Yield = 1 cinnamon roll per kid; 1 nutrient-dense muffin and 1 coffee per mama
Prep time = however long it takes to get yourself and kid(s) out of the house
Total time = At least an hour; ideally two.

Ingredients
- Local coffee shop or bakery
- At least one other mama
- Homemade cinnamon rolls
- Mama muffin
- Quality coffee with your favorite accoutrements
- Time

Instructions
1. Locate a bakery or coffee shop in your area with an inviting, "stay as long as you'd like" atmosphere, offering baked goods made from scratch. Either focus on the gathering for nourishment or, if you have more bandwidth, ensure the baking philosophy and/or ingredients align with your values and needs.
2. Figure out how your baby's nap/play schedule coincides with that of other moms and their babes and, ideally, patronize the shop when it's not morning rush hour (so you don't feel anxious about potentially loud babies, utter chaos, or taking up space for a while).
3. Order your favorite beverage (decaf is equally delish, if you're avoiding caffeine while breastfeeding) and be grateful that someone else is preparing it for you.
4. Order cinnamon rolls for your kids and a mama muffin (or some kind of baked good full of nutrients) for yourself.
5. Enjoy the community of other moms, their kids, and others who frequent the shop (because it's way better than being alone at home).
6. Sip coffee slowly.
7. Watch your toddler or baby get messy with food.
8. Lick the icing off your kids' fingers and faces.
9. Be present and be thankful.
10. Embed this activity into your weekly ritual. Y'all need each other.
11. Bring home the energy of connection; ideally, it will improve your partnership, as well.

CHAPTER 25

Recipe for Disagreement

I was raised in a home where the air of disagreement coated every conversation and unspoken word. We sisters simply accepted that most of our parents' conversations would end in discord. I assumed it was an Italian thing because my dad had a short fuse and a loud voice (which I also inherited). I wrongly assumed the Finnish were just quiet but, in reality, my mom had chosen her silence (not in my DNA).

By high school, in the last of 14 houses we had cycled through, there was a major dispute about the kitchen sink. My dad was a contractor who had designed and built hundreds of kitchens in tract homes, custom homes, remodels, and many of our own homes. Now he was remodeling our kitchen to improve its function. Evidently, he didn't ask my mom (who cooked 90% of our meals) for her opinion regarding the placement of kitchen cabinets, or whether to punch out an opening between the kitchen and dining room for passing food. Or anything about the sink.

Mom wanted a cobalt blue ceramic sink—a color of deep ocean. Dad said it would be an eyesore; Mom said it would accent the monochromatic wood which was everywhere. I noticed it would match the blue windmills hand-painted onto Mom's antique Dutch canister set.

The sink situation was a window into the depths of melancholy inside Mom. And Dad's objection was the door already closed to his feelings for her. It was the last big argument I remember Mom winning. After that, she went back into withdrawal.

I never liked disagreeing with either of my parents, nor did I suppress what mattered to me. I maintained my integrity by not asking for opinions or permission. As the middle daughter, I navigated my way into most everything that interested me. I just did things—at first, responsible, perfectionist things. If my father disagreed, he'd tell me I was making a mistake; if he agreed, I never knew. Mom would ask questions to understand why on Earth I would want to (fill in the blank); whether or not she agreed, she made a point to support me.

Later, in my own partnered life, my husband and I tended to agree on most things *eventually*. If we didn't, we'd just let the other one do whatever it was. As with my father, I wasn't usually seeking approval, but what I wanted (deep down) was my husband's understanding and belief in me. I'd never learned how to ask for that.

So, when Chris wanted to become a musician, supporting his passion was just what I did *inherently*. It meant he'd be working more nights. Secretly, I hoped he'd quit waiting tables at night to open his schedule for performances and private gigs, then take a day job. Instead, he asked coworkers to trade or cover his shifts on nights when shows conflicted. After a year or so, he found a steady rhythm with a mix of evening shows and restaurant work. And a habit of booking everything he was offered.

Monday nights became the one night he consistently didn't work or play music—we declared it our family night. I finished studying by late afternoon to enjoy our evening. On those occasions, I found an extra bounce in my step while moving about the kitchen, concocting slightly more creative meals because, well, my partner loved flavor. It was a treat to embellish elk burgers with minced garlic, shallots, ground coriander, and Worcestershire sauce, adding a side of sauteed shrooms. Chris would whip up his classic Caesar dressing, smashing and separating anchovies in the bottom of my favorite handmade ceramic bowl using two forks in synchronistic, well-seasoned strokes. I smiled as he squeezed lemons atop our vintage glass juicer, then carefully added olive oil and Dijon just using just his eyes and experience to measure. Sometimes, he'd fire up our small grill while I filleted zucchini lengthwise to layer between the burgers and to toast the locally made Challah buns. It was too much work just for the kids and me, so I was elated when Chris and I cooked together.

Chris's finishing touches on meals were the icing on the cake. On those Mondays, I was reminded how much I missed his well-seasoned palate during the rest of the week when I needed a taste-tester (and an extra hand) to balance a tahini sauce or to zest my pancake batter. During our decade of good times, that's how we worked—I was the idea-maker and head chef; he was the executor with a twist. Plus, he helped wash dishes.

Though our kitchen synchronicity reflected my ideal activity, I was thrown off whenever Chris tried to be sexually playful while I navigated the peak of mothering *and* cooking at the witching hour. I grew both easily annoyed by his untimely advances and acutely guilty that I wasn't in the mood. For goodness' sake, how could I be sexy in the old yoga pants I'd worn for three consecutive days, with unkempt hair, and my hands full of garlicky-anchovy-Dijon-romaine? I just wanted to place a homemade, delicious dinner on the table before a toddler meltdown destroyed all the effort we'd invested into the meal. Serve food with love. I didn't want my groove spoiled by kitchen caresses—I preferred to have the counters cleaned and dishes done before any of that nonsense.

Over the months and years, I shrugged him off too many times, until his playfulness withered into listlessness. Soon enough, I cooked alone while he moved despondently across the yard while playing badminton with our son, our daughter at his feet picking dandelions. He stopped coming inside to help, stopped asking me to relax in the hammock with him for a few minutes while the home fries were baking.

My love for kitchen creations oscillated from passion to pointlessness to obsession. From the kitchen counter, I looked up between chopping pistachios and shaving pecorino to curse the wall and artwork—a glutinous pile of bread, fruit, and cheese on a silver platter—that separated me from my family outside. I reasoned that a kitchen wall remodel would solve the problem of distance between us—I thought watching my family in the yard from my meal-prep location would bring some joy. Chris argued that if I would just order take-out, we'd be able to hang out together while our son soared off the swing in costume and our cheeky daughter harassed the cat. Our disagreement was as absurd—and as revealing—as the blue ceramic sink standoff.

Anyway, he was tired of home improvements (and my cooking). And I never liked hammocks (they were boring and uncomfortable).

In all practicality, I couldn't imagine how take-out would improve our family life; there was literally *one* take-out spot in our town—the salty-cheesy pizza we ordered after our Aylee's birth. To order anything else, one of us would have to drive 10–12 minutes to and from Hailey—plus time to pay and pick up food—to retrieve sub-par noodles or sushi our kids wouldn't eat, so I'd have to make a second meal, anyway. In those 25–30 minutes, I could save us $50 by making homecooked black bean tacos with organic veggies and local goat cheese. Beyond our economic state and the stark difference in quality, one of us still would be alone with the kids while the other dealt with food. Hence, I believed his argument was illogical.

About every six months, the same disagreement resurfaced—not necessarily about Monday night dinners or take-out, but about perspectives. He wanted his wife to relax, be playful and spend time with him while food magically appeared; I wanted him to support my joy and ethics in providing local, seasonal, sustainable food high in phytochemicals for our rapidly growing and developing children, overworked husband, and me.

He wanted me to change my food values, and I wanted him to change his routine.

He wanted me to chill out and put out, and I wanted him to be on board instead of checked out.

He wanted me to "just get a job," and I wanted him to get a day job.

He said I was asking him to *be someone else*, fearing I no longer honored who he was at his core. I said he was asking me to *change who I was*, no longer respecting my passionate views of the world.

He reasoned if I were working a 40-hour per week job, he could reduce his work to three nights a week (still probably weekends) and we'd have more time together. I replied that I was already working a full-time job as a mom, a part-time job as a freelance writer, a full-time grad student, and soon I'd be making money in a career I loved.

He remained enthusiastic about high-quality, hand-crafted food at work, yet belittled the same standards I placed on food at home. I continued to prioritize my values over breakfast, coffee, lunch, snacks, treats, and dinner, while hoping one meal one day would stir his appetite for my food infatuation.

Chris was tired and dismissed his intense vow to work every day for that house for as long as needed; I didn't want to work that much for someone else. He prided himself on not being "the norm" though our problems were perfectly common. I felt like I was missing out on life—family life, social life, outdoor life—*because* he was adamant about "being different." He was the one who'd desired a family, pushed for a mortgage we couldn't afford, and wanted the fancy bikes, trucks, fire pits, campers, hot tubs, and vacations everyone else had. His dream was the American Dream, similar to most people he tried not to be like.

Contentious circles.

Anyway, it was exhausting just imagining a life more exhausting than the one we already led, with even less time together than what we already had. As it was, I could carve my own hours around Chris's schedule and the kids' needs; and I'd continue to do so once I started my own nutrition practice. Flexibility and time to live life—that's what I envisioned. Paradoxically, that's what Chris said he loved about restaurant work.

Yet, even when I expressed appreciation for his efforts for our family, to remodel the house, and to be with our kids while I attended grad school, I felt criticized for pursuing aspirations that felt right for me. I didn't care about Things—I just wanted to fill my life with what I loved so I had more to give. In the immense effort and pressure to turn my career into something Chris surely would see as a benefit to him as well, I plowed ahead full force.

I continued to show up as a woman who wanted more for herself and her family.

If Chris said, "Thank you." I didn't feel thanked.

I might have said, "I appreciate you," but it probably didn't register as authentic.

The weight of our different perspectives quashed his words and mine so that we did not agree to disagree. We simply disagreed.

RECIPE for DISAGREEMENT

It's hard to argue about a truly delish salad. This version is my take on Chris's table-side classic that is garlicky, lemony, not too fishy, light, and perfectly creamy even without the egg. The pistachios and sun-dried tomatoes pay homage to the Caesar Salad from Ketchum's revered restaurant, The Evergreen, of our past life. Add quality protein to balance the meal.

Classic Caesar Salad
Yield = 6 servings as a side dish
Prep time = 15 minutes

Ingredients for Dressing
- 4 fresh anchovy fillets (or 6 packed in oil, drained)
- 1-2 garlic cloves
- 2 tbsp freshly squeezed lemon juice
- 2 tsp Dijon mustard
- 2 tsp organic Worcestershire sauce
- ½ c unrefined extra virgin olive oil from a glass container
- 1 egg yolk from a pasture-raised hen (optional)

Ingredients for Salad
- 1 ½ heads romaine lettuce
- 1 small head radicchio (optional)
- 10-12 sun-dried tomatoes (if they're dry and crunchy, omit)
- 3 tbsp pistachios
- 1/3 c grated pecorino Romano
- Toasted artisan breadcrumbs (optional—don't mess up this recipe with packaged breadcrumbs). See Panzanella recipe (chapter 21) for breadcrumb instructions.
- Freshly ground black pepper

Instructions
1. If you're making your own breadcrumbs out of delicious artisan bread, prepare them first.
2. Prepare dressing. In a large, wide bowl use two forks to mince the anchovies and garlic clove. Add the remainder of the dressing ingredients and mix well with a fork. If you're adding an egg yolk, do so now. Mix thoroughly. Set aside.
3. Prepare salad ingredients. Wash and chop lettuce and radicchio. Slice sun-dried tomatoes into thin strips. Rough-chop pistachios. Finely grate pecorino Romano.
4. Add lettuce, cheese, pistachios, and sun-dried tomatoes to the dressing in the bowl and toss together with hands (or salad tongs) until well coated. Add croutons (if using) and toss 1-2 more times.
5. Serve immediately with freshly cracked pepper.

CHAPTER 26

Recipe for Disappointment

Sourdough breadmaking is the perfect activity to observe whether chemistry and environment are "off"—even slightly. The dough changes shape, intensity, and essence. The same was true of our marriage.

My first sourdough loaves were almost perfect. I paid attention to every detail, organized my day around the multi-hour effect of dough rising, and controlled temperatures in different rooms in the house or oven to optimize the ambiance for the developing dough. I was eager to invest time and effort, devote attention to the unfolding of the process, witness the subtle nuances from start to finish.

Making sourdough helped me feel the pulse of life alongside the active culture in a cyclical, Circadian manner that seemed to make time slow down, like when you're first in love. As in the beginning when our relationship was easy and we had all the time in the world, I naively assumed I was a natural baker.

Then breadmaking turned sour—the weather changed and so did the perfect place to incubate. I grew less interested in consistency, and more impatient when my life revolved around the need to cultivate the bread. I often tried to force dough to rise: I mixed yeast with warm water, added more flour and a bit of sugar, then folded into the flat, sticky leaven to salvage a couple of pizza crusts, at the very least. I did whatever it took to save the dough and turn it into *something* edible—an exasperating process—and often wondered why I even gave a damn anymore. It would have been easier to just buy bread or (dare I say?) the pizza down the street.

But I was a dreamer, after all; I couldn't let go of the image. Surely, my idyllic visions of our life—I mean those domed, golden loaves—would fill the house like the successful early efforts and delicious moments of pure warmth. Toasty on the outside, delicate goodness within. Spread with grass-fed butter. A sprinkle of sea salt. Homemade jam or pesto.

In the beginning, such was our daily bread.

I knew sourdough baking wasn't the best use of my time, but it slowed me down and culminated in a different outcome each time, one that begged me to evaluate the process. In the rest of my life, there was no scientific method for lovemaking and definitely no clear formula for marriage saving. The disappointing, squat loaves that turned heavy and dull brown evoked an inner disappointment and struggle to start anew. As I tried to reignite my starter, I wondered how my life had come to a point where I'd spend so much time and effort on *bread*, but very little effort on my relationship.

Aiming to make perfect bread again, I focused on problem solving and experimenting. Eventually, with some insight and subtle shifts, the bacteria revitalized! The intentional effort resulted in something tasty, whether flat or lofty, dense or porous—it didn't matter. Breadmaking became exciting again.

Similarly, to figure out what was at the core of our deflated affection, mechanical interaction, and passive (or aggressive) verbal exchanges, I saw that one root cause of our lackluster lives was lack of attention.

Right. My attention was focused 99% on our kids, studies, food, and community work. Very little attention to myself—for years, I hadn't even looked in the mirror, let alone changed my slovenly, ragged pre-children outfits, which coupled as pajamas and study attire. Leftover time devoted to my husband? Almost nil.

Recipe for Disappointment

It was like neglecting my sourdough starter: when I didn't have time for it, it was pushed to the back of the fridge. Chilled, the fermentation ceased. There, it could wait.

But *we* couldn't wait any longer.

While home together during the day, Chris waited as I turned out sourdough and term papers, dinner, and tended to our babies. Our conversations dried up, like days-old crust. We grew cold like the dinners that parents of young kids eat after getting up from the table six times to refill waters, fetch the ketchup, cut the veggie burger into smaller pieces, then rinse the wet rag to wipe the mess baby #2 made after picking up the spork kiddo #1 just dropped on the floor.

I could warm cold meals in the toaster oven and leftover coffee on the stove (though I rarely bothered), and I could warm my heart with a glass of wine (a rare occasion). But I couldn't butter him up (without sex) and could barely warm him up with a touching kid moment. I no longer softened to his wordless guitar strumming that only mildly distracted me from the animosity hanging in the air like the aftermath of burnt toast. There was no quick fix for years of decline. We were resisting both change and restoration.

Thus entangled, we endured.

Each afternoon around 3:30, panicked in the face of time ticking, and always behind on my reading or research, I'd hear the garage door open beneath my "study tower." Husband and kids were home from their daytime adventure—time to switch shifts. Legs tightly crossed into eagle pose, shoulders up to my ears, shallow breaths, and fingers frantically typing as if wired on caffeine (yet wasn't), I'd rush to write two more sentences or cite one more reference before my love-muffins burst in. Sometimes Chris would come upstairs, but rarely with a smile or a delightful story about their day. He might inform me which kid had a Band-Aid and why, or a tummy ache, though it was unclear why. He seldom inquired about my day, never asked what I was learning or whether I was enjoying my courses or teachers. With a resigned shrug, he withdrew to dress for work.

But I—I was greeted by two pairs of sparkling eyes! Filled up by Daddy's attention, my kids peeled me away from the computer. They were infinitely refreshing and a healing salve to overcome any melancholic visage or distant exchange that just exited the room.

These dramatic neuroendocrine shifts from the stress of intense study and feeling pretty dang high on the dream path, to a burned-out mom with depleted cortisol; from science student—memorizing the enzymes needed to convert niacin to its active form in cellular respiration, understanding the rate-limiting steps of the Kreb's cycle, and the function of adrenocorticotropic hormone—to horsie for small children to climb on, a shoulder to wail on, and a mama to rely on. These abrupt changes occurred daily and I appreciated the seemingly opposing roles of hungry student and satiated mama. Truly, I had energy for only those two things.

In the fifth trimester, my graduate program required peer nutrition consultations—our first round of assessments on real humans. A nutrition autopsy, without a scalpel. My partner was well-versed in personalized healing after surviving a debilitating disease state. With four kids, Emily had found the strength to pull herself off the IVs and multiple meds of ineffective Western treatment. In contrast, I felt uncomfortable for what I wrongly presumed to be a lifetime of excellent health.

At first, Emily was unsure what to "do" with me. My food and beverage intake were ideal. I slept like a rock (except while nursing). I was active enough. My metabolism seemed fine. I had no physical pain. My nutrition-focused physical exam produced no noteworthy signs to improve. I had no labs for her to review because I'd had no reason to request labs from my physician. On paper, I was the textbook picture of wellness.

Naturally, I was flummoxed when she indicated I might be nutrient-deficient and energy-depleted. I'd never considered such a thing! Was it even possible to be deficient while eating a well-rounded diet consisting of tons of plant-based foods, 90% of which were organic, the rest non-GMO or sustainably grown by local farmers and harvested in season, including hunted meat?

Emily said something much nicer than this, but I recall, "Women with issues like yours seek medical help, often resulting in a depression or anxiety diagnoses and the consumption of pharmaceutical drugs." Well, I wasn't interested in a medical diagnosis, and I certainly didn't want to become part of the

preposterous percentage of American women my a
anti-depressants. *Hell, no. I will do this on my own—n⌄*

Knowledge was at my fingertips. After all, I was 1
how the body functions at a cellular level and which a
states, organ dysfunctions, genetic predispositions, medications,
and lifestyle factors contribute to nutrient insufficiencies (and,
subsequently, chronic disease), and which could be healed by
nutrients (without big pharma) and lifestyle (no Band-Aids).

Investigating potential nutrient-deficiency issues, the effects
of stress kept surfacing in my brain. I'd always chalked up my
volatile attitude to stress and learned behavior (from stressed
parents). Apparently, that wasn't the whole picture: there was
normal life stress and there was chronic stress.

Stress, a natural response to internal or external stressors
(often *beneficial*), is not a medically recognized condition. It's
an inherent function of the body, requiring alterations to endure
it, notably, the regulation of cortisol—a hormone that, when
constantly elevated, leads to inflammation, blood sugar dysregulation, oxidative stress, energy dysregulation, thyroid and sex
hormone dysfunction, nutrient depletion (um, hello?), and more.

I'd already learned that "chronic stress" is a major underlying cause of disease. Countless peer-reviewed studies link
chronic stress to 21st century conditions like mental health
issues; impaired weight maintenance; disordered sleep; neurode-
generation; chronic pain; gut dysfunction; allergies; suppressed
immunity; and cancer.

Oh, geez. That explains a lot. Our modern world celebrates
women who "do it all," but at what expense? Marital problems.
Messed up hormones. Medications. Autoimmune disease.
Insanity. Illness.

Shoot. Was I on that path?

I dove into the research rabbit hole (while trying not to freak
out). I learned of genetic predispositions to stress. Apparently,
when a pregnant mother is stressed or depressed (similar effects
in the body), the fetus undergoes reprogramming while in the
womb; genes are altered before and after birth and affected by
early life environment, nurturing, and life circumstances. One
outcome of early life stress is elevated levels of baseline cortisol. In other words, fetuses and babies growing in stressful

conditions exhibit a higher level of stress *as their norm* compared with those who are grow up in calm environments.

Wait—*what!?* Without blame (Mom and Dad, I love you no matter what), I was both biologically and behaviorally predestined to be a stress-case thanks to my genetic make-up, personality, and childhood. Stress was embedded into my cellular matrix, DNA, and habits.

I thought back on earlier women in my ancestry—Gramma Day's upbringing on a rural Idaho farm, sent away with her twin sister as young teens to care for their crippled grandmother who had dementia. Gramma Truppi, born into immigrant poverty in the Bronx with ten other Catholic children, six of whom died young.

How could I, in this modern life of privilege, be more stressed than they were? Was the abundance of choices, overwhelm of information, and keeping up with the Joneses our collective evolution of societal stress? Could generations of penury, adversity, and loss be contributing somehow to my own ill-being? Had my own stressors—stacked atop potential genetic predispositions and the body's inherent desire to balance physical, mental, and emotional stress—collectively caused *nutrient depletion*? In me? An otherwise healthy person.

The cool thing about nutrition, though, is that every bite of food provides an opportunity to change our DNA. Yep, it's true. If you don't believe me, read the work of Deepak Chopra. I heard him say just that in a keynote address at a nutrition and integrative health conference. His words resonate.

But then, Emily's nutrient recommendations were all supplements (eek!): B-complex, magnesium, vitamin C, vitamin D, and adaptogenic herbs. Oh, and sea salt on my food. She proffered that I needed to reduce stress to replete nutrients and, to do so, she suggested taking specific nutrients to help mitigate the effects of my long-term stress. A catch-22.

I opposed supplements as adamantly as I rejected the pharmaceutical industry. That prenatal pill conundrum was my first experience with a well-marketed solution to our food system, health system, and cultural eating problems. Further, I saw the unregulated industry as a side hustle for stay-at-home moms and the bread and butter of health food stores. The over-priced,

Recipe for Disappointment

lab-designed pills were for people who didn't have the knowledge, time, or desire to care for themselves through diet and lifestyle. Supps were totally fine for others, but I was not one of those people.

For a week, I pouted about the idea of supplementation. Couldn't I receive all the vitamins and minerals I needed from my food? I researched that, too. Guess what? Globally, our food is grown in depleted soil. Even though a sweet potato is a sweet potato and will produce the same nutrients in every sweet potato (and the same for cantaloupe or fish or milk), the levels will vary depending on soil quality, season, geographical location, monocropping, and a bunch of other factors like when the food is picked, how it's ripened (and, of course, pesticides). Even people living off their own "organic" farms (and sometimes using organic pesticides) may experience nutrient insufficiencies thanks to the overwhelming burdens the body must balance (it's called "allostatic load").

So even "healthy" humans can be depleted. Today, virtually everyone needs supplements (and/or pharmaceuticals). Hats off to agribusiness and capitalism.

Plus, no amount of yoga, deep breathing, meditation, sleep, exercise, or mental health therapy would "cure" my emotional unpredictability without enriching my nervous system with nutrients I couldn't acquire or replenish just from food. Fine. I'd try a supplement. But just one, to start.

Where to begin? Emily suggested a B-vitamin complex. Turns out, when you exist in a constantly elevated state of "fight-or-flight," the gut is unable to make enough B vitamins to supply energy to the rest of the body and also the body utilizes B vitamins from the diet more quickly so cells can make energy that is quickly depleted in the stress state. It's like B-vitamin wasting. Plus, multiple factors affect B-vitamin status and utilization—medications, poor gut function, inflammation—and since they're required for, like, *everything* related to energy and cell function, stressed-out, tired people also tend to have gut problems and systemic inflammation. Then they medicate (which stresses their bodies, makes them tired, and depletes nutrients). Are you picking up what I'm putting down? Like applying pesticides to fix a problem, the pests adapt (ah, Nature), and more pesticides are needed. Ugh, Science.

Emily pointed out a handful of my symptoms related to B-vitamin insufficiency. I thought it was just "mom brain" but no. Apathy, fatigue, irritability, inability to relax, shallow breaths, and brain fog were signs that I could be headed toward depression, autoimmunity, cognitive decline, cancer, and heart problems (thanks to nutrient deficiency). I'd always figured my mom's family had cognitive decline due to old age, bad water and, in Gramma Day's case, too many prescribed medications. I'd assumed my dad's family had heart problems simply because they were Italian with off-the-charts cholesterol levels. No one could explain my sister's cancer.

In my research, I learned that when you're deep in your own dark hole and burning the candle at both ends, it's physiologically, chemically, and energetically impossible to find peace in your soul, creative thought in your brain, deep breaths in your lungs, or relaxation in your reproductive organs. The body is designed to put each of those functions (and more) on the back burner during stress. I call it, "burnout" though the World Health Organization definition differs. My definition of burnout is surviving while smoldering and not realizing it. And, that was me, so....

Anyway, I calculated nutrients from my meals and, sadly, concluded that no matter how many chickpeas, nuts, avocados, mushrooms, or wild meats and fish I was eating, there weren't enough B vitamins for my depleted cells. *Shoot.*

First supp: high quality B-complex down the hatch. Just one food-derived version, though the bottle recommended two. Within a couple of days, I was greeting the day with less annoyance and exhaustion was lifted. My husband still saw me as cranky and inflexible (and I'd been conditioned to believe I was), which was slightly disappointing, but the uplifting feelings were noticeable to me. I found moments of peace, and it was my intention to cultivate more.

Next up: magnesium—depleted during stress, required for energy production and hundreds of other functions. No amount of seeds and nuts, beans and leafy greens, quinoa and millet, could supply my body with the magnesium I needed to chill the fuck out. Bring on the magnesium.

Then: adaptogens (one at a time because I like to test and assess them individually). Ashwagandha first (ooh, that one was noticeable). Rhodiola next (nope, provoked anxiety in me). And so on....

Finally: vitamin C. It's super depleted under stress.

Within a couple of months, my attitude shifted as my mental and physical capacities improved. I looked forward to nights alone with just my kids—without resentment. My son was our Billy goat, butting his way into everything, incessantly active, adventurous, tenacious and, thankfully for me, he ate everything (despite his little-boy resistance to being amenable). My daughter was like a sweet peach of summer—soft on the outside but easily wounded by a hand who held her too tight, sweet all the way through to her tough core (and took cues from her big brother to eat what he ate). I enjoyed watching their idiosyncrasies unfold.

We three became a synchronized unit, intuitively responsive to each other's needs. My children were as tuned into my energies as I was to theirs—they played together quietly when Mama was on edge; cowered when it had been hours since I'd taken my last deep breath; cuddled me when tears finally welled up enough to spill over into the light of day; threw their heads back in infectious laughter when Mama reverted to silliness to combat stress; snuggled with me every night, their limbs strewn atop my tired body in perfect pretzel configuration.

And my husband? Long after I went to bed with the kids, he slept in our bed alone. I knew we wouldn't last if that continued. Hard as it was to peel myself away from our precious children, I was emotionally ready to tackle a massive effort I'd half-ignored: save my relationship. I would attend to my husband as I had attended to my sourdough. My now-nourished brain and lonely heart urged me not to wait any longer.

Of course, I analyzed the shit out of the situation. How could I pull myself away from the two humans on Earth who loved me unconditionally while the man I chose as my partner was loving me less and less and absent more and more? It was another distressing endeavor.

And it was *freakin' hard!* Here's a snapshot of how poorly this endeavor turned out: I'd put kids to bed and fall asleep with them as my catnap. I'd set my alarm to wake around 9:30 or 10:00 pm to study, write, wash dishes, or whatever else still needed to be accomplished. I'd wonder if Chris would return home before Aylee woke up for the first time. Or the second time. Each time she woke, I'd lie with her until she fell back to sleep. Sometimes, I was so exhausted I'd fall asleep again, nestled between my sweet babes, comfortable and guilty. And remain there until morning.

Other nights, I busted ass to get my coursework finished so at least *that* stress would be lessened. But I never knew when Chris would be home; he never knew if I'd be awake; I didn't know if he'd be exhausted and ready to sleep or if he'd been drinking and wanting to make love; I was too burned out for the latter, regardless; we were too awkwardly disconnected for me to muster up the energy for intimacy 95% of the time, despite knowing how much it mattered; it was difficult for me to shift from late-night study about phytonutrients or the pathophysiology of liver disease to late-night kinky chemistry; often I chose to go to bed before hearing from him, so I didn't have to wrangle with any of the above; and some nights he chose not to come home at all or communicate about where he was.

Simultaneously, Chris grew tired of not knowing whether I'd respond to a text or even be awake—he was disappointed when I didn't answer. He assured me, if he didn't come home, it was because he was being safe by not getting behind the wheel—and that he'd never fail on his daddy duties. As promised, if I needed him home by 9:00 am so I could take an exam, he showed up right on time.

And just in time for sourdough French toast.

RECIPE for DISAPPOINTMENT

French toast has the potential to be the ultimate comfort food. For me, with my nutritionist-mom mind, it must be intentionally created with the finest ingredients. I add an extra egg to increase nutrients, warm spices to soothe, and the essence of citrus to uplift.

Sourdough French Toast
Yield = 4 servings
Prep time = 5 minutes
Total time = 25 minutes

Ingredients
- 8-10 slices of slightly aged sourdough of the artisan variety
- 4 eggs from pasture-raised hens
- ¾-1 c organic whole milk or plant-based milk
- Small pour of vanilla extract
- Several dashes of cardamom, cinnamon, ginger and/or nutmeg
- Freshly grated ginger (optional)
- Zest from a grapefruit or orange (optional)
- Freshly ground vanilla bean sea salt (yes, this exists) or a pinch of sea salt
- Coconut oil for the pan

Optional Toppings
- High-quality butter or ghee
- Berry or fruit compote or preserves
- Sliced bananas or seasonal fruit
- Almond, peanut, or other nut butter
- Maple syrup, ginger syrup, or honey
- Whipped coconut cream

Instructions
1. Slice the sourdough into ½" thick pieces.
2. Crack eggs into a pie plate or shallow dish, then whisk to combine whites and yolks.
3. Add milk, spices, ginger, zest, and salt. Whisk together with eggs.
4. Place slices of bread into the mixture in one layer. Allow to soak up the mixture for 1-2 minutes.
5. Meanwhile, heat a cast iron skillet to medium and add a couple of teaspoons of coconut oil. Evenly coat the skillet with the oil.
6. Turn the bread so the other side can soak up the mixture for another 1-2 minutes.
7. When the skillet is heated and the bread is saturated (good, old bread won't become soggy), transfer each slice to the skillet. Grill until the bottom is golden brown and a spatula can easily slip underneath to flip it over. Repeat on the other side, then remove from skillet.
8. While round 1 is toasting, add more bread slices to the egg/milk/spice mixture. Flip over the bread in the pie plate when you flip over the French toast on the skillet.
9. Add more coconut oil to skillet, spreading evenly. Repeat steps 3-8.
10. Garnish warm French toast with your favorite toppings.

CHAPTER 27

Recipe for Determination

What I couldn't cure with supplements, comfort food, super food, or meditation was the emphasis of not sacrificing my food values while living on a shoestring. To others—even my husband—I may have seemed obsessive about whole foods and homemade meals but, truthfully, our financial constraints played a massive role in my food decisions. I pledged to obtain as many nutrients as possible from real food and spend less on food eaten out. I rationalized this methodology also would result fewer supplements (assuming I was also prioritizing activities to maintain my health) and limit unnecessary expenses of health care.

Some form of chronic pain, I sensed a constant dull ache in my body from the pressure of counting every penny, though I'd become an expert at doing so. Scarcity of funds consumed my analytical mind almost more than studying, and ate at my emotional wellbeing at least as much as my crumbling marriage. Our bank account was the source of blame, shame, criticism, overwhelm, and frustration, yet also fueled my desire for a career shift. Our financial predicament became the source of seemingly every decision, thought, and action I made for years.

Thankfully, I was revitalized by lectures on the pathophysiology of autoimmune disease; peer reviewed articles on the role of a nutritionist in a team effort to help individuals overcome mental health *dis*-ease; and an understanding of healing power of glutamine on the gut lining. Little snippets connecting humankind, the earth, and science further propelled me to persevere. My classmates, teachers, and friends encouraged me. My mom and Jaclyn believed in me.

Even Avery, who wiggled in my lap as I finished typing sentences, loved being with Mama at her desk. As a toddler, he fondled the waxy leaves of the plant than cascaded toward the floor, pointed to dead flies on the windowsill, and marveled at the reflection of light through the glass bagua ball that was supposed to bring prosperity. Aylee moved through her exploratory phases by rearranging my flashcards in patterns across the floor and making houses out of my books. My children were a constant reminder that my efforts were for them, too. For us. Our family.

Uncomfortable spending any of Chris's hard-earned money or student loan money on myself—no haircuts or teeth cleaning, no replacing holey and stained maternity and nursing clothes, no yoga punch cards or hemp milk lattes. I needed to earn just enough spending money to keep me from suffocating from inadequacy.

Even before Aylee or grad classes, freelance writing was a side hustle. I interviewed farmers, ranchers, bakers, chefs, and others in the expansive food system to learn their stories and share them. With my map in the passenger seat, I'd drive off the beaten path in search of watermelon farms, heirloom cherry orchards, permaculture operations, and disappearing pieces of agricultural history. On these adventures, my potty-training son was my co-pilot, so we stopped often (to pee), enduring 114-degree weather and faded signs telling of miners and pioneers on some of the loneliest roads in Idaho. I hoped he'd absorb a trifle of Mama's free spirit and enthusiasm for exploring. Ultimately, freelance writing didn't pay enough for the effort involved. When kid number two was on her way, I had to find something else.

Recipe for Determination

I started working at a food sustainability center in trade for raw honey, pasture-raised chicken eggs, garlic scapes, fresh greens, and more. I redesigned and painted the vacuous, crooked old building, which had once housed equipment for the US Forest Service. The idea behind the budding food sustainability business had been to create an epicenter of local food life, where farmers, chefs, and community members would gather around long tables with a five-course meal prepared by local chefs. They served up seasonal veggies sauteed with foraged roots, pasture-raised beef sliders, and fresh local fruit à la something-or-other. As I helped organize the space and define the mission, vision, definition of sustainability, and a credo for ethical sourcing, my ideas were met with resistance from the owners. I was deeply connected to their original idea for the center, then equally frustrated when it was deemed too idealistic and, sadly, rather unsustainable.

I tried other work, too, such as filling in at the health club's spa and teaching yoga. Both endeavors took away precious time from my family and home life and, since neither paid particularly well (and brought on unnecessary stress), I let go of those side gigs, too.

Through it all, I found my people and passion in community volunteer work. It started when I helped our local food bank with a data-collection project. This two-year project on food insecurity and accessibility culminated in a multi-day workshop, which uncovered a complicated matrix of inequality and collective needs. We discussed the many challenges of the food system, the socioeconomic failings of school food, and, importantly, what we could do to incite positive change. We didn't talk nutrition specifically, but we toiled over people's food needs, beliefs, capabilities, and the intricate, integrated, often discombobulated efforts that sprouted out of others' desires to grow, provide, include, serve. Multiple concepts broadened my grad school studies; other topics echoed my values in sustainable agriculture, contested my definition of "local," and confirmed how food is the single, most fundamental matrix connecting all humans on Earth and with Earth.

One popular consensus was that idealism had no place in community food—at least, not in a mountain town where growing food at 5500+ feet challenged access to food and all but eliminated the discussion about quality or purity. From my own ample research—and a surety that the only explanation for my sister's cancer and death was chemicals—I'd come to understand that pesticides and other chemicals were at the root of many (quite possibly most) modern human and environmental ailments despite cited academic studies promoted to prove otherwise. It pained me to think our community was serving these "tainted conventional foods"—processed products and also food grown right down the road from us—to locals who already suffered symptoms of the Standard American Diet and struggled with the severe inequalities between haves and have-nots.

The concerted effort of so many people coming together fueled my desire to help make a difference. Ten of us formed a food council and determined priority steps and committees to oversee the topics of utmost concern. I showed up. Every week. Every month. For years. This community food system work was like a prebiotic in my gut, laying the rich, fertile soil upon which everything else could grow. More importantly, I'd found a group of people who saw the world as I did, who shared the same passions, and who respected and supported one another through our actions. My experiences were heard; my opinions were validated. I hadn't realized how desperately I craved a reminder that I was on the right path and doing something useful.

Yoda might say, "Change the system we must!" The way we grow food now—all over the world—feeds the people, yet at a terrible cost. The current methods are making us weak and sick. Our food system has been globalized, challenging the ability for community food to be localized. Through a mapping exercise, we found our "local" food spanned a several-hundred-mile radius. Our county—with only five small towns—relied heavily on farmers from Idaho's "banana belt" climate at a lower elevation and elsewhere. Otherwise, there wouldn't be enough food year-round for the locals, let alone the tourists and second-home owners. Further data indicated our sparsely populated county was the ninth most expensive county in the *nation*.

We knew we could devise a better way to feed our community and improve our food system.

Our next exercise was to map out the course of action to tackle food distribution and transportation, massive food waste, shoddy school lunches, the need for political reform, and food insecurity. Ultimately, the council decided to start with food and nutrition education as a campaign toward resilience. Yay! Finally, my graduate work would have real-life significance!

I was one of two food council members not associated with a non-profit, our local government, or a university. I stayed on with deepened fervor to understand the food system and participate in positive change. Still, I felt small compared with those who had organizations behind their names, affluence to make a difference with their dollars, and the power to be heard. Plus, they were paid to attend meetings and follow through with the work.

Unpaid, I worked tirelessly for the cause which, unfortunately, added more contention at home. And as I understood more about the complicated food web, it became clear that my own family was food insecure.

Upwards of 40% of the families in our valley—a statistic that matched counties nationwide—simply needed to know they would have food to eat that night. But I needed to eat a chemical-free dinner. I was at a point in which I couldn't even think about eating at the local taco shop without asking about their sourcing and sustainability. Many nights at home, we ate rice and beans, and you can be sure it was organic brown rice with local, organic beans, and made from scratch via sprouting (to reduce anti-nutrients and improve digestion and absorption of all the nutrients consumed in the meal). Only later did I learn about arsenic in brown rice.

I feared we'd reached a point where I'd have to buy cheap, toxic, nutrient-poor food. If there were a name for this kind of eating obsession, it might be "egetexia," Latin for "fear of a condition as a result of chemicals." There isn't. I just made it up. At any rate, I suffered from it.

What really bothered me, more than knowledge about the thousands of toxins in our air, soil, and water affecting every single living organism on Earth *as a result of human greed and thoughtlessness*, was that toxin-free food had become a high-priced privilege.

Affording organic food is no longer possible for so many. By prioritizing consciously cultivated, biodynamic, and sustainable food from smaller farms and back yards, can we collectively improve the system? And quality food, with its huge health impact, also generates less waste and more harmony with nature. All that is what I wanted to pontificate.

Dubbed a "food snob" by friends and family, I nevertheless persisted in procuring quality food and supporting local farmers and producers. Somehow, I conjured up money to buy local, raw goat yogurt and eggs from pasture-raised hens (each costing three times that of their conventional counterparts) raised by people I trusted to farm the way Mother Nature intended. I was buying some of the most expensive food in our state while living in the most expensive place in the state. It was the cost of living true to my values.

Well, no wonder it's financially hard to live here! We native Idahoans pride ourselves on appreciating the simple life in tune with our vast and varied natural surroundings, on being free from the pressures of living up to our nation's norm. But the state is deadlocked in agribusiness and commodity crop economy—in which I cannot bring myself to partake. The massive, sprayed potato and sugar beet farms mostly are off the beaten path, hidden behind expansive landscape, or relatively unobtrusive to the naked eye. Occasionally, a dairy farm backs up to the highway, offering a glimpse of cows cramped side-by-side, stifled by each other and the urine-saturated mud beneath their hooves. Smelling them from miles away, I deplore the rampant destruction of our land, the depletion of our precious water, the pollution of our air. (And, of course, I cannot bring myself to drink that milk or eat cheese or yogurt made from it.)

Most of these ag-atrocities are downstream from us, though quite in our backyard. Our valley is tucked between mountain ranges, luscious with chemically manicured lawns even during drought (veiled behind thick walls of planted trees). An architect's dream, with custom estates stretched over acres of once-wild land, sagebrush razed, and wildlife displaced from their natural homes. Besides overt affluence, this beautiful, idyllic mountain life is wrought with unimaginable, unforgivable waste and reeks of toxic load.

I wasn't a part of that caste. Those people paid my husband to serve them and play music for them. They paid my

Recipe for Determination

friends—builders, designers, landscape architects, outfitters, bike mechanics, fishing guides, gallery directors, realtors, teachers, massage therapists, nurses, doctors. Everyone in the construction, restaurant, resort, and recreation business. Blue-collar workers and service industry employees aplenty! Yet, "those people" also funded non-profits (lots of them) that gave us and our kids more. They paid my peers on the food council. But they didn't pay me...not yet.

Though I loved the volunteer work, it contributed to our dire situation. One day I set aside my pride and asked for help procuring food, though I couldn't bring myself to tell my husband what I was doing. Food punch card in hand, I entered the food bank facility where I had volunteered many times. Only, that time, I entered through the front door. In the produce section, there was garlic grown at food bank's farm out the canyon. I'd helped harvest vegetables there many times with my kids, and I knew the food was not sprayed. I took one head of garlic. On the pantry shelves, I found only one organic, nonperishable food: oats. I took a bag.

Knowing I had only a few dollars to buy food for my family that week, I still could not bring myself to accept food that was not organic or non-GMO, at the very least. I could not accept conventionally grown vegetables—not even "the clean fifteen" foods I knew still contributed to a system wreaking havoc on our environment; harming farm workers; depleting the human gut microbiome; contributing to chronic disease.

"Clean" food, a buzz word for food without toxins (which basically no longer exists—I've researched that, too), also insinuates privilege, higher prices, perhaps fanaticism. In fact, "clean" foods should be the dirtiest foods grown naturally in diverse soil, versus toxic foods in neat, unsoiled rows devoid of the very rich earth and microorganisms required for plants to thrive. The more we engage with rich dirt, the healthier we become. Or, as with the hygiene hypothesis, the more we disinfect nature, the sicker we become.

I left with a mostly empty cart and a heart sick with emotional turmoil. What was more shameful—being penniless or refusing food offered to me? What was worse for my wellbeing—the physical pain of distress, or a few chemicals from commodity foods? Regardless, I knew others needed the food more than I did and would be more grateful for it than I could be at that juncture in my food journey.

A week later, I went back to the food bank to try again. I experienced the same resistance, and heightened shame.

I needed another method to my madness.

RECIPE for DETERMINATION

To stay atop my nutrition and subdue symptoms of burnout, I created these date balls using spicy, fatty, chocolatey, and naturally sweet ingredients that offer a specific nutrient combo to support the stress response. Yes, the ingredients are always organic (and more expensive) and, yes, buying them contributes to globalized agriculture, but I try not to stress about those factors. Using bulk ingredients, they're still cheaper than many prepackaged "energy bars." Making them also helped me appreciate the abundances in my life. Recipe adapted from "Feeding the Young Athlete", by Cynthia Lair (Readers to Eaters, 2012).

Nutty Spicy Date Balls
Yield = 12-15 balls
Prep time = 20 minutes

Ingredients
- ½ c raw cashews
- ¾ c pitted, raw dates
- ¼ c raw sunflower seed butter
- ¼ c raw cocoa powder
- Zest from 1 orange
- 2 tsp freshly grated ginger (skin removed)
- ¼ tsp ground turmeric
- ½ tsp ground cinnamon
- Hint of ground black pepper
- Pinch of sea salt

Instructions
1. Pulse cashews in food processor until they begin to resemble course flour and start to become creamy. No need to soak them.
2. Add the dates, sunflower seed butter, cocoa powder, orange zest, spices, and salt to the food processor. Pulse several times, scraping down the sides each time.
3. Continue pulsing until the mixture binds together and forms a ball.
4. With moist hands (I like to rub coconut oil on my palms), roll the mixture into 1-inch balls.
5. Meditate while rolling balls.
6. If you're super stressed, smash one! Then gently roll it back into a lovely sphere.
7. Close your eyes. Bite into a nutty date ball. Notice the beautiful combination of flavors, textures, spices, sweetness, umami.
8. Take a deep inhale, then exhale slowly.
9. Find gratitude for one thing. Just one.
10. Store in an airtight container in the fridge for up to a week, though they may not last that long.

CHAPTER 28

Recipe for Data Collection

As Dr. Suess says, I had a "brain in my head and feet in my shoes." With this reminder, I set forth to figure out how to eat high-quality, toxin-free, whole foods from local farmers who gave a hoot, while feeding a family of four on a seriously small budget in an unusually expensive locale.

I had to treat scarcity like an experiment. Since it aligned with some of the community assessment data collection I'd helped work on, as well as my grad school studies, it didn't seem altogether bizarre to conduct my own affordable family food research. In my extra time.

I opened a new excel spreadsheet to start organizing my thoughts and budget. I created a list of all the foods I purchased regularly, grouped them into weekly, monthly, and quarterly purchases, regardless of whether the item was perishable or could be stored. I listed the grocery stores in my town; the big-box stores in the city; a couple of online shops, which I used irregularly due to packaging, delivery fees, and fuel waste; places where I procured fresh fruit and veggies, plus a few locally made products I didn't have time to make myself (like mustard).

Each time I shopped, I scrutinized the price of every item at every location, saving receipts so I could enter amounts into my spreadsheet. In the excel doc, I entered prices for each purchased item. Not surprisingly, our family-owned grocery store asked the highest prices (on average)—though they also donated more money to our community and paid employees higher wages than chain stores. They probably also had higher property taxes. So, I still shopped the sales there and bought locally made items (like herbal hand salve).

Each time we drove to the city to hit up Costco, WinCo, and TJ Maxx, I became edgy, blood pumping extra hard, with only my breath to calm my nerves. I avoided Costco on food demo days so my kids weren't coaxed by aromatic won tons and chicken fingers—food they'd never heard of and the packaged versions of which I didn't want in their bodies. Mostly, on weekdays the aisles were easier to navigate and people were scarce, so I could hyperventilate slightly less.

Even with Costco's expanding array of "healthier" foods, I avoided organic kid snacks and squeezy packs (I could make those at home with less sugar); prepared granola (cheaper to make at home with more protein to boot); hummus in plastic containers (wasteful and easy to make); and almost every frozen meal. I splurged once or twice on organic spinach ravioli (a beast of an effort to make from scratch) and always organic chips and salsa for Chris (even though they were packaged in plastic). Otherwise, I stuck to my list: organic quinoa; non-GMO avocado oil in a glass bottle; organic canned, crushed tomatoes; organic frozen blueberries, broccoli, and peas; organic butter and peanut butter. You get the picture.

WinCo—an employee-owned discount grocery store—was a whirlwind. The first time I went in there I almost threw up. The store is designed to usher people along as if in a food maze, with 12-foot-tall racks of items lining both sides of every aisle and nowhere to go but forward. It was more overwhelming than Costco because instead of large cases of food, the individual items were packed together like knick-knacks at a flea market with packaging and promises that enticed customers. There, I took deep breaths. Lots of deep breaths. *Focus on the bulk bins, remember? Just find organic grains, fill your bags and scoot.* There were exactly 11 items in WinCo at one point that checked my "standards" boxes—the foods I would consume without anxiety and willingly feed to my family. I purchased only the items more affordable than in our expensive town. They were still luxury items: coconut water, Kashi crackers, bulk organic basmati rice, plus non-food items like Band-Aids. But since I never knew what would be available, shopping there was aggravating and inefficient. A waste of time equaled a waste of money.

Then off to TJ Maxx, where I focused on reusable kitchen essentials that were Earth-friendly and would save me money in just a few uses. I found BPA-free food bags with dinosaurs shouting "Eat Me" or plant graphics on them; silicone spatulas; bamboo serving utensils; cast-iron skillets. Once in a while, I could find a bulk bag of pink Himalayan sea salt or unrefined olive oil from a small farm in Spain (safe enough even without labeling, since the EU has banned thousands of pesticides used widely in the US, and heavily restricts use of many others). I bought one item at a time every four months or so when we trekked to the city to shop. I kept to my list, avoided aisles with scented dish soap or candles (typically toxic), and bought only what we absolutely needed. No new kitchen towels, succulent pots, or bamboo salt dish.

The anxiety I felt in TJ Maxx was triggered by the contradiction of buying eco-conscious products made all over the world at a big box store. I wondered whether the companies I patronized would benefit in any way from my purchases, and I guessed probably not. My mind went into a justifying frenzy, settling on the fact that these products were available at a last-ditch price point for thrifty folks like me. I had no idea about the carbon footprint, and I kept to items without plastic packaging. Again, I hoped my own financial scarcity would be short-lived, justifying that I supported as many small businesses and farmers as possible.

The last-stop shop: online purchases. I didn't love this idea, but was there really an environmental difference between buying from Amazon and buying from Costco? An ethical one, perhaps.... When I assessed prices on Amazon, they were higher than other locations on my grocery route. Great! I didn't have to buy food from the largest online retailer in the world.

From Azure Standard (a smallish online market delivering bulk, organic foods) I purchased breadmaking flour, dried cherries, macadamia nuts and a few other foods I couldn't find locally. Over time, their prices increased (and so did the delivery fee), making this option less viable (though I do miss quinoa flour and giant vats of peanut butter). Eventually, I checked that grocer off my list.

The final pieces of my pantry puzzle were the most rewarding: community food and farmers. In the summer and fall, I volunteered in our food bank's two community gardens in exchange for vegetables (since my own garden was the pits). My kids caught grasshoppers or made umbrellas out of Swiss chard, while I helped plant seeds, pull weeds, and harvest. I frequented the farmers market for the non-veggie items. A nonnegotiable requirement for my inner peace and sanity—even though I couldn't afford most of the summer berries (and I avoided peaches that I knew were sprayed)—I attended weekly and bought dried beans (one type each week), raw goat yogurt, elderberry syrup, and whatever I needed to supplement my garden volunteer work. I also treated myself to one baked delight from my baker friend's booth: a nut-date-coconut bar or something similarly decadent.

Soon, I knew all the market prices, and while I would have loved to buy from each of the farmers, I narrowed my focus to two or three—the cream of the crop. They honored the land, took care of their animals, and created truly sustainable systems that made my heart sing. I trusted them, believed in them, and supported them with the few dollars I had. Surprisingly and thankfully, many of their products were the most affordable. (That has, of course, changed.)

The entire food procuring endeavor was beastly and, perhaps to onlookers, an obsession. The point was: organization and forethought were essential. I was saving money where I could, which assuaged my guilt for choosing to study instead of earning wages at an uninspiring job. When Chris told me to stop worrying so much about money, I didn't understand that he meant I'd gone too far. I thought I was helping.

Once home with affordable groceries that met my standards, I felt proud as I looked around at what I'd accomplished with some determination and grit. I felt rich surrounded by bags of organic grain, flats of ripe tomatoes, and hand-labeled bags of black beans. My kids bailed on helping me put things away, but it was meditative for me and I often found myself smiling while rearranging the cupboards and fridge. I felt safe knowing I had an array of good food, and this conscientious effort helped me feel food secure. I did not know then how sanity-saving my well-stocked pantry would prove to be later on.

Despite saving sometimes hundreds of dollars each month, and though the effort was well worth the reward of quality food, my noble endeavor created deeper strains on our family life. Chris's increasing discontent at my fixations became an anathema to my joy. The crevices in his frown grew deeper, his gaze fell upon the view outside, with shoulders bent forward as if to shield his heart. He stopped accompanying me on trips to the city to grocery shop and, instead, chose to stay home with the kids.

Slowly, I started to feel all my efforts were frivolous, that grad school had been a terrible decision, that my passion for food systems, whole foods cooking on a budget, and human and environmental nutrition were splitting us apart. Once again, my ambitious mission—with a strategy for my family's happiness, health, and finances—had turned sour. Clearly, what mattered to me did not matter to my husband. The only way out of this chaos was to finish grad school and start making my own money.

RECIPE for DATA COLLECTION

Grocery shopping in bulk can be utterly exhausting. Worse, when you get home, you have no idea what to cook. And you're probably tired. Rather than order take out (expensive) or reheating prepared food (not my ideal), I became adept at making a simple meal with what I brought home from the shopping excursion. Here's one easy, affordable dinner idea. Omnivores, feel free to swap meat for beans.

Quinoa, Broccoli & Bean Bowl
Yield = 4 servings
Prep time = 20 minutes

Ingredients
- 1 c dry quinoa
- 2 c veggie broth
- Olive oil
- 1-2 cans of your favorite beans (I like white or black beans in this recipe)
- 1 package of fresh or frozen broccoli florets
- Garlic powder, cumin, salt, pepper to taste
- Cheddar or parmesan cheese
- Avocado
- Salsa

Instructions
1. Prepare the quinoa according to the package instructions using either water or broth. It will take about 20 minutes to cook.
2. Add olive oil to a medium pot with lid. Heat on medium, then add broccoli florets. Cover.
3. Open the canned beans and strain the liquid. Add beans to the broccoli pot with a bit of fresh water. Add your favorite spices, stir, cover, and heat until warm and broccoli is bright green, about 6-8 minutes.
4. Prepare toppings. Grate cheese. Slice an avocado. Pull out the salsa. Maybe some chips, if you feel so inspired.
5. Add some spices to the quinoa, if you'd like, and fluff. Then add quinoa to bowls along with the broccoli, beans, and avocado. Top with cheese, avocado, and salsa.
6. Sit down with your family. Acknowledge your gratitude for everyone's support of your food procurement endeavors.
7. Be grateful for simple, wholesome, homemade meals eaten together.

CHAPTER 29

Recipe for Dixie Debauchery

When one of my closest friends, Rosa, planned a trip to New Orleans to celebrate her 40th birthday, I leapt at the chance to go. I took out a bit more money in student loans that term so I could attend, though I could not convince Chris to come. He didn't think it was financially wise (or perhaps, another resistance) but he encouraged me. He knew I needed to get out of the study tower and our home where I'd been sequestered for many years (while he got his social fix at work many nights per week).

Aylee had just turned two and was no longer nursing. My mom had recently moved to town, an unplanned surprise that changed everything for me. Her presence further opened doors to possibility. For the first time in five years, I was free to travel solo.

To New Orleans! NOLA, the ideal US city to experience a melting pot of European, African, Caribbean, and Latin flavors and traditions. I would be swept away by strings and horns, intoxicated by Creole cooking, and awakened by street revelry. I desperately needed to be whisked away from my reality for a spell, transported into a timeless intersection of dark history, voodoo, and magic—a culture I'd sensed only vicariously through historic novels and licentious movies. Dramatic backgrounds of old cemeteries, ornate balconies entwined with flowering botanicals, and uneven cobblestone streets winding through light and shadows....

I needed to let loose!

Rosa rented an incredible 18th-century house-turned-Airbnb in the Marigny. Its colossal pillars spoke of extravagance compared with the shotgun houses that later sprang up around it. Located on North Rampart Street, it was only two blocks from the co-op (essential for a traveling nutritionist) and three blocks from St. Roch Market (culinary invitation to my soul). The neighborhood was abundant with talismans tucked into cracked windowpanes, faded plastic beads dripping from trees, flowering bushes, eyeballs and such in lieu of doorbells, and peeling wrought-iron fences. Though we'd arrived just after Mardi Gras, I sensed the decor was permanent.

We filed in from Los Angeles, Oregon, and Idaho. When our friends from Atlanta showed up with fresh eggs and produce from their local farmers' market, a few bottles of bourbon, and a dozen instruments, the good times were full-on.

Music and food anchored our activities. Both had been pivotal in my life, and both had lost their luster along mundane rhythms of small-town Idaho family life. I'd lost my taste for rock, folk, bluegrass, funk, while attuned to whatever classic country or pop song my husband was learning to sing and play. I'd given up the night life and my posse of fun-loving foodies to motherhood. Hence, the camaraderie was intoxicating, the cocktails uplifting, and the food brought me back to Earth as we toggled between satiation and exhaustion.

It had been six years since I'd lived in a city, and though I was a total outsider, how refreshing was the artistry! Whether showing off or truly authentic didn't matter—creative performers and visual artists captivated us onlookers. Street art spoke truth, exposed myth, and gave insight to a sense of place that tourists otherwise may not begin to comprehend.

I was in New Orleans to celebrate and relax, but I'd forgotten how to be free, or to be me. I resisted letting go. Uncomfortable in the humidity and in my own skin, I struggled to find my inner funk and my outer expression. Even when seated front and center, accessible to the sweat and pulse of the band, with a glass of wine in hand, I felt out of sync. In the past, I'd dive right into the experience. Surely, I was just a bit rusty.

The next day, we ventured over to Magazine Street to lunch at the James Beard award-winning restaurant, Shaya. Nothing about it overtly spoke "N'awlens" though there was shrimp and fried chicken on the menu. The ambiance was cool and clean, and the swank prevailed in the simple descriptions of every mouthwatering dish on the Israeli-inspired menu, of which many names eluded me. Gastronomic obsession was evident in the puffy bread emerging from the wood-fired oven, the mysterious "Tunisian spices" and *babkeh* (pistachios).

We ordered a dozen items that awakened my taste buds, the way I'd wanted my body to feel the night before. My homemade everything paled in comparison to the intentional creations that came out of that kitchen. Food complexity and convention transformed creatively through passion. *Passion*! It used to underlie the very essence of my being, my zest for living. Purposeful food, a creative cocktail, and a meaningful meal—the sensory world I'd been missing in Idaho, which lacked a thriving food scene.

The Sazarac blew my mind, too! Whatever was in it (and I did ask), it was devoid of the peaty mustiness I detested from rye whiskey and it definitely lacked Peychaud's with red food coloring number #40 (I would have noticed). Perhaps they made their own bitters. Anyway, the licorice-infused absinthe was distinct—a fave from my Bohemian days in Europe—with a twist of citrus. Since having kids, I'd hadn't been drinking much. In fact, I'd vowed never to drink alone, which was 90% of my evenings for at least five years (plus, not drinking saved us money). So I wanted my beverage to be perfectly balanced and worth every penny. I ordered another.

I perked up. Exalted by food and drink, the medicine connected me to the blissful moment. Finally, I felt *alive!* Sustenance of the spirit was literally bursting out of every dark corner and from under every streetlight in New Orleans: crooked tombstones in once-orderly lines; haphazard rhythms of too many stringed instruments and egos; and nature everywhere! Magnolias, bursting with blossoms, scattered delicate petals over well-worn steps. Sidewalks were tripped up by rising roots. Nothing tidy prevailed. Life *emerged* into disobedient beauty.

We ate our way through late-night Bananas Fosters and wee-morning beignets and chicory coffee. Twice we visited St. Roch Market, once for deep-fried Haitian plantain chips and rice and again for vegan falafel bowls with kimchi. When the others reveled in Creole shrimp and grits from my friend's favorite restaurant, I wandered far in search of a menu that didn't include allergenic crustaceans. No kitchen I tried would accommodate a shrimp allergy, so I returned empty handed to the family-style table with my friends and chose to drink my dinner that night.

This holed-up mom yearning for quasi-tamed debauchery (compared to my twenties) and imbibed temptation was jolted from a long, unintentional hibernation into a lucid, alluring dream. Magic really did exist in New Orleans beneath bushes, brass, and booze, waiting for me to discover it. My comatose, curious, and creative spirit had stirred.

The following few days relaxing into old and new friendships further revitalized me. Then just when I thought I couldn't feel lighter, an intense rain pounded me down. I smiled as it washed over me, droplets soaking my hair and clothes, dripping down my bare arms in a sort of baptismal rebirth. Nature's power to both create and diffuse cacophony. *Even in chaos, there is balance.*

I vowed to recreate that life balance in my own chaos at home! Or else, I might drown in it.

RECIPE for DIXIE DEBAUCHERY

Rice and beans are an ideal foundation for experimenting with new flavors from other cultures. I'm not adept at southern cooking, but this recipe makes it easy to pretend. It's also a nutritionally complete meal and naturally shellfish-free!

Cajun Beans, Sausage & Collards with Rice
Yield = 6-8 servings
Prep time = 1 day to soak beans & rice (or 10 minutes to gather canned ingredients)
Total time = 1 day + 60 minutes actual cooking time

Ingredients
- 2 c dried kidney beans (or 3 cans prepared kidney beans)
- 2 c white rice
- 7 cloves garlic
- 3 ½-4 c veggie (or chicken) stock
- 1 tbsp whole cumin seeds
- 3 tbsp extra virgin olive oil
- 1 yellow onion
- 2 large tomatoes, diced (or a 14-oz can diced tomatoes)
- 2-4 tsp Cajun spice mix (or to taste)
- A couple of Andouille sausages (optional) or 1 ocally sourced, sustainably raised and home-spiced sausages from your favorite farmer
- 1 bunch collards, ribs removed
- Sea salt and pepper to taste

Instructions
1. The night before, rinse and soak both the beans and rice in separate bowls.
2. Rinse, then cook the beans with 3 garlic cloves and cumin seeds for 45-55 minutes or until beans are soft. Alternatively, open and rinse canned beans.
3. Rinse and cook the rice with 3 ½ c veggie stock for 20-25 minutes. If you didn't soak the rice, rinse then cook with 4 c stock and cook for about 30 minutes.
4. Prepare the veggies. Dice the onion. Mince the remaining 4 garlic cloves. Dice tomatoes and reserve their juices (or open can of tomatoes). Wash collards, remove ribs, then slice into "ribbons".
5. Slice sausages into desired thickness. If using fresh sausage, crumble into large pieces.
6. In a large cast iron or stainless-steel sauté pot/pan with lid, heat olive oil to medium and add onions. Stir to coat with oil. Cover and let simmer for a few minutes, until onions are translucent. Add spices, stirring for about 30 seconds. Add garlic and stir another 30 seconds. Add tomatoes and juices. Add 2 c beans and sausages. Stir. Cover.
7. Go make yourself a Sazarac. Mmmm...
8. Add collards to the veggies, bean, and sausage mixture. Cook for 5 minutes.
9. Adjust spices to taste.
10. Scoop rice into bowls and top with the bean, veggie, and sausage mixture. Enjoy as is or add fresh herbs or other favorite toppings.

CHAPTER 30

Recipe for Desire

It was all too easy to return to my anxious, lonely, glass-half-empty behaviors as I studied for finals, then entered my last term of grad school. Buried under the layers of school, kids, and house duties were transitory moments of pondering how different my life had become from the one I envisioned. No wonder the years had flown by with monotony and triviality—my calendar and kitchen sink were always full of the mundane.

Five days in New Orleans had reignited my desire to explore and a sense of wanting more. It was *in* me, this inherent need to be rattled by experiences. The adventure could be brief. Go anywhere that would feed my soul. Frequently.

The reckless "footloose-and-fancy-free" younger version of me on the road to nowhere while irresponsibly trashing my body for the sake of a good time was no longer me. But I could be the fun-loving, light-hearted, adventurous mom-and-bad-ass-entrepreneur who sweeps her kids away to discover the world! In reality, I felt stuck. *Grounded*. Like a plane that can't lift off during the storm. I sought clarity, or a single moment of joy to break the power that life's minutiae held over me.

After a bit of assessment, I postulated that nutritionally, I seemed fine. Something in my *mind* was off. I struggled to connect my desire to be revived with the motivation to *do* something about it.

As my elation faded a little more each day I was home, an epiphany struck me: when my new musician friend Lily, whom I'd met in NOLA, shared her whole-hemp extract with me, my entire body shifted into a state of relaxation and contentment. It was like the mind-body bliss one feels after the perfect Hatha yoga and meditation class. Picture a wilted flower resurrected by rain and sunshine. Well, like the *Cannabis* plant itself (its healing potential just rising up through the misconceptions), it helped me open up. One sublingual dropperful of non-hallucinogenic hemp plant—cannabidiol, cannabigerol, and its entourage of nutrients—changed something in my brain and body. My shoulders fell gently away from my ears; my scapulae drew toward each other, opening space for my heart; my spine straightened, bringing my chin slightly closer to my neck; my breathing slowed to a deeper, even rhythm.

I looked into Lily's eyes and saw her, heard her, sat in heightened awareness with her while my mind-chatter quieted. I felt like a whole human, not fragments patched together. I surrendered to a novel feeling of being both present and relaxed. As in one a fleeting but fruitful meditation, I sensed by body connect to my mind, and I was attuned to my mind-body in the room. I was not just existing but really coming into the moment, into myself again, with clarity. The experience was controlled and peaceful.

I have described this feeling as my brain finally "turning on" after who knows how long, retrieving capacities that had been switched off by my chronic state of "fight or flight". In less than 60 seconds, I realized I'd *known* in my analytical mind I was a stress case—volatile and irritated, focused on "how great it would be someday" when life would be rosy again. But from that moment, a certain emotional, energetic *clarity* emerged to reveal that simply being aware and attuned to the present could change everything.

Here's why: our bodies make two cannabinoids called *endocannabinoids*. One is "anandamide" (N-arachidonoylethanolamine), a hormone named for the Sanskrit word "ananda," which means "internal bliss." *Um, hello!* We release it naturally during pleasure-reward activities such as sex, running, thrill-seeking, or while using certain pleasure-center drugs. The other endocannabinoid, 2-AG (or 2-Arachidonoylglycerol) is a potent activator or inhibitor of neurotransmitters. Its primary role is to protect the brain and modulate learning, memory, mood, and more. Both endocannabinoids—and, in fact, our entire endocannabinoid system (ECS)—are key to the functioning of the central nervous system, as well as the regulation of mood, appetite, addiction, energy metabolism, pain, inflammation, stress, anxiety, and depression.

Bingo!

Not until I experienced the "aha" of non-psychoactive hemp did I fully understand the connection between my own symptoms of overwhelm—low blood pressure, shallow breath, flatlined cortisol—as imbalances of alternating chronic stress, anxiety, and depression. The craziest part was not how my *body* responded to stress—which I'd already remedied, in part—but how my *brain* was affected: my inability to make decisions, forgetfulness, irritability, disordered mood, and poor regulation of emotions.

Unlike after smoking pot, there was no "coming down" or fogginess (and no cravings for crunchy or salty). Instead, my consciousness remained acute. A single plant supplement had kick-started both my body's natural endocannabinoid sensors and my mental motivation to *become* the person I wanted to be. (Turns out, that's because the ECS is the body's balancing system. When it's malnourished, we're out of whack.) What really blew me away was that I'd been studying how nutrients from food were the sustenance required for the body's many systems to function. But the ECS wasn't yet in textbooks and, as far as was known, it could be repleted only by *Cannabis*, though other foods and nutrients certainly play a secondary role in its function or malfunction.

I was struck by the irony: Earth Mama discovers ancient plant wisdom connection in city known for alchemy. *I found my juju in the center of voodoo.* Brass horns, bayous, beignets, imbibed spirits—and a non-psychoactive plant—conjured vitality in me.

After researching the company, the growing methods of the hemp, and assuring quality of the extract, I ordered some.

I started to restore the awareness in my brain that I could do anything I put my mind to.

And, desperate to find a similar revitalization in my marriage, with the man I loved, I impulsively did the crazy and irresponsible: I pulled out my credit card and booked two flights *back* to New Orleans...for Chris and me! My cousin's wedding was scheduled there in a couple of months, but this extravagance would not be just to "a trip" to hang with my often obnoxiously loud yet incredibly awesome Italian family. I counted on New Orleans to rekindle something in *us* in stolen moments away. How long could we keep going with the monotony? And my mom, who knew Chris and I were suffering, was happy for more quality time with her grandchildren.

I booked an Airbnb in the back of an upstairs art gallery far from the hotel where many of my family members were staying. Two rusty and rickety single-speed bikes became our weekend chariots. Chris seemed more out of place than I'd felt last time; he looked around nervously as if he didn't want to stare yet wanted to ensure we were safe. But, hey—we had a map and a destination! We pedaled south to meet my family on the upper balcony of a macaw-colored joint on Frenchman's boasting the best po' boy sandos in town (I opted out). The night was young, and the street was just filling up with musicians, tourists, and locals.

After a couple of hours of booming Truppi voices, Chris and I embarked on our own night-life adventure; we meandered, allowing ourselves to be lured in by music and wine. I knew where the night might go, though, and had some adolescent anticipation about where he might attempt to be passionate. While it didn't take long for us to release the frustrations of parenthood and diurnal tasks, still we weren't gazing longingly into each other's eyes or slipping fingers into sensitive crevices of each other's bodies.

At least, I wasn't. Speaking plainly, I recoiled from public display, and I was never very comfortable with intimacy. I guess that's what happens when your "first" and "second" were rape (yes, #Me Too), and your role models were parents who sat stonily across the room from each other. I feared "letting go," and

Recipe for Desire

even though I had fallen in love with this man, my moments of true surrender in intimacy were few.

Late into the night, weary from traveling and exploring (and expecting), we biked back to our artsy studio, cutting through the muggy breeze mostly in silence except for the rhythmic squeaking of our rusty bikes. The humid air stuck to my skin and curls in my hair, as if preparing me for the very different perspiration soon to come.

And, yes, there was absolute passion when we made love! I delighted in feeling him beside me, inside me, with me. But through the caressing and adoring, something was always amiss. Was it me, unable to allow myself to let go fully? Did my overly questioning mind (once again) usurp my full attention from the beautiful moment as I wondered whether we were truly connected? *Is it simply a much-needed vacation and overdue sex?*

I did not question whether *he* might be the one holding back because, over the years, Chris continued to tell me he wanted to hold his wife, to be close. He wanted me to *be* with him, for us to be available to hold each other regularly. Like other tired, chronically stressed moms, I had next to no libido after being needed and clung to constantly by our children. I was filled up by their love and affection.

In the morning, I woke early to work on a comprehensive stool analysis critique (sexy!) that was due. The tiny room made it impossible to sit anywhere other than next to the bed. The sound of my typing was like an alarm clock. Chris stirred, looked at me, rolled his eyes, and turned away.

The next day, I took Chris to Shaya, though the atmosphere seemed less invigorating. We sampled a traditional Sazarac (with red food dye #40) at Arnaud's French 75. We sought out a tiki bar recommended by our bread-baking friend, Sean. NOLA wasn't as carefree as before. I wanted to know the origin and story of every food ingredient; Chris just wanted to taste it. I wanted to boogie freely; he wanted to dance intimately as a couple. I, to be scooped up in the art scene; he, to appreciate it from afar. I flirted with the poet typing about dreams on his vintage typewriter, while Chris was enticed by a new hat to wear while performing. Life burst around every corner, but I was restrained. *Is he too?* Instead of being open to what could unfold for us, I held my breath as Chris tugged me along through air thick with obligation and tangled up in reservation.

The night of my cousin's wedding in an ornate Greek Orthodox church, what *seemed like* true love evoked memories of our early true love. I caught myself projecting what their life experience would become in the chaos of raising kids, holding jobs, balancing finances, untold conflicts, and the distant memory of youthful adoration. Love changes. That's why people speak of the honeymoon *phase*.

I had grown to appreciate my husband as a father and the breadwinner; he still wanted the intimate passion we'd had as young lovers. I wanted him to see our deep-seated love, as parents and life partners. He wanted something more physical. How disparately we had changed.

After the reception, we meandered through the now-familiar streets in the Second Line celebration. Chris and I said goodbye to my family, then hit up two more clubs en route to the waterfront for a final round of powdered beignets. I savored my chicory-infused coffee—bold, earthy, and rounded out by a bit of sweetness. It was closing time and empty except for us. Or like us.

As we left New Orleans, our sugar-dusted marriage seemed, like the beignets, mostly fried worked dough. As with the photo at In-N-Out burger years before, in our photos at Café du Monde, we *appeared* happy together. Me in a vintage polka dot dress and cropped mustard cardigan, he in a loosened tie and new fedora. Spent, yet relatively content.

RECIPE for DESIRE

On only a few occasions my husband made the classic New Orleans dessert, Bananas Foster, at home. It had been a specialty tableside in his fine dining experience, and it was incredibly satisfying for me to witness him preparing this flamboyant and decadent dessert. It tastes amazing, too!

Bananas Foster
Yield = 4 servings
Prep time = 5 minutes
Total time = 15 minutes

Ingredients
- 4 firm bananas (not too green, not too ripe)
- ½ stick grass fed butter (or ghee)
- ¾ c cane sugar (oy!)
- 1 tbsp + a splash more of blackstrap molasses
- ½ tsp cinnamon
- ¼ c banana liqueur
- ¼ c dark rum
- 4 scoops organic vanilla bean ice cream
- Sprinkle of cinnamon

Tools
- Sauté pan or skillet with rims
- Long-handled lighter

Instructions
1. Prepare bananas. Peel and cut the bananas in half widthwise and then again lengthwise, as if filleting a fish. Set aside.
2. Add butter, sugar, molasses, and cinnamon to a skillet with rims OR a sauté pan and turn to low heat. Stir until the sugar dissolves.
3. Add the banana liqueur. Stir.
4. Add the bananas, stirring into liquid until soft. When bananas begin to brown, add the rum.
5. When the rum heats up in the pan, tilt the pan and light the rum with a long-handled lighter. The flames will go out automatically once the alcohol burns off.
6. Divide bananas into four bowls.
7. Add a scoop of ice cream and a sprinkle of cinnamon. Then pour the sugary liquid evenly in each bowl, smothering the ice cream and bananas.
8. Revel in the deliciousness.

CHAPTER 31

Recipe for Disaster

I don't know why I believed we would be different after that getaway. Naturally, everything quickly returned to "normal," each of us unable to dote on the other around endless priorities and needs. In my last months of coursework, I powered through Advanced Lab Assessment (grueling), Clinical Strategies II (with eight more "mock" clients), and Practice Management (ethics, forms, legal forms, more forms).

Mostly, I had summer fever. Ideal weather called me to hike, play in the woods with my kids, and escape into the backcountry. Sunshine pulled me to simplify, release a few "to dos" on my never-ending list, create moments of calm away from the heaviness of home life.

Chris's summer schedule became almost unbearable. Having built a rep around town as a professional, crowd-pleasing musician with a beautiful voice, his "days off" (our supposed pre-planned family days) were booked solid with gigs. I completely grasped the need to network, to say yes, to build relationships in his heart-driven new venture (but, for cryin' out loud, all I wanted was that same support and understanding for following my own dream).

Clean Food, Messy Life

I continued planning excursions around Chris's schedule when I'd have the kids. Sometimes, we'd travel north into the mountains when Chris had shows in private backcountry locations. On those occasions, Chris would show up well into the night—after I'd pitched the tent, unpacked gear, laid out beds, dressed cold kids, re-dressed wet or muddy kids, cooked, fed kids, cleaned dishes—more than once in a rainstorm. It was hard to stay awake after putting kids to sleep, but "that one night" after the sky cleared, I forced myself to emerge for a bit of peace with my friends gathered around the fire. Around midnight when we ran out of dry wood, Chris swooped in from work with firewood, chocolate, wine, and live music. Everyone cheered for our knight in shining armor. I wished I could have been as enthusiastic. Instead, I found myself resenting his lighthearted ease and scowling with exhaustion from dealing with diapers and tears and bike crashes and cooking under questionable shelter.

To add to our challenges that summer, a registered-dietician-to-be was living with us during her rotation at our local hospital. We needed the money. She needed a place to live because she was kicked out of her summer rental (I soon figured out why). I already felt like a mentally imbalanced stress case, but with the addition of her volatile energy, anxiety, poor habits, and some unexpected emotional and physical needs, I was ever more uncomfortable in my own home.

She was kind, though. Rachel acknowledged my overwhelm and was the only one I can remember who thoughtfully made dinner for my kids and me one night—Asian chicken noodles and veggies. Unfortunately, my values got in the way and I couldn't eat it. I called her to inquire about the chicken (was it organic?). I didn't, however, ask about the quality of noodles or vegetables. I'd already seen her preferences on the shelves in the cupboard: white sugar, white flour, Ritz crackers, potato chips. Rachel was studying nutrition for her RD exams, helping people with their diets, and she prepared nutrient-poor food for herself. In many ways, I couldn't relate to her *at all*. She wondered why she was so stressed, was bloated all the time, and couldn't lose weight. She'd never heard of adaptogenic herbs, small-intestinal bacterial overgrowth, or the role of the microbiome in weight regulation. We were in totally different worlds experiencing similar dysfunctions.

Rachel was also a mirror, reflecting my own volatility, fragility and downright misery. Annoyed all the time, often angry, I yelled at my kids when I should have held them. I slammed doors. I'm sure my face was a perma-scowl. I could see why others stopped hanging out with me. The food, supplements, volunteer work, and my studies—all efforts to find happiness—couldn't deter me from becoming someone I loathed. Still, living with an RD-to-be helped me deeply ground into my vision in functional nutrition and confirmed that I didn't need the understanding or approval of the systemic medical perspective. I felt relieved that IVs, pharmaceuticals, and Western ways were not my competition. I needed to find *my* people.

In August, I passed my comprehensive exam. I was officially an alumna of Maryland University of Integrative Health! I closed the computer and looked around the fun room. My smile waned. *Where is the fun?* No one was there to celebrate with me; no accolades, gowns, ceremonies, or confetti. I wanted *some* form of merriment! I'm sure Chris acknowledged the completion of my goal, but I cannot remember his words. There was no embrace, no dinner, card, or Mason jar of wildflowers.

I had just spent *six years* pursuing a master's degree in science and nutrition—what a triumph! I truly was proud. I was empowered to give, to serve. I'd done what I'd set out to do, and I valued every milestone in the process, held up by my children, my family, friends, and peers…while my marriage crumbled around me.

So, I planned my own graduation celebration. About a dozen of us ladies hiked miles into a canyon in search of alpine lakes. No cell phones, no dudes or kids, just girl talk, trail food, bubbly, and mountain vistas. These women reminded me how strong I truly was and acknowledged how much I had accomplished. Though I didn't see them often enough, they'd been the women supporting and encouraging me during the past five years of early motherhood, changing careers, and navigating family, financial, and marital challenges. They knew me, believed in me, and inspired me to keep going.

I kept going.

I was on my path and could envision the top, but with *no clue* how to get there. So many obstacles to overcome: I hadn't defined my niche; I was unsure how to distinguish myself as a functional nutritionist from health coaches, registered dietitians, and everything in between; there was no wellness center in the valley with which I could collaborate—only solo practitioners. And since Idaho licensed only dietitians (who have different areas of study and requirements than nutritionists in the integrative field), I could not even order functional labs for my upcoming clients. Also, I had no idea how to be an entrepreneur and feared starting a business on my own—the learning curve, the financial investment, and becoming even more isolated. Anxious to find a community of colleagues who wouldn't look at me blankly when I mentioned secretory IgA, glutathione, or methylated B-vitamins, I hoped my endless networking efforts in the valley would present an opportunity.

And they did. A few food council members and I pitched a year-long project for me to be an AmeriCorps member. I was to research the need for nutrition education in our valley; develop and implement a program based on results; and ensure it would be sustained long term. It was poverty pay and even I called it "volunteer work" but it was an income, nevertheless. Plus, it would culminate with a chunk of money to pay down student loans. Importantly, it was something meaningful in my local community and in tandem with my network of food folks.

The contract was a 30-hour per week steppingstone that gave me the breathing room (or so I thought) to start my clinical work at the same time. In my "spare" time, I registered my business, outlined offerings for clients, created a logo, designed and launched my website, and started marketing my first course—a four-week family nutrition program. I hosted events to create buzz and build a mailing list. I offered a hemp sampling and informational evening at my house. I taught a sugar and cortisol class in a local farm-to-fork restaurant owned by friends. I spoke about stress-related disease at the high-end health club where I used to work. I presented about functional nutrition and its role in wellbeing at a local functional doctor's office. I started writing a monthly nutrition column, "A Nutrition Mission," in our local newspaper.

Recipe for Disaster

I was crazy busy, in over my head, and felt I didn't know enough. I desperately missed the guidance from my grad peers and professors, the constant learning. So I signed up to work with a nutritionist mentor in Maryland to pursue national board certification. I knew the effort still would not result in licensure in Idaho (and would cost more money, *eek!*), but the internship provided the tools I needed to grow in my clinical work and gave me a trusted community to lean on. Plus, all the hours dedicated to the AmeriCorps work, my family nutrition course, my column, and my clients applied toward the mentorship requirements. Notably, I'd added even more to my plate (I couldn't help it!), as I was required to attend weekly lectures, webinars, mentor meetings, and check-ins with fellow post-graduate nutritionists on the same track. It meant more study, more work, more time.

Well on my way toward my vision (and burnout), on New Year's Day I went into the University of Idaho Extension office, where I was given desk space to work on the AmeriCorps project. Chris and our kids were home with my sister, Jaclyn, and her family, while I was working. Alone. For a moment, I lamented what I was doing, but quickly reminded myself that I was striving for something and so, I persisted. I was behind in my preparations for a kids' camp on Martin Luther King, Jr. Day. I still had to map out the first nutrition lesson at a preschool set to occur that Friday for 125 kids. My family nutrition program was starting the following week. I had a talk to prepare, and I had an article due.

I was a mess and could hardly keep it all straight. Naturally, for each project, I kept an excel spreadsheet to organize the food and ingredients, shopping list, a budget outline, activities, and lists of materials to prepare. Separate word documents held lesson overviews, parent take-home sheets, kid take-home activities, and recipes (accounting for allergies and age). I made PowerPoint presentations for a couple of the events and for my course. Designed business cards. Created sign-up sheets. Wrote consent forms. Figured out the tech to livestream lectures. And ensured my HIPAA-secure client relations program was ready to go with automated scheduling, forms, registration, and billing options. I had a daily to do list, as well, to stay atop the ridiculous number of details.

I could have patted myself on the back for keeping it all straight, figuring it all out, doing all the things. Instead, I cried. I'd bitten off more than I could chew. All that impact—what I thought I wanted—and I was a fucking disaster.

No time for self-pity. I straightened up, wiped my tears, and mapped out the week at home to ensure my kids would be well fed, clothed, bathed, nursed, and ready for preschool, or a day with dad, or at home while I worked. I planned all our meals, a shopping list, lunch boxes, and (I almost forgot!) Aylee's first birthday party.

I had to stay focused, or shit would hit the fan.

Or worse.

One Thursday night after putting my daughter back to bed for the second time, I was downstairs in the kitchen separating orange fig sesame bites into the next day's nutrition lesson box and into additional freezer bags for subsequent lessons while making kale pesto for dipping tofu sticks and freezing individual bags of ingredients for the Leprechaun smoothie lesson. I was also baking spinach-and-feta egg cups for my own family breakfast and high-protein muffins for snacks to get us through the weekend (I mean, the oven was already on, so I figured I should keep on cookin'). The sourdough starter was fermenting for pizza night, and so I doubled the pesto batch for our traditional movie night meal.

Yep, I had the next day's lunch covered, too: for me, a salad with leftover roasted veggies and black beans on top with a lime-avocado dressing, and all the fixin's for Chris to make black bean quesadillas with chopped roasted veggies for the kids while I was working. There was leftover quinoa for Saturday's soup, which I would make with squash cooked and frozen from fall (I'd pulled it out to defrost) and which would double as part of the base for the homemade mac and cheese sauce I'd be making next Monday at the Martin Luther King Day kid camp. No, mac and cheese wasn't Dr. King's favorite meal, but I thought it would wow the kids alongside his favored black-eyed peas, sweet potatoes, and collard greens (which we'd also be making).

Finally, I divided frozen collards and bananas into four weeks of smoothie prep for the preschool lessons, then closed the freezer and looked around. I'd turned our kitchen into a cluttered a prep space. The counters were littered with ingredient lists and labeled grocery bags; cutting boards and knives; veggie ribs and tips; cork trivets and potholders. The sink was full of dirty bowls, measuring cups, and Cuisinart blades, which I would absolutely wash before retiring for the night and, ideally, before one of my babes woke again.

Once my happy place where our small children sat at my feet playing with wooden spoons as I chopped veggies to downtempo music, our kitchen had become a late-night food prep workstation, silent but for my mind-chatter and an occasional deep sigh. I'd become a fanatical food mom. And the simple, meaningful life I'd envisioned had become a messy, complicated catastrophe. I pondered the irony of this while reviewing recipe ideas for my Simplify Family Nutrition program. *Ha!*

As I put away the last of the prepped food, covered the still-warm muffins with beeswax, and closed the dishwasher, Chris came home and entered the kitchen. Exhausted from being a playful dad all day and on his feet for eight hours at work, he glanced at my tired eyes, food-stained apron, and clean countertop (except for the lists).

No words. He went upstairs to bed, and I wept again.

RECIPE for DISASTER

There is something fundamentally satisfying about throwing a bunch of healthy foods into a blender, drowning out all the chaos with the noise of the engine, and watching the cacophony meld into a unified color of nourishing goodness. Then, the quietude after pureeing, the focus while pouring green goodness into a jar.... I created this recipe for the "calcium" lesson in my early childhood nutrition program, NECTAR & POLLEN. I was delighted that most toddlers loved it!

Leprechaun Smoothie
Yield = 2-3 servings
Prep time = 7 minutes

Ingredients
- 1 c collard greens (chopped or frozen)
- 4-6 oz plain yogurt
- 1 banana
- ½ avocado
- ½ c full-pulp orange juice
- ½ c water
- Handful of mint leaves
- Dash or three of cinnamon

Optional green ingredients to add sometimes
- Green juice of choice
- Hemp protein powder
- Another protein powder free of sugars or isolates
- Adaptogens, such as maca, mushrooms, etc.
- Spirulina
- Chlorella
- Ginger

Instructions
1. Add all ingredients to a high-speed blender (using any emotion necessary).
2. Blend until creamy, at least 30 seconds (while meditating).
3. Pour into mason jars (with intention).
4. Enjoy immediately (along with a few deep breaths).

CHAPTER 32

Recipe for Driving Everyone Nuts

Nutritionist moms with Type-A personalities (or maybe just me) have the potential to go off the deep end because, well, we analyze every single food decision. Every. Single. One. I couldn't get out of my own head—I knew "all the things I should be eating and feeding" my kids. If I didn't know, I'd research, ask, experiment—or whatever I needed to do to make a more informed choice. I know it sounds like it made life harder by knowing more, but (I'd convinced myself) I could meal plan better and cook with ease because I had such confidence in what I was doing.

I don't remember anyone calling me out on my preoccupations with food quality though, most likely, I was incapable of hearing. I reigned over the kitchen most nights and every morning and during the day, too—even when I wasn't there to cook, I'd executed a meal plan. Yeah, I was the diet dictator. The food fanatic. The plate police. In retrospect, I fucked up a lot. At home, and in public. While I was having a blast coordinating the food circus in my head, I was driving everyone around me mad. Driving people away.

Take the skate park incident. When Avery was five, he entered a skateboard competition. He'd been riding for a few years—since his "coming-of-age gift" when he decided to stop breastfeeding (I saw it more like a no-more-boob-bribe). Regardless, we spent a lot of time at the skate park. He was as fixated on sports as I was on food, so we humored his interest in the competition.

In an oversized pirate vest cinched together with a wide, black belt, soccer shorts, and Converse shoes with flames, Avery competed in the youngest age group, then begged us to stay until the awards. We sat for hours in the dry summer heat and, after running out of the snacks and coconut water I'd toted with us for what I thought would be a short event, we were hungry. While I nursed Aylee in the shade, Chris took Avery to grab lunch. They returned with deli sandwiches and drinks. Which is when everything went downhill.

Chris thoughtfully allowed Avery to choose his own drink as a celebratory gesture for Avery's first competition. I later learned Chris had vetoed Gatorade (knowing I disagreed with marketing processed beverages to athletes) but said yes to V8 Splash Tropical. Of course, the first thing I did was read the nutrition label. The second ingredient: high fructose corn syrup with whopping 36 grams of added sugar in one bottle! *Seriously?* Also "natural flavoring" (it's still unclear what that means), red 40 (argh!), and sucralose (an artificial sweetener).

"Chris, Avery *cannot* drink that! What were you *thinking?*" I reacted, much louder than I realized. People turned to look at me.

"Just let him have some. It's not going to kill him...." Chris kept his cool, even tone with clenched teeth while his face welled with fury.

"*No!* I'm sorry. It's just *not good* for him." I looked at Avery. "Bud, this drink is not healthy for you. I can't let you have it." I took it from my son's grip. Avery burst into tears. Everyone kept staring. I stuck to my guns. I would *not* introduce artificial food to my blossoming child. More than my adversity to consumption of unnatural ingredients, I didn't want to teach him those kinds of beverages are okay even sometimes. They're not. Forget the food dye and lack of nutrients—I knew too much about the ill-effects of excess sugar intake. I had *just* researched and taught a class to high school students about sugar and mass marketing to teens, with ads targeting children as young as age two. V8 Splash symbolized everything I was against; it was at the core of American disease.

And I'd totally ruined the moment, as I'd done many times before (and after) with my reactions to conventional ice cream, store-bought birthday cake, 99% of Halloween candy, the suggestion to bribe potty-training toddlers with M&M's.... You get the picture. I'd also demeaned my husband, shamed myself, and disappointed my son. In public.

Just thinking about the masses buying cheap, processed food for convenience further isolated me. I could no longer relate to my culture, let alone my own family, and I criticized myself for that, too. I hungered to be around people who were like me and wondered if there were any.

Not long after the regrettable skate park moment, I signed up for a five-week course, Cultivating Emotional Balance. Chris was unusually supportive. I learned about my triggers and took baby steps to respond instead of react to them (and silently celebrated my progress). During the full-day sessions, I found ways to forgive myself and find peace. However, the happiness piece underlying the teachings did not materialize. At home, I was overwhelmed by all the ways I wanted to improve. Negativity and discontent followed me around like twin shadows. I tried to meditate; adopted a gratitude practice; started working with a mental health therapist. So much pressure. Something was eating me alive.

I could feel better only when away from the house—the proverbial box closing in on me. I took to nature. In autumn, the kids and I crunched leaves under our boots beneath the barren aspens. In winter, we bundled in layers of wool and feathers to marvel at the magic of sunshine sparkling on crystallized snow. In spring, we rode bikes out the canyon, observing each budding sign of renewal. These small excursions provided my psyche with sustenance crucial to managing co-existence with the mundane. I could return home to appreciate more of the little things that otherwise drove me crazy.

Clean Food, Messy Life

The problem was that my food obsessions followed me everywhere, too. I thought I was being mindful. I sought peace in my kitchen and in my purpose. I chose coffee mugs based on how they felt in my hands. I planted herbs based on the energetics of a certain pot and deliberately placed them in the health or wealth corner of a windowsill. I strove for spaciousness on kitchen countertops, plates and bowls spaced evenly on open cupboards, and the perfect garnishes on recipes. I prepared lunches or snacks for every excursion (because, hello, cheaper and better), considering what we'd eaten for breakfast and what was on the menu for dinner. I calculated the number of fruits and veggies we consumed each day. I accounted for every color in the rainbow, including brown and white. I minimized simple starches and maximized whole foods. My Weekly Meals Chart with beautiful pictures hand-drawn in crayon created expectations for my kids and kept meals simple for me: soup and salad Sundays, tacos on Tuesdays, one-pot Wednesdays.... And it worked. The kids helped me change up ingredients based on seasons and sales, so we didn't get bored with the same ol' same ol'.

The mindful eating workbook I filled out for a class in grad school pointed toward eating disorder. I disagreed. I felt as if I was standing in my vision of food idealism.

If it weren't for the coffee, the passion, and the perfectionism (and probably the supplements), I might have exhausted myself from all those details. Instead, I was energized to create impeccable menu for longer road trips, with meals checking all the nutrient and satisfaction boxes I'd created in my head. With all the extra packing, preparing, details, and directions for road trips, though, getting out of the house always utter chaos. Add the food frenzy, and the well-orchestrated plan I'd envisioned inevitably boiled over with frustration.

Until…one Thanksgiving, our annual drive to SoCal to visit Chris's family, when I wanted the pre-trip intensity to be different. Armed with emotional balance tools, ashwagandha and hemp extract, I also had a game plan my therapist and I devised. Instead of burdening my husband with road trip food minutiae, I reminded myself how much I loved the organizing, planning, and execution. Lists in hand, I grocery shopped with intention. Instead of getting mad at Chris for playing his guitar while I

Recipe for Driving Everyone Nuts

packed up the car on my own, I lovingly placed the small cooler (with dinner) up front and the large cooler (with tomorrow's breakfast and lunch) in the back with the suitcases and gear.

What a relief not to rearrange everything Chris had packed in his attempt to be helpful! What a change from the major anxiety triggered by my food fixations! And, for once, I was not late (shocking). Five minutes before we needed to leave, I announced, "Okay, kids! Let's put on our shoes!"

Chris stopped strumming and looked at his watch. Then he looked at me, dumbfounded. "Don't you need help packing the car?"

"Nope. It's done. We're ready to go except for your bag." Chris placed his guitar on its hook and raced upstairs to *finish packing. Ha!* I fed the cat, scooped up the kids, buckled them into the car, and waited in the driver's seat until Chris joined us. He rushed into the garage, loaded up his bag right where I'd left a space for it, and we pulled out of the driveway *on time* to attend the Lantern Walk at Avery's school before leaving town.

As the gate closed behind us, Chris looked at me. "You're so *relaxed*. Are you stoned or something?"

"No, dude. It's the new me," I said, fucking proud of myself and annoyed that he thought I needed drugs in order to get my shit together.

Future trips—family visits, weddings, baby showers—were all on me. I'd become accustomed to solo trips with kids. However, after one visit with my dad and his wife in Arizona, I'd had enough. The three of us drove 14-hours south in one day without ipads, car movies, nor books on tape (because even the CD player was busted in our old Land Rover). We sang Waldorf and campfire songs, and played "I-spy", "guess the animal", and "road trip bingo." We toured the Grand Canyon and Zion on the way home (and enjoyed ourselves). But I wanted my husband and co-pilot with us. I wanted the kids' dad to enjoy these moments. I wanted him to appreciate the immense effort I'd invested into planning such amazing trips, all the details dialed in. Including our diet, which complemented every part of the journey.

When the opportunity arose, I presented an ideal *family* adventure to Chris: a trip to Bend, Oregon—one of our favorite places to visit during the good' ol times—then to Ashland for our friend Maureen's, wedding. I promised to be as spontaneous as possible and approach the trip with a childlike sense of wonder at the unknown, like the food-writing-road-trips of old! We'd frolic in ferns and splash in puddles! Taste life! Eat it up! I couldn't wait!

But no, Chris wouldn't entertain the idea of coming with the kids and me. *Someone* needed to stay home and work to pay the bills and buy the gas I'd need to travel. Hm. Freedom to travel was the very reason I chose work I could take anywhere, to meet with clients virtually, to pine over research and recommendations in the wee hours after putting kids to bed. Chris, on the other hand, now embodied the very persona he loathed—inflexible, tied down, and in a funk (like everyone else he professed not to emulate). He was unwilling to take time off work to live—at least, not with us. Or, maybe, not with *me*.

Fine. I would go. Chris practically ushered us out, while I reasoned we'd all have a lot more fun without a curmudgeon dad in tow. Deeply bothered by his decision to stay home, though, I considered whether regular breaks from each other might be good for us. Some marriages seemed to operate well that way. I proposed not to make Chris feel bad for his decision. The kids and I would leave in a good mood, come home refreshed, and accept what our life had become.

In the days preceding our trip, I moved around the house like a woman on a mission, relocating sunglasses from the laundry room to the car, printing directions (no GPS) to lay on the passenger seat, stacking sneakers, sandals, stuffies (which cannot be replaced on the road) in grocery totes, and watering my beloved plants (lest Chris forget). Intentional deep breaths reminded me (again) that I loved trip planning, and to look at my lists for suitcases, gear, car-games, and emergency tools. Last, but not least, *food*—divided, as ever, into meals, snacks, and beverages because I could not (would not) buy costly, poor quality trail mix at a gas station. Yes, part of road-tripping was the unknown of roadside potty breaks and snacking from farm stands, it's just *harder* when driving solo with two kids relying on Mama for everything.

Recipe for Driving Everyone Nuts

Being ready to offer food when my kids and I needed it bolstered the freedom I craved (militant as it seemed). Packing *exactly* what nourishment we would consume each day on the road meant we could stop whenever and wherever we wanted without being at the beck-and-call of highway intersection truck stops or fast food anything that would make us feel like shit (me, mentally; all of us, physically). Of course, I packed the enzymes and tummy soother herbs, anyway.

Plus, I loved planning food surprises! I cherished the memory of the look on guests' faces when Travel Guide Jamie offered hot chocolate and mugs in the cool morning fog at the peak of a five-mile hike in an abandoned cow shelter in the Swiss mountains. The thanks I received when supplying ice-chilled mint-and-melon balls for the afternoon roadside break on a 20-mile bike ride in the sea-salt heat of a San Juan Island summer. I wanted my kids to smile in the same delighted-and-thankful way as privileged guests on a luxurious trip.

Hence, I supplanted the notion of being a food control freak with being food *enthusiastic*. My aim was not to drive people nuts, but to delight people with figs, goat cheese, and candied nuts! It was all a matter of perspective (my therapist assured me).

Memoir purists may not delight in the following details, but ingénue-foodie moms may appreciate knowing what this nutritionist mama packs for a road trip with young kids. I spent days refining my road trip meal list, which I carried with me everywhere. Here goes:

In Bento boxes I packed kids' lunches—salami, Havarti, and kale pesto sandwiches on my homemade sourdough bread (and my own adult version piled with arugula in a stainless-steel container). Sides—grapes, sliced red peppers, and chocolate-covered almonds. I kept organic bars, fruit leather, trail mix, and ginger chews up front and at the ready. The back cooler was packed with more snacks—yogurt, hard-boiled eggs, green smoothies in reusable BPA-free pouches, and homemade monster cookies as well as all the ingredients for meal number two (dinner). In the shade of a park (or somewhere the kids could run around), I'd repack the Bento boxes with a mackerel salad, crackers, olives, cherry tomatoes, carrots, hummus, and kraut.

I thanked myself.

Clean Food, Messy Life

In the back of the old Land Rover, was a black milk crate, aka my mobile pantry containing extra food and drinks for the week: typically, granola, more trail mix, boxed dairy alternatives, dried fruit, oranges and apples, nut butter, honey, rice cakes, seaweed, popcorn (often homemade), and dark chocolate something. Beverages ranged from kombucha to coconut water, or sometimes organic-juice boxes left over from last year's birthday party. For me, a supply of dairy-free creamer and usually a dairy-free cold-brew.

Rooted in quality assurance and nutrient balance, but also in presentation and pleasure, planned nourishment was also road-trip "food freedom" without worry. It was our ticket to flexibility with what we *might* find along the way. We could stop for pie when the sign said "homemade." We'd definitely visit my favorite bakery in Bend (twice) to indulge in Ocean Rolls, the most amazing pastry I've eaten anywhere in the US. We'd often cook with friends we visited, and occasionally splurge on a well-crafted meal eaten out.

I was truly looking forward to the drive, and my heart sang when my kids asked, "Mama, what's for lunch!?" They loved my road trip food, and always gobbled it up.

RECIPE for DRIVING EVERYONE NUTS

My version of "tuna salad" is made with mackerel or sardines, which are much lower in mercury. For your own meal, add the mackerel salad atop a bed of greens. Let kids help select crackers, veggies, and fruit. Save cookies as a surprise for after the 54th time the kids have asked "how much longer?"

Road Trip Bento Boxes
Yield = 2 kid lunches + mom's salad
Total time = 20 minutes

Ingredients
- 1 can mackerel
- 1 small carrot, grated
- 1 stalk celery, finely chopped
- 2 tbsp fresh parsley, chopped
- 2-3 tbsp sauerkraut, chopped (without brine)
- A tbsp or so raw sunflower seeds
- 2-3 tbsp hummus and/or mayo and/or mustard
- A huge handful of mixed greens
- Whole grain crackers
- Cherry tomatoes, sweet peppers, or other veggie of choice
- Avocado slices
- Olives
- Colorful fresh fruit of choice
- Something sweet, such as figs or dates

Instructions
1. Scoop the mackerel into a bowl with some of the oil and mash.
2. Prep carrots, celery, parsley, and kraut, then add to the bowl. Add sunflower seeds. Fold together with mackerel to combine. Add hummus or mayonnaise if you're a traditionalist. Dijon mustard is a house fave—just a little. Don't make the salad too runny or it will be messy in the bento box.
3. Pack bento boxes for kids. Add mackerel salad to one bento section, then crackers, cherry tomatoes, peppers, olives, avocado, fresh fruit, dates, etc. to the rest of the bento box sections.
4. Pack a salad for yourself. In your favorite reusable to-go container, add mixed greens and top with mackerel salad. Add the same veggies, olives, etc. to your salad. Add extra seeds/nuts, kraut, or anything else you'd like. Dressing optional. Pack fruit for yourself in a separate container.
5. Save treats for later—if you pack them in the bento box, most kids eat them first. Kids are so excited to have a cookie or brownie about the time you're also craving one.
6. Remember to pack sporks and napkins!

CHAPTER 33
Recipe for Despair

Our little darlings, now three and six, were growing ever more curious about the world around them, but Dad's daytime play schedule was interrupted often due to scheduling gigs, meetings with potential clients, practicing new songs for his playlist, wrestling with speakers and wires and strings. Chris's schedule became irregular, making afternoons trickier. Some days he left at 3:30, other days sooner, and some evenings he was home until 5:00 or so. Flexibility and focus became even more important in my schedule.

Without consistency, I was jarred by midafternoon transitions leaping from an overbooked workday to mom life, from heady analyzing and organizing to heart-centered patience and tenderness. To shake off the to-do's—creating handouts, client recommendations, text for my newspaper column—I developed a survival ritual: hole up in the laundry room, take a few deep breaths, drop some hemp extract under my tongue, relax my shoulders and jaw, express gratitude for one thing, reset my intentions…reenter the kitchen with my mom game on.

Even so, "the witching hour" was far from tranquil. The kids were tired from preschool, camp, or a full Dad-day; or riled up if they didn't have enough outside time. I was stiff from sitting on my butt in front of a computer screen and needed to move my body. The atmosphere was ripe with volatility. Remaining in our home meant my brain was hijacked by work: endless pressure, text messages, all the things I hadn't yet accomplished. And the effort it took to be a good mom. Getting out meant replacing the never-ending lists with the kid time and fresh air to clear my head. We'd escape from endless pressure by riding bikes around the canyon loop, exploring the dusty hillside trails above the house, or attempting to garden in hard, clay soil. Back home, I was refreshed enough for some batch cooking, planning our upcoming weekend adventure, or reading books with my children.

I could never escape or surrender to monotonous loneliness. While scooping batter into parchment muffin cups or stirring the squash soup, my mind often wandering to the life I dreamed about in Hailey, where friends would randomly stop over to say hi upon biking home from the grocery. I'd invite them to stay for dinner, and we'd fill each other's souls and bellies while our kids played. But that wasn't possible in my life as I knew it. *Would it ever change?*

Then change occurred. That fall, the restaurant where Chris worked closed. His boss was pooped after more than 30 years in the business. She wanted to live her life with fewer commitments. We could certainly relate to that. To me, the universe was listening! My hopes soared, and I failed at suppressing my excitement.

"Babe, this is your chance to branch out into something new!" I suggested daytime work with one of the non-profit athletic organizations or the county recreation district, reminding him of the many organizational and professional talents he possessed, not to mention his love of games. "Remember, you said you don't want to miss out on our kids' events? You love being active! You're great with kids."

Again, he resisted, and it was unclear why. I'm sure there was fear, but all Chris could say was, "I'll figure it out."

Perhaps the universe headed to Chris's call, as well. Simultaneously our friend Joel, from the Evergreen restaurant, a wine friend, and so much more, opened a new restaurant. My husband was his first recruit. I would have been annoyed except

Recipe for Despair

for three things: 1. the café was located in Hailey; 2. Joel wanted his restaurant to fill the niche of real food for locals, with from-scratch meals, and food sourced from regional farmers; and 3. the joint would be open *during the day*.

Holy shishkabobs! Is it too good to be true?

I was pumped to help the restaurant thrive! I helped connect Joel and his chef with my favorite producers—sourdough from our one-and-only artisan baker; eggs from the pasture-raised-chicken farmer; microgreens from the small, budding farm in "the triangle"; grass-fed beef from the rancher down the road. With a healthy menu from unforgettably rich breakfasts to simple quiche, superfood salads with dreamy sauces to crafty sandwiches with pickled radishes on artisan breads, it was just what our town needed.

That job for Chris also meant I'd cut my workday by a couple of hours so I could pick up kids after school. I was happy to do that. Less work, more time together? It was an easy choice.

We had endured, bided our time, bit our tongues, rolled our eyes, walked on eggshells. And now things were unfolding for us. For the first time in 15 years (six years with kids), we spent evenings together, had family time. Some afternoons, he'd come home and I'd pop out for a run while he caught up with the kids. After, we'd enjoy dinner together. *Together!*

That routine brought more good times. One evening, I was invited last minute to a movie and beer with girlfriends. Not only was I *able* to go, but Chris *encouraged* me to go! He happily stayed home with our kids so I could have girl time. Other days, I encouraged him to mountain bike with Sean while I prepared dinner; then he'd be home to eat with us. Sometimes Sean came, too. Evening excursions around the loop included all *four* of us.

Better still, we invited friends (and their kids) over for dinner, reveling in the still-warm fall air and backyard leisure activities that previously had seemed like a far-fetched illusion. Even if I still found myself in the kitchen prepping food and washing dishes while others were playing, I was far from alone. Other moms and dads joined me, brought me a cocktail, helped dress the salad or slice the quiche. I was steeped in vitality and happiness.

Joy! It was real: change of jobs, change of pace, together time. Ease and flow.

And it was ripped out from underneath my like a bad tablecloth trick. Apparently, the south valley was too small to support a quality breakfast and lunch restaurant—too many people commuted north to work. They wanted to-go coffee and a pastry or a slice of quiche to enjoy in morning traffic. Others delighted in the gourmet coffee and delish breakfast, then occupied seats for hours, typing away on their computers. I did that.

The new restaurant's vibe was good, but without a liquor license, few in-house diners, and low check totals, the vision was unsustainable. Plan B: stop serving breakfast and lunch altogether and serve only dinner. *Shoot!* The restaurant closed for a few weeks to reinvent itself.

By Christmas, we'd reverted to our old, familiar routine. The blip on my hope journey weakened as my husband's night schedule filled up again with restaurant work, regular shows, and holiday gigs. And again, we high-fived each other mid-afternoon and talked kid logistics before he left and I became the permanent, solo night parent. I sighed a lot. Lost the pep in my step. Snubbed the supposed magic of the winter holiday season. Bah, humbug.

In moments of pause, I clung to a conversation we'd while I drank coffee at the restaurant before the changes. During a lull, Chris sat with me for a few minutes and surprised me with his reflections. "Trup, I see how working during the day benefits us… Soon Avery will be playing sports after school and traveling for weekend tournaments. I don't want to miss those things." As I soaked it in, he continued, "I also understand the convenience of living and working in the same town where our kids go to school. So, I want you to know I'm open to living up here someday. Not now, but someday.…"

Those words kept me optimistic about us. I was desperate to believe we'd be okay. Selfishly, I hoped he'd burn out from his current night schedule sooner than later, recall how lovely it had been to work during the day and be with his family at night. I prayed we'd find a way to recommit to the sweet life we'd experienced for those few peaceful, happy months. Adaptation to our former routine indicated nothing would change, yet I clung to the potential of something better for us.

RECIPE for DESPAIR

A few leftover veggies, a bit of cheese and some eggs, and you've got the makings of a quiche—the perfect meal for supplying your body with plenty of nutrients while you're going through a rough time. The crust makes this meal feel like you're eating a pastry, too, which is soul-soothing. It's super versatile, so don't overthink ingredients. Here's one possible combination.

Simple Quiche
Yield = 6-8 slices
Prep time = 40-70 minutes (because the crust needs to chill)
Total time = 75-105 minutes

Crust Ingredients
- ½ c whole wheat pastry flour
- ½ c white pastry flour
- 6 tbsp cold butter or coconut oil (or a combination)
- ¼ tsp sea salt
- 4-6 tbsp cold water

Filling Ingredients
- 1 ½ c leftover cooked veggies, such as Brussels sprouts and roasted potatoes
- Some leftover salmon or sausage
- ¼ c minced herbs
- ½ c cheese of choice
- 6-7 eggs from pasture raised chickens or ducks
- ¼ c unsweetened milk of choice
- A sprinkle of salt and pepper
- 1 Roma tomato

Instructions
1. Make the crust. Add flour, salt, and butter/coconut oil to a food processor. Pulse a few times to begin to blend. Then slowly add cold water to the food processor, 1 tbsp at a time, pulsing each time. The dough is ready when it forms a ball and when not too sticky. If too dry and crumbly, add more water.
2. Using your hands, form dough into a firm ball. Refrigerate for 30-60 minutes. Roll out dough on a floured surface; then lay into an 8" or 9" pie plate, trimming the top edges.
3. Preheat the oven to 375 degrees F.
4. Prepare the filling. Chop leftover potatoes, Brussels sprouts, salmon (or whatever you have on hand) into bite-sized pieces. Chop herbs. Grate or crumble cheese.
5. Add the veggies, meat, and herbs evenly to the pie crust. Sprinkle with cheese.
6. In a bowl or large measuring cup, whisk the eggs. Then add milk, mixing again. Pour the eggs/milk over the veggies/meat/cheese until well covered.
7. Slice the tomato and gently lay the slices on top.
8. Bake 30-40 minutes (depending on the size of the pie plate) until the center of the quiche is no longer jiggly and the edges of the crust and tops of the eggs turn golden brown.
9. Let cool slightly before slicing and serving.

CHAPTER 34

Recipe for Depth

My birthday in late February offers the perfect opportunity to escape the dead of winter chill and wearisome routine. For my 40th birthday, I planned an extended weekend celebration—ladies only (no surprise there)—at a remote Idaho hot springs resort only a couple of hours away. My girlfriends traveled from California, Oregon, Washington, and also from our valley. We rented a quirky cabin for 12 with ceiling lines at every possible angle and stairs in haphazard places. A back-deck hot tub was fed by warm mineral water touted to be the deepest source in the country. The kitchen was unusually spacious and up to date—the icing on the cake for this birthday girl!

I'd frequented that magical hot springs for years, thanks to my mom, whose family had cabins there when she was a child. It was called Paradise even in Mom's day, and I grew up hearing her stories about the people who'd been coming there since before paved roads or paid advertising. Even in the earliest days, the hot springs was a sanctuary between remote mining towns where workers rested their horses and bones. Generations later, it was still a refuge for the working class drinking Red Bulls or coming straight from a triple shift driving an 18-wheeler, as well as for a bunch of down-to-earth, overwhelmed, ski-town mamas.

Beyond my familial roots, I felt spiritually connected to the mineral waters. It was more than a haven for soaking my skin while breathing clean mountain air; with no cell service or internet, the off-grid healing called to me. I was drawn to the water under the full moon, new moon, rain, snow, and sunlight to help me tune out the noise and turn inward. A true respite.

The nearest grocery store was more than an hour away. The nearest foodie market was more like two hours away, while the little one-pump town six miles up the road offered a smoky bar and a small convenience store that did not tempt my tummy. So visiting the hot springs necessitated planning a menu for three days for 12 women. I was burning the candle at both ends, true, but like finding a way to travel, I always carved out time to meal plan. Knowing everyone's dietary preferences and needs, of course, my Excel shopping list ensured our meals would cover vegan, vegetarian, pescatarian, and omnivorous diets and offer dairy-, nut- and gluten-free options.

Two feet of snow dumped on the first day of our getaway, so we cozied up in the cabin eating simple snacks—hummus and fresh broccoli, carrots, and peppers, plus ancient grain chips and guac—while everyone trickled in. We dipped in the private hot tub, poured French sauvignon blanc, and eventually made our way to the kitchen to prep dinner. On the menu: a spread of wild Bristol Bay salmon (from a fishmonger who lived in our valley) marinated in an orange-ginger-maple marinade, accompanied by roasted asparagus, Caesar salad with pistachios, sun-dried tomatoes, and shaved pecorino, and my homemade crusty sourdough bread.

By the time dinner was ready and everyone had arrived safely, we gathered around the kitchen island, poured Oregon pinot noir, and dished up our plates. Many of the ladies had never previously met, though they'd heard about each other for years. While standing in a circle around the food and each other, the girls took turns sharing how and when they first met me. Kristen, during sorority rush on the first day of undergrad then reconnecting several times in Sun Valley; Naomi, while studying abroad in France and then living together there for six months

Recipe for Depth

before I moved to Idaho; Sarah and Nicki, my hiking besties from our roaring 20s as single ladies in Sun Valley (and our kids were now growing up together); Rosa, while purchasing artwork from me for a client, and we became fast friends; Maureen, while in Portland, became such a close friend that she later entrusted me as a home-birth buddy for her daughter (even before I liked children).

The other women were newer friends—we navigated our 30s together, plucking gray hairs and contemplating whether Botox was or was not natural; commiserated about our husbands not understanding mom-worries; complained about food-stained yoga tank tops when slipping away for a Sunday morning class; caught each other's eyes to acknowledge sweet interactions between our beautiful yet whacky children. We leaned on each other through deaths, difficulties, amusements, and births, putting our kids first and ourselves (and often husbands) last.

In my estimation, the food paled in comparison to the company and the overwhelming love I felt while reliving the experiences I'd shared with those beautiful women. We survived frat parties and being hustled in the streets of Tangiers. We ate *profiteroles* in Paris cafés and picked mountaintop wildflowers. We hula hooped at Bluegrass shows and boogied in dive bars. We shared stories well into the night, accompanied by Kentucky bourbon on ice and a dark chocolate bar medley of crystallized ginger, salted caramel, and mint. And played a random game of Cards Against Humanity.

In the morning, we dragged ourselves into the kitchen with our hangovers to toss together the birth-day quiche: Brussels sprouts, shrooms, and sheep feta plopped into glutinous and gluten-free crusts, local eggs and milk, and adorned with sliced tomatoes. By the time the coffee was ready, so was the oven. We dressed up fair-trade French-press brew with a smattering of creamers and raw, local honey (sourced from the U-pick blueberries-and-bees farmer just up the road from the resort). I plated my homemade vegan banana bread with walnuts, sesame seeds, and cacao nibs. We had some cut-up grapefruit, kiwi, and bananas (not at all seasonal or local, I realize). We hydrated with filtered, mineral-rich spring water…and more coffee.

Clean Food, Messy Life

Having eaten, there was more relaxing and reveling on the docket! We walked up the hill in our suits and snow boots to lounge in the natural hot springs pool, where we soaked until our tummies told us it was time for lunch—a lighter soup-and-salad fare. Soup: pureed carrot, pumpkin, red lentil, and coconut cream soup with Moroccan spices and my homemade veggie stock, garnished with avocados, cilantro, and plain, Greek yogurt. Salad: a simple quinoa-tabouleh-esque salad with parsley, cucumber, pumpkin seeds, lemon juice, olive oil, and cumin. Not too early for birthday wine, either!

By midafternoon, we needed either a nap or some exercise. Opting for the latter we laced up our boots, zipped up our puffy coats, bundled up in beanies and mittens, and trekked up the peaceful canyon in the deep snow. Arm-in-arm with tiny crystals sifting down around us, time seemed to stop. We had no worries, nowhere else to be. Beauty, nourishment, and friendship cocooned us. I wanted to remain in that idyllic snow-globe moment forever.

It was mealtime again when we returned to the cabin. My birthday dinner was a French-Italian-inspired smorgasbord (yes, I know, that's a German word) of my fave artisan goat, sheep, and cow cheeses; soppresatta, salami, and prosciutto; olives, figs, and grapes; pesto (my own), onion marmalade (my friend's), and butter (local, supposedly grass-fed) to accompany crusty walnut-raisin bread (from the local bakery). Veggies were offered in a mixed-greens salad with rosemary roasted potatoes, blanched green beans, capers, and a lemon-shallot-tarragon-garlic-olive oil dressing. Aaand...some French and Italian wines, light to dark. Spoiled we were with such a gastronomic epitome.

Remember, I didn't love cake, so I rang in the big 4-0 with chocolate peanut butter pie in pecan-date crust. And a bourbon cocktail with a twist of citrus. There might have been some weed.

Snowed in, sated, and silly, we contemplated how each of us could take home some of the good vibes. We marveled at how much we'd all needed to disconnect from life to connect with each other and, in doing so, how easily we'd cultivated a deep camaraderie in only two days. Weary before we'd arrived, we were fully satiated from bonding in the healing water, in the woods and, of course, around the kitchen table. We found peace

Recipe for Depth

in letting go of all the to-dos and don'ts and distractions, so we could simply be. I was soul-nourished and grateful to be my authentic self with women who honored and held each other, just as we were.

When prompted to share goals for my 40th year, I came up with these: to generate magnetic energy through mindfulness, meditation, and visioning; to strengthen my body again through physical challenges; to cultivate positive emotions so I could move away from the ordinary and toward the extraordinary. As I spoke, somehow I trusted a powerful shift of energy would bring new perspective to my life, to ambitions that had been compromised during my marriage, to habits that had built a wall around my heart, and to behaviors that had invited frustration and indifference.

I vowed not to live the next decade in disappointment and disconnect, but in the creation of joy and contentment. I wanted to rediscover my appetite for life with a strong conviction to cultivate more depth and meaningful experiences. I was ready to grow, unfurl, blossom. And I was still committed to reconnecting with my husband, though I wasn't sure how.

In a roundabout way, I was to get my wish.

RECIPE for DEPTH

A charcuterie board may not be the most economical, earth-conscious, or healthy meal on the planet, but it certainly is indulgent! "Charcuterie" is French for "meat"—the focus of this meal—with infinite options, as you'll see. A spread of meat, cheese, fruit, veggies, and dips epitomizes my love affair with European lifestyle—slowing down, reveling, relaxing, enjoying the moment.

French-Inspired Charcuterie Board
Yield = 8-10 buffet-style servings
Prep time = 30 minutes

Ingredients
- Aperitif, such as kir or vermouth
- White wine, such as a sauvignon blanc or chenin blanc
- 3 different cured meats, such as smoked salmon, prosciutto, salami
- 3 artisan cheese varieties that pair well with the meats
- Pink wine, such as a rosé
- 3 fruits, such as grapes, fresh figs, and apricots
- 3 fresh veggies, such as tomatoes, cucumbers, and arugula
- 3 pickled goodies, such as cornichons, capers, and olives
- Red wine, such as a pinot noir or a cabernet franc
- 2-3 spreads, such as olive tapenade, pesto, and onion marmalade
- 2-3 artisan breads and/or whole grain crackers
- Digestif, such as Cognac or fruity liqueurs
- 2-3 desserts, such as pot de crème, macarons, lavender shortbread or, simply, chocolate
- Raw, roasted, or candied nuts
- Water, perhaps infused with cucumber, lemon, or mint

Instructions
1. Line up all the beverages in order of when you'll consume them.
2. Lay out all smorgasbord foods in an artistic manner, grouped by themes on different platters.
3. Meats and cheese pairings together, adorned with sides, such as grapes, and pickled food like cornichons. Create 2-3 platters of combinations.
4. Breads and spreads go well with sliced veggies, dried fruits, and olives.
5. Desserts pair well with berries and raw or candied nuts. Place them away from the rest of the meal as a temptation and reminder not to overeat the charcuterie board.
6. Take your time. Eat and drink with pleasure. Enjoy your company.

Décor & Ambiance
- French subway or café music.
- French-inspired linens, with patterns such as the fleur-de-lis, country stripes, or toile de jouy.
- Tall candles in silver or gold candlesticks (whichever match the linens better).
- Wild and colorful flowers and leaves.
- Simple platters that highlight the food over the décor, like wooden boards or white ceramic.
- Small plates and a collection of antique forks, spoons, and knives for serving.
- A collection of liquor, wine, and water glasses.

CHAPTER 35

Recipe for Dramatic Moments

#1

Coming out of the woods and back into reality always is somewhat jolting. Starting the first week of my 40s with a positive outlook—knowing it would be jam-packed with back-to-back nutrition consultations, loads of paperwork, mentorship lectures, volunteer meetings, and mom duties—would require a massive effort. No time to pause or divert my attention, no space in my schedule for a kitchen accident or a sick kiddo.

There certainly was no time for working on my marriage. *Shoot.* I vowed to carve out together time in the following week. We needed it. But something else had been brewing, and it didn't care that I was busy. Nothing could have prepared me for that Thursday night conversation.

When Chris came home late after work, we were both exhausted, but he seemed even more so than usual. We went upstairs to our bedroom, propped our pillows against the headboard, only a space apart yet incredibly distant. I looked at Chris as he stared vacantly at the shuttered bay window and asked him what was up. He flatly replied, "It would be best for all of us if you moved out."

"What!?" I was blindsided. While searching for more useful words, instant cacophony inside my head blocked my analytical mind while the hope in my heart was suddenly smothered. Chris remained silent, and I could only muster up the question, "What do you mean, best for *all* of us?"

"Trup, we've gone in circles for years. We have different needs and desires. I don't want to resent your passions, but I simply have no interest in them. And I don't want our unhappiness to rub off on our kids."

Woah. He finally said what I knew to be true. I countered, "Babe, I just came home from a weekend with 12 women who shared discontent in their marriages. What we're going through is *not unique*! This time in life is *fucking hard*. You're giving up and we haven't even tried!"

"I just can't see how this can work." He still hadn't looked at me.

"Are you in love with someone else?" I blurted out.

"No!" He finally turned to meet my gaze. "I'm just not happy."

I wasn't happy either, but I also didn't want to *give up!*

Searching desperately for what else to say, thoughts raced through my brain. Our totally *opposite* assessments about how to repair our marriage loomed crystal clear. How had I been too busy to notice the depth of his misery and distance? I thought pursuing my dream would have positive effects on *all* of us. Clearly, my efforts had backfired. When I reached my goals, Chris would not be waiting on the mountaintop with a picnic, and everything would be not sunny and delightful.

Before we could discuss anything further, Aylee woke up crying, as she often did, and I went to the kids' room to soothe her. I fell asleep there.

#2

I held myself together the next morning while waking up with our children, struggled through teaching a nutrition class about vitamin-D-rich foods (of which there are few) to preschoolers (complete with a frittata I'd made), followed by a meeting with the director of programming at our community

Recipe for Dramatic Moments

YMCA. I deflected my pain during the highway drive up and back down the valley until arriving late morning at the University Extension office in Hailey. Thankfully, I was the only one who worked there on Fridays—I was desperate for the quiet space. After locking the door behind me, I collapsed on the floor where no one could see me below the window. Finally, I cried.

Of course, I'd been trying to hold myself together inside for years, though not very successfully.

Then I called Rosa, who had recently divorced. Just the last weekend at the hot springs, we'd talked about the time when she'd badly wanted a relationship as seemingly *easy* as Chris's and mine. She was not surprised to see how complicated it had become because, well, we humans are complicated. And life is complicated. Over the phone, she grounded me, reminded me I was a freakin' amazing manifestor and I could create anything I wanted! I'd done it plenty of times before. I was doing it right then. I'd witnessed *her* grab her dreams by the horns after splitting with her husband.

So would I.

The pep talk had been good but had not mended my punctured heart.

I acknowledged what I'd already lost. I'd lost out on dinners and campouts because I was miserable. I'd lost my love for running because it elevated my anxiety. I'd lost my gusto to explore and experience life with my partner, because even when I carved out time in my own busy life, he didn't want to partake. I'd lost invitations to anywhere because married couples didn't ask miserable moms whose husbands didn't come for happy hour or game night. I'd lost my confidence because I'd suppressed it beneath guilt and ambition.

What I'd really lost was my sense of Self. I'd become someone I didn't recognize or want to be, living in a place that didn't resonate with me, married to a man who no longer cared about what I cared about, nor exerted effort to find our love again.

I'd also gained. Two beautiful children. Innumerable life experiences that showed me I loved being a mom more than imaginable. Time in the woods to find perspective. Time on my mat to reflect. An insane amount of biochemistry and nutrition knowledge. A desire to know myself again. A renewed interest in my potential in this life. Confidence in my personal and career goals.

Something else struck me, as suddenly as summer hail: even though I loved my husband, I didn't *need* him. I never really did. I wanted him—*of course* I wanted us to experience this crazy life together!—but our bond was never about that mushy "you complete me" bullshit. I'd always felt like a whole person and thought of him as one, too. But my wholeness had deflated as a result of us together. And so had his.

My lungs hurt from attempts to draw in air between wailings, my throat weak from inability to find the words to express my emotions, my nostrils raw from filling tissues. After a few half-hearted attempts at accomplishing trivial tasks, and with puffy eyes, I looked around my office, which doubled as a 4-H storeroom. I observed the gorilla racks of random items: cheap blenders stored in their boxes, bins of toxic Teflon cookware, plastic utensils, disposable napkins, and Dixie cups. Here was a university-run office priding itself on its mission for human connection to animal husbandry, native plants, and community education, and I was surrounded by a storeroom of cheaply made, disposable, commodity items used for outdated classes on food preparation and inaccurate information about health, while the employees planned an end-of-the-year celebration with hot dogs and Mountain Dew.

And I was a multi-degreed nature lover teaching small children about food by touching spiky, fat cucumbers and pulling peas from the greenhouse vines, while their teachers prepared chicken nuggets and animal crackers.

What am I even doing here?

Fixated on my own ideologies, I had desired to make a difference in people's lives and in our community. I'd felt compelled to acquire an understanding of how our internal and external environments are intricately related, then help others puzzle through their own connections between nature, food, and health, while simultaneously inviting them to live more harmoniously with their mind-body and our planet. Whew.

That was what I was doing. And absolutely, I was living true to myself.

Recipe for Dramatic Moments

#3

I slowly pulled myself together. I needed to prepare for my new client, who also happened to be our neighbor,

I'd met Kate only once, on Christmas day while I was walking my daughter to sleep in the BOB stroller. She had looked weak and was unable to catch her breath, even on the flat part of our road. When I asked if she was okay, she told me of her recent diagnosis with an unidentifiable cancer, chronic fatigue syndrome, and fibromyalgia. On top of that, she was also deeply depressed about her health, and fear of the unknown was squashing her faith that she could heal. Eventually, we set up a consult.

Upon settling in her living room for our initial consult, I told Kate how proud I was that she reached out for help. Her doctor knew the importance of food yet lacked the time and knowledge to specify functional foods for her needs. They both hoped I could help. I hoped so too.

Although worn down by my own personal tragedy, I couldn't take my focus from this amazing woman's angst and anxiety. Kate's condition and needs were exactly why I had studied the science of nutrition. After 90 minutes of discussing her narrative and a nutrition-focused physical exam, and hours previously spent analyzing her intake forms and lab work, symptoms, dietary and gut distress, I suspected gastrointestinal disharmony was afflicting her brain, sucking her energy, and contributing to her tumor growth. We developed a plan for lab work, food, mindfulness, and mental uplift.

Having gathered my belongings to head home before Chris left for his show up north, I opened her door as Kate commented, "I'm sure your family is waiting for you!"

I burst into tears.

"Oh, honey!" she cried, hugging me tight.

My professors had cautioned against sharing too much of our own lives with clients, but in that moment I shared about the previous night's trauma. Kate was incredulous that I'd been able to focus on the session for her. Without realizing it, she in turn helped me see that my heart was pure: despite my marriage despair, I could still gift my love and knowledge to help others get their lives back.

(Post script: And she did. After working together for a while, Kate became cancer-free and was thriving, thanks in large part to my suspicion of small intestinal bacterial overgrowth hijacking her gut, brain, and immune function.)

That afternoon as I walked tall up our driveway and Chris backed his truck out of the garage, our interaction was short and awkward. We had little to say.

I was asleep with the kids when he arrived home that night.

#4

Next morning after breakfast, we bundled up in our puffy coats and Chris and I took the kids out for a chilly neighborhood walk. I was shaking, but not from the cold. Chris took my arm, an unusual gesture for him, and said, choking back tears, "I don't want to break up our family."

Well, that was unexpected. And lovely.

Normally the overly verbose one, I remained quiet as he continued, "It took me asking you to leave to realize I still love you. I don't want to let go of us."

So, we'd slipped to the bottom in tandem, found our footing separately, and Chris was extending a hand to help us both climb out together. Maybe this was a new path for solid ground, a first step back to the top of the flowery alpine mountain where we'd first blessed our marriage and our life together.

I felt hopeful. In fairness, I revealed my insights. "I've been thinking, too. Honestly, your declaration made me realize I don't need you, though I very much love you, too. I still want you to be my partner and husband, but to stay married, we *must* figure out how to reconnect."

Chris agreed. "How?" he asked.

I had a couple of ideas that would help me, personally, though I knew I was asking a lot of him. "Well, first you agree to make friends with *one* dad who has kids our kids' ages. I don't care who you choose—it's easy for me to become friends with most people, so I'm not worried about being friends with his wife. We need to spend time with other couples, other families, so you can see that our challenges are normal and also have a dad to talk to about them."

Recipe for Dramatic Moments

"Okaaay...," was all Chris said, as I continued.

"Second, for the sake of our relationship *and* our family life, will you *please* stop working weekends?" We'd exhausted the conversation about changing careers, so it seemed a reasonable request to enjoy our favorite activities on weekends together. "Maybe, *just maybe*, sometimes we can hike, camp, bike, and explore with whichever family you choose to invite into our lives."

I was surprised how quickly he agreed! Those two requests made a lot of sense to him.

"Now, what can I do for you?" I asked. I knew the answer, of course. More sex.

"I want to feel close to my wife." I reminded him of all the ways I'd been trying, and of the ways he either resisted or didn't make the effort. Nonetheless, I agreed to do more, find more spontaneity, more spark in order to enjoy other aspects of our lives again.

"Is that all?" I asked. Chris nodded and pulled me closer as our kids rode their bikes in circles in front of us, oblivious to what their parents were experiencing, yet surely aware.

Anyway, we agreed to try. We would show our kids we loved each other. Since we'd both concluded we truly did, it was refreshing to be on the same page about prioritizing *us*.

For him, though, couples counseling still was out of the question.

RECIPE for DRAMATIC MOMENTS

Vitamin D supports our bones and immune system, as well as our mood. It's primarily available from sunshine, and hard to obtain from foods. The foods we tasted in the preschool class—eggs, salmon, and Swiss cheese—make a delicious frittata chock-full of other nutrients to support mental wellbeing, the stress response, gut-brain health, and the endocannabinoid system. Note: I promote whole, raw milk, though I know that's controversial to many.

Sunshine Frittata
Yield = 6-8 slices
Prep time = 10 minutes
Total time = 35 minutes

Ingredients
- ¾ c shiitake mushrooms
- Butter or oil for the skillet
- 7-8 eggs from pasture raised chickens
- ¼ c whole cow milk or vitamin-D fortified milk of choice
- 3 oz cooked, canned, or smoked wild salmon
- 1 ½ c fresh spinach leaves or ½ c frozen spinach
- A few sprigs of your favorite fresh herb (parsley, thyme, etc.)
- A few oz Swiss or Emmental cheese
- Avocado
- Sauerkraut

Instructions
1. Clean and chop the mushrooms, then place them in the sunshine to absorb vitamin D (studies show this is possible with some shrooms, like shiitake!).
2. Preheat oven to 400 F.
3. Whisk the eggs and milk together in a bowl.
4. Cut the salmon into bite-sized pieces.
5. Chop the spinach and herbs.
6. Shred or cube the Swiss cheese (for some reason, Swiss and Emmental appear to have trace amounts of vitamin D).
7. Melt butter on medium-low in a cast iron skillet with at least 1" sides, coating the sides when the butter melts.
8. Sauté the spinach for 1-2 minutes. Add the shrooms and sauté for 1-2 minutes more. Turn off the heat. Add a drizzle more oil, if needed, to ensure the skillet is well coated.
9. Sprinkle the herbs, salmon, and cheese over the spinach and shrooms. Pour the egg and milk mixture on top.
10. Bake in the oven, uncovered, for about 25 minutes, depending on the size of your skillet and the thickness of the egg mixture. When the middle is no longer liquidy, it's ready!
11. Serve slices with a side of avocado and a spoonful of your favorite kraut.

CHAPTER 36

Recipe for Dutch Oven Baking

A lightness replaced much of our tension and Chris and I found ourselves wanting to hang out together.

Making changes was tough, though. My spring calendar was overfilled with weekly lessons for my preschool program, more clients than I could handle with a three-month wait list, and milestones to meet with my post-grad school mentorship. Chris was still working or playing music five to six nights each week.

Even so, a series of visitors and school fundraisers provided opportunities for a few date nights. First, my friend Ashley came from Seattle to celebrate her 40th birthday party (and brought her foodie friends). We all dressed up in neon and scrunchies for an 80s' night, met Ash and her costumed entourage for sushi, and boogied all night in our high-top sneakers. A few weeks later, we adjusted belt buckles and shit-kickers for a Hoedown fundraiser. After that, we positioned raffle tables and yard games for the coffee shop game night (where Chris played music). Finally, we busted out flip-flops and beer steins at the local dive bar's live music and fundraiser raffle (where Chris and his band played).

Those social gatherings, plus spring school festivals, were exactly the events that Chris and I had always enjoyed together: costumes, music and games, food and drink, good people, and a reason to celebrate. Most events centered around our kids and their small Waldorf school, where many parents had become my close friends. I was over the moon to be out in public *at night* with my husband, our kids, and an amazing community of like-minded folks whom we adored.

Enjoying family life for the first time in years, my belief in us grew. Precious family time was scarce, though. I was traveling a lot: Phoenix to be with my dad at the Mayo Clinic during open-heart surgery; Boise for a conference for the AmeriCorps work; Cincinnati for the Farm to Cafeteria Conference; Austin for a 3-day hemp conference. Even road travel with our kids to meet up with family at Craters of the Moon and friends at Yellowstone.

I had anticipated a lighter summer load as my weekly lessons ended, but that's not what happened. I'd said yes to other things, of course. I created and taught a 5-day seasonal Food and Senses kids' camp for preadolescent girls to develop a healthy relationship with food. I helped organize an inaugural 12-week Veggie Prescription program with our local food bank and the hospital. I attended weekly garden sessions where I guided participants to improve food habits and whole cooking skills to offset their diabetes (in exchange for a basket of seasonal veggies). These programs were a refreshing break from paperwork and computer work yet required a lot of time and effort.

The outlook for Chris's schedule seemed hopeful at first, too. His boss was incredibly understanding about shifting to a weekday schedule so he could spend more time with his family. Not surprisingly, though, being available on weekends was a magnet for more shows, so his music life picked up. His band was offered gigs they couldn't pass up, Chris committed to a regular Monday night show (our *one* family night!) in the lounge at Ketchum's new 4-star hotel, plus performances at bars, a country club, wedding receptions, and private events. Like me, he couldn't say no.

Thankfully, and true to his word (with a little nudging), Chris accompanied the kids and me on the first campout of the season in late May. It was my friend Aly's annual birthday

Recipe for Dutch Oven Baking

celebration at our favorite alpine lake. The kickoff weekend at the lodge included races, so we moms ran the 5k while the dads played with the kids at the finish line. In previous years, I'd scrambled to find someone to watch our wandering kids, while Chris would drive up early to run the half marathon, then drive home midday for work. That year, he was there *with our kids*, and I ran *with my friends*, worry-free.

And he camped with us! All 25 of us.

It was a flashback to a decade prior: as Chris tried to hang with the guys, the same look settled on his face and in his eyes, that question of whether he could ever fit in or if he even wanted to. I watched him do his thing: bring out the games, which drew a few people to play intimate, yet competitive, frisbee. That was who Chris was, inside. Playful.

And I joined in between pauses with my own camping passion: experimenting with Dutch oven baking! Aly's birthday inspired one of the other moms to turn out a chocolate cake in her Dutchie (delish!) and I went for fudgy brownies (yummm…).

Chris was either having fun or he drank more than I realized because he mustered up the confidence to bust out his guitar that evening, again bringing himself more fully to the group. I watched with hope and I prayed (in my way) that this relaxing social weekend in the mountains would fuel his fire for more. With that thought lingering, I leaned over to place dark chocolate on a cinnamon graham cracker. The back of my long puffy coat brushed the flame of a camping heater. I was literally on fire the very moment Chris sang Bruce Springsteen's "Oooh, I'm On Fire…." I'd have to be careful what I asked for!

Unfortunately, big groups were still not his jam. But he *did* choose a dad he wanted to befriend—Avery's best friend's father. That was awesome for me because I adored the wife/mom—Mandy had already become a good friend. Plus, this family was always up for adventure, *and* they prioritized gourmet cooking while camping—I vowed to love them forever.

We swore this family to secrecy when introducing them to our favorite camping spot, located over a treacherous pass and less than an hour from home. Privately, we called it "Moose Meadow" thanks to the Bullwinkle whose grass-chomping woke us from our under-the-stars slumber in the bed of Chris's pick-up a decade prior. It was the same meadow where we were married and, without fail, it provided us with quietude and gratitude for Mother Nature.

Our kids ran around blissfully in the woods, the dads cracked microbrews, and Mandy corked a bottle of wine for us ladies. Chris was a firepit maestro, so he rebuilt the stone ring and collected firewood while Aylee and I picked wildflowers to adorn the rickety pop-up table, which I'd covered with a stained lemon-colored gingham tablecloth. Our friends prepared their open-flame specialty: seafood paella. They went all out with calamari (for my sake, mollusks—not shrimp!), Andouille sausage, veggies, rice, saffron, and even organic bone broth.

The entire process spanned two relaxing hours, and I marveled at how Mandy and Mike, as a couple, moved in tandem through the steps harmoniously, effortlessly. When one of them attended to a scraped knee or checked out the magical features of a light-saber stick, the other seamlessly took over, stirring the veggies and rice and broth over the fire. An onlooker might see nothing noteworthy. But to me, their synchronization was true love. I was a bit envious of their seemingly perfect bond, especially over food. As I set the flowers on the table in the center of the speckled blue enamelware, I felt alive and warm with joy in the moment, like a perfect, simple life. I was thankful even for the hard shit that got us there.

The next morning, I managed to botch it up with a breakfast stint at the campfire and my two-hour Dutch-oven coffee cake project.

To me, camping was the perfect opportunity for a cooking endeavor because, hey, we were reveling in outdoor activities and the slow life. But as I prepared to light the 25 coals (seven for the bottom, eighteen on top) in the charcoal chimney, I poured some white gas (Chris's suggestion) onto the coals and managed to light myself on fire again! I dropped a few F-bombs and swore to make coals the old-fashioned way next time. Chris rolled his eyes at my mishap, while Mandy attended to the small burn on my leg. I cursed at the char on my favorite camping jeans, but inside I was hurt—actually, livid that my husband didn't ask if I was okay or needed help. I tried to shake off my frustration

Recipe for Dutch Oven Baking

while lining the Dutchie with parchment paper, placing it near the coals, and preparing the rest of the area for a clean, safe experience.

While the coals heated, I worked on the batter (alone). I placed butter in a metal bowl and perched the bowl on a rock adjacent to the fire. I gathered the remainder of the ingredients as the butter melted then mixed the wet ingredients before adding the dry. Finally, I gently folded in dried, wild blueberries. By then, the coals were ready, so I organized them around the Dutchie to begin heating it up.

I paused. Located my coffee. Closed my eyes. Took a sip. Opened my eyes to take in the scene in front of me—an idyllic blend of humans cohabitating with nature. But that time, I felt separate from them. I sighed and returned to the task at hand: pour the batter into the Dutchie, place the lid, add the remaining coals on top. Then I prepared the topping: another bowl near the fire to melt butter; the accompanying oats, pecans, molasses, cardamom, and sea salt.

No time to sit and enjoy. I could tell everyone was already hungry, so I quickly whipped up scrambled eggs with leftover paella to keep our tummies happy. Then, I topped off my cold coffee and joined the rest of the adults around the fire while our kids, in their fleece pajamas, played dirt hockey with sticks and rocks. I'd forgotten to set a timer or even look at a clock, so the coffee-cake readiness became our morning guessing game. I shuffled coals, drank more coffee, watched our kids build their own pretend fires and felt my anxiety building. We'd had no agenda during paella prep the night before, but now we were in a hurry to hike before the sun beat down too hot. My blissful food project had become a source of tension as Chris began to mill around the campsite picking up shoes and hats and gloves littered around the campsite, but mostly avoiding eye contact.

Anxious that I was screwing up the morning, I got up from my 5-minutes of pause to fill the water packs in our Camelbacks, gather snacks, and check for the essential Swiss army knife, bear whistle, bandana, first-aid kit, and layers. I changed kids from cozy pants to hiking shorts and applied sunscreen, bug spray, and hats. I readied myself, too.

Surely 25 minutes has passed? I peeked at the coffee cake—it was somewhat mushy in the middle. *Perfect!* I quickly added the topping, and carefully replaced the lid. I rearranged coals and took the final sip of my cold coffee, now gritty with grounds. I knew the cake needed about 10 more minutes. Overcaffeinated and anxious, I went to the car for some calming hemp extract. I applied Tiger Balm to mosquito bites on one kid's body. Assessed a scratch left by a misplaced rock on the other's leg. Mama kisses.

Back to the Dutchie. I opened the lid to check—the cake looked good and smelled amazing! That time, the aroma of cinnamon wafted into the morning air, beckoning the kids to see what had transformed inside. I slid a knife into the center, and it came out clean. Perfect. *Whew.*

More waiting…. The coffee cake needed to cool.

Did I enjoy the activity as much as my friends enjoyed their paella-making? No. It was impossible to enjoy the cake, or to shift back to the contentment and ease I'd felt the night before. I tried, but I couldn't get there. It was frustrating. Like my life.

Like a microcosm of my inner transformation, campfire baking required intention, planning, commitment, an ability to assuage stress, a shitload of patience, and hope for an outcome that would benefit everyone. Like preparing blueberry coffee cake in the woods, small efforts toward cultivating inner joy seemed entirely my own affair.

My husband didn't care about my nutrition work, and he'd made it clear he also had no interest in baking outdoors together. Once again—how could I be where I'd envisioned myself, yet so far from *who* I wanted to be?

I carried the disappointment with me while we hiked. Turned out, that was our last weekend campout with friends.

Once back home, requests for both public and private music gigs flowed in. Chris chose building a music career over spending weekends with his wife and kids. I understood because I'd chosen to focus on my work, every day, for years. I was building a business doing what I loved, and it was time for Chris to do the same. I encouraged his every effort, despite the continued strain on our life and happiness. While I hadn't earned his support for my dream, I would not get in the way of his.

RECIPE for DUTCH OVEN BAKING

A delicious Dutch oven meal can be so rewarding, particularly after dedicating a ton of effort to the endeavor! If you don't have an outdoor Dutch oven set-up, you can still make this coffee cake at home in a ceramic or cast-iron Dutch oven, as described below. This recipe is based on Sheila Mills' Klinkhammer Coffee Cake, a Salmon River favorite from her "Outdoor Dutch Oven Cookbook."

Dutch Oven Blueberry Coffee Cake
Yield = 10-12 pieces
Prep time = 15 minutes
Total time = 60 minutes

Batter Ingredients
- 1 c turbinado sugar
- 1 ¼ c each whole wheat flour and choice of buckwheat, oat, or quinoa flour
- 1 tbsp baking powder
- ½ tsp sea salt
- ¼ tsp baking soda
- 1 ripe banana
- 2 eggs from pasture-raised chickens
- ½ c unsalted butter, melted
- 1 c each milk and plain yogurt of choice
- 1 tsp pure vanilla extract

Topping Ingredients
- ¾ c sugar
- ¼ c butter
- 2 tbsp molasses
- 1 tsp each ground cinnamon and ground cardamom
- ¾ c chopped pecans
- ¾ c dried blueberries

Instructions
1. Preheat oven to 350 F.
2. Line a Dutch oven with parchment paper.
3. Mix dry batter ingredients in a large bowl. Make a well in the middle.
4. In another bowl, mash the banana. Add the eggs and whisk with the banana. Add the melted butter, plus milk, yogurt, and vanilla.
5. Add wet ingredients to the dry, mixing slowly, gently. Don't over mix.
6. Pour the batter into prepared Dutch Oven. Cover. Bake for 35 minutes.
7. Make the topping. While the cake is baking, melt the remainder of the butter in a small pot. Turn off heat, add the rest of the ingredients, and mix everything together.
8. After 35 minutes, remove the Dutchie from the oven and sprinkle the topping over the cake. Replace the lid. Bake 5-10 minutes more, until a knife inserted into the center comes out clean.
9. Cool at least 5 minutes (ideally longer if you can stand to!) before cutting into the cake. Serve with coffee.

CHAPTER 37

Recipe for Disagreements

One of the things I love about cooking is that I don't feel pressure to cook better than anyone else, no need to adorn a meal with fancy garnishes (but, yes, garnishes), no egotistical desire to put on a show. Cooking simply is the culmination of all the things I love—seasonal fresh food; experimentation with herbs, spices, and cultural recipes; taste, texture, and presentation details; and the sensory unfolding of an age-old process into creating a meal I am proud to serve and eat. Cooking is my escape from perfectionism, my creative outlet, and how I find my flow. It's my earthy gift. My love language.

It's also a game. Like figuring out how to use leftover rice, wilting lettuce, and the peanut sauce my kids wouldn't eat because it was too spicy. Or, motivated by meal planning strategies, challenging myself to combine every color of the fruit and veggie rainbow into daily meals and snacks, with plant-based foods balanced by the right amount of protein and fats. *Have we consumed enough calcium on days without yogurt? What about iron on vegetarian days? Does a sprinkle of chia, hemp, or sunflower seeds offer enough daily omega-3s?*

Clean Food, Messy Life

As the days unfolded, I was mostly okay with the fact that my husband (and others in my life) could not fathom the food game I played. It was always *game on*, yet never about competition (though it would have been infinitely more fun with two or more players).

Knowing so much about the role of food and nutrients in the body—and obviously caring deeply about wellness—I couldn't shut off my brain from strategizing. Some might call it OCD, orthorexia nervosa, or a pastime of control. In my mind, home, and marriage, food had ceased to be recreational. To maintain my sanity, I needed to think of another activity for Chris and me to enjoy together—something not food related at all. Meet him where he was. Be playful.

I grew up playing card games with my family, so was skilled at Pinochle and Rummy; board games were downright fun. When I started playing poker regularly with friends, Chris came mainly for the liquor, elk stew, and to dress up in themed costumes. Otherwise, he preferred lawn games and pushing himself to run or bike to the top of a mountain over sitting for hours with card strategies.

Scrabble was the perfect game for Chris and me, and the only board game he seemed to enjoy. With its simple approach, it was anyone's game. I used to joke that Scrabble was the only board game my husband could beat me at, as if we were tracking or if it mattered. I was the linguist, avid reader, and writer; hence my ego always wanted me to win. He was more strategic and simply played a better game. It had been years since we'd last indulged—too long to remember.

One night after the kids were asleep and (miraculously) both of us were home, I suggested we play Scrabble downstairs—not upstairs in the fun room, which had become my sacred space. The living room was more about us and reflected our story, milestones, growing family, the changes in our professional lives. It exemplified our evolution, our remodeled life. Its huge windows overlooking the south valley, the fireplace flanked by my beloved pots of geraniums, umbrella trees, succulents, and my favorite piece of artwork—a large pastel watercolor of a lily by a quasi-famous French artist. Though the living room also felt like the music room (Chris's room)—with the baby grand piano, a

Recipe for Disagreements

djembe, and wall-mounted stringed instruments including several guitars and a ukulele—it was where I'd held our angelic daughter for the first time and where we witnessed our son transition from kicking a soccer ball to building LEGOs. It also had witnessed numerous arguments.

Unlike the kitchen, which had become a space reflecting the delicate balance between function and dysfunction (the broken clock on the stove and the coffee grinder that needed a knife jabbed into the hole to work), the living room was, in fact, the family room, a place where we/I could relax (sometimes) together.

As we set out the Scrabble board and tiles, Chris said, without addressing me directly, "Hopefully you don't get pissed off if you lose, like usual." Not the greatest mood setter.

Because my goal was to *enjoy* time together, I replied calmly, "Well, one reason I like playing Scrabble with you is that we can't predict the winner. Besides, you know I get fired up with board game competition...." *Should I remind him he'd once adored that about me?*

An hour in, the score was basically tied until Chris blocked my spot with a 7-letter word: popcorn (go figure!). Game freakin' over! It would have been impossible to catch up. Huffing while trying to control myself, I spewed a few profanities and yelled, "Why did you have to *steal* my spot?" Likely, I punctuated it with a long, exasperated sigh.

He looked up, sat back against the couch, and replied, "You're always so negative."

Woah. Pause. Deep breath. *I am always so negative?* Inhale. Long pause. Exhale. Nope. Not true. Wholeheartedly, I disagreed.

I looked across the board at the man who hadn't smiled seemingly for years calling out absolutes about *my* negativity. Me. The one trying to find ways for us to have fun together. The one making suggestions about how to reconnect. Who enjoyed her work and her kids. Who woke up every morning to practice yoga and gratitude. Who had been in therapy for three years to understand that our marital problems did not hinge solely on my critical behaviors or passionate personality.

I never claimed to be perfect at anything. Ever. *How's that for absolutes?*

Shockingly, I didn't overreact to his remark. I had learned a few things about being triggered, so I did something I'd never done before—I said nothing and made no inappropriate gestures. Instead, I simply left the room. In the kitchen, I turned on the stove to heat water for Cup of Calm tea. Between inhales and exhales, I remembered that I was awesome (often).

With my tea in hand, I walked back into the living room, sat on my poof, and said, in as neutral a tone as possible, "Chris, I'm not *always* negative. That's an unfair statement." Then I shared the compliments I'd received *that very afternoon* at my local food systems meeting. My colleagues expressed how much they enjoyed working with me because my optimism was refreshing and, therefore, I was refreshing to be around.

So there.

"Seriously," I continued, "for the first dozen years of our life together, did you really peg me as negative?" I knew I wasn't. Like anyone, I'd brooded occasionally, but I used to be super fun and up for anything! Chris didn't answer. "Look," I said after a long pause, "I'm sorry everything has been so difficult lately. I'm sorry for any snarky side comments about how shitty our life has turned out. I'm sorry I'm so critical of seemingly everything."

"Thank you," was his reply.

"There are many things I appreciate and I'm trying hard to focus on them." I shared a snapshot of all the little things I was doing to become a better version of myself—all the changes I'd made in sincere attempt to raise our children without the same household friction in which I had been raised. I desperately wanted him to notice how I had improved, to acknowledge the years of effort I had put in to better myself.

Chris remained subdued, slumped back against the couch. No effort to reply. Personal patterns are hard to break. Over the years, I realized, he'd created an idea of me, and he was sticking to it. His perceptions were like petrified wood. Solid.

"I'm not sure what to say," was all he could say. *Well, fuck that!* Now I was annoyed.

A fleeting thought arose: none of my efforts mattered if they weren't starkly obvious to him. Unable to hear what the other meant, see what the other wanted, we were incapable of

Recipe for Disagreements

going deeper to source the fears or loneliness or longing buried beneath layers of blame and heartache. *Oomph*.

"Well, I'm not sure what else to do...." I replied. And, since the game was over, we started cleaning it up. In silence.

Being on edge is how my husband and I had evolved to survive around each other. The result was a negative aura all around both of us (not just me). Everything inside me objected to being defeated by something I knew we could change. Okay then. I would create *more* positive thoughts in my mind, speak those thoughts more often, and the trickle-down effect of a more positive version of me would infuse my partner, our home, our family. I'd keep trying.

One thought kept pestering me: how was it that I could be authentically positive around other people, but not around Chris? I was beginning to understand how the magnitude of his disengagement affected me. While working on myself, in isolation, I'd been made to believe *I was the problem*; but now I saw *I could also be the solution*. I was nothing if not persistent!

The new strategy? With a clear lens, I would forgive myself as I'd been, commit to how I'd like to be, and start anew. I would consciously act like the person I truly was, deep down. Be the changemaker. The new Ms. Positive Pants would help us both win. But would the effort work if Chris sat back, disengaged?

I wanted him to walk the Game of Life with me or, at least, meet me part way. The end game was still *our* Happiness!

RECIPE for DISAGREEMENTS

I'm not a huge popcorn fan, so I was surprised when one year Chris bought a vintage-inspired popcorn machine for himself for my birthday (I bought myself a vintage blender). Since having kids, homemade popcorn has been well worth the effort—it's easy for me to make with heirloom popcorn and we love changing up the toppings each time. Chris still prefers popcorn from the machine. Agree to disagree.

Stovetop Popcorn with 3 Toppings
Yield = 4 servings
Time = 10-20 minutes

Ingredients
- 3 tbsp coconut oil
- ½ c popcorn kernels
- 2-3 tbsp melted, grass-fed unsalted butter

Toppings
Mexican churro
- 6 tbsp coconut sugar
- 4 tbsp cinnamon
- 1 tbsp cocoa powder
- 1 ½ tsp sea salt

Rosemary, sea salt, & dried porcini mushroom
- 3 tbsp dried rosemary
- 6 pieces of dried porcini mushrooms
- 3 tsp sea salt + a dash of black pepper

Savory kale, garlic, & nutritional yeast
- 1-2 c kale chips
- ½ tsp garlic salt
- 1 ½ tsp nutritional yeast

Instructions
1. Make the toppings.
2. Mexican churro. Add all ingredients to a bowl and mix until well blended.
3. Rosemary, sea salt, porcini mushroom. Add ingredients to a food processor. Pulse until blended.
4. Kale, garlic, nutritional yeast. Add ingredients to a food processor. Pulse until blended.
5. Make the popcorn.
6. Add coconut oil to a large pot with lid. Add 3 popcorn kernels.
7. Cover and cook on medium-high until the 3 kernels pop. Remove the popped kernels. Remove pot from heat. Add the rest of the kernels and cover. Wait 30 seconds.
8. Return pot to heat and shake from time to time (to prevent burning) until all (most) kernels have popped, about 10 minutes.
9. Turn off heat, shake again, but keep lid on for 2 more minutes.
10. Drizzle popcorn with melted butter and mix to coat. Then, add your favorite topping and enjoy.

CHAPTER 38

Recipe for Divine Intervention

To become a better wife/mom/human would require a major transformation. My soul was conflicted, my mind frenzied, my life messy. My normally indomitable spirit was suffocating in a grayed-out misery of helplessness. Everything in my life felt off—even the good stuff. I thought I would benefit from some divine intervention, but since miracles are scarce and I didn't know how to ask for one, I took matters into my own hands. Unsure what path to take, I tried every which way.

I sought clarity through various mindful morning routines, supposedly *the thing* separating the rest of us from highly successful people. Meditation. Breathwork. Journaling. Reading. Yoga.

Sitting still to quiet the mind without expectation would benefit people like me. (I'd read a bunch of peer-reviewed studies on the topic. My therapist suggested it. It was a tool discussed during the Cultivating Emotional Balance course.) Carving out time to *sit still* turned out to be nearly impossible. Most days, I struggled to wake early enough for even a few minutes of alone time before a kid came downstairs.

Clean Food, Messy Life

Sometimes I practiced a meditation technique—adding up to dozens, over the years—to "tune in", but rarely did I feel elevated afterward. Mostly, I was frustrated with myself for doing it wrong or being unable to capture a glimpse of higher awareness. Sometimes I sat on my red-striped pillow to simply find my breath, but ten minutes was not enough time to steady my shallow, uneven breathing, let alone clear the mental disarray of my diminishing marriage or fragmented mama-life (must make breakfast, help a kiddo go pee, take a shower). Sometimes I simply wrote a few lines of gratitude or loving kindness in my journal, but it seemed impossible to carry those feelings through the day. Sometimes I picked up books by Thich Nhat Hanh, Sharon Salzburg, and a bunch of Zen monks, yogis, and swamis, yet couldn't focus on reading them in their entirety. Most of the time I was so unsettled in futile sitting postures and ill attempts at clearing my mind, that it seemed the only thing left to do was move my body out of the discomfort. Through asana, I breathed into the nooks and crannies of my joints, organs, cells. While I allowed my body to move freely, I felt far from free.

My Jesus loving friend asserted that I was disconnected with some higher being she called God, but I was still apprehensive about such a revelation. Still, her conviction was strong, and she showed up like an angel in a particularly dark moment, so I tried to become curious about my belief in a higher life force. My version of the divine was always nature, so I resolved to find magic outside myself, in how flowers transformed into fruit and how seeds were nourished by the soil, sun, and water which, in turn, also nourished humans and other animals. That helped a little. I tried to see the same beauty inside, but no light shined in there.

The only spiritual ritual I could truly understand or rely on was my post-morning-session coffee ritual. It was the one thing that warmed me and lifted me out of my glacial state—icy and submerged. (I hated that version of me.) Energetically, I thanked the farmers, the beans, the delivery truck drivers, the caffeine, the bitterness, the sweet and creamy stuff I mixed in.

Pragmatically, I analyzed how I'd come to be so cold: I was *doing* too much. That was my *modus operandi*, my fiery constitution, my ancestry—even my last name literally translates into "too much." So yeah, I was cursed. I'd stowed the world I wanted on the back burner; the life I wanted was pushed aside the many

Recipe for Divine Intervention

cast irons on the flames. I fixated on not burning it all down. Instead of forgiving my actions, unkind words, or demeaning thoughts, I began seeing how I projected layers of self-blame and criticism outwardly in hurtful, hateful ways. I tried to let go of last week, yesterday, and that last inappropriate thing I said aloud or to myself. All I sensed was noise. My unsettled thoughts usurped my "soul voice." I sat in paralysis analysis for 10, 20, even 60 minutes on some occasions. Bearing the weight of a world that consumed me, and overwhelmed by it all, I felt myself crumbling.

I wanted to believe the daily work was helping in some small way, yet the failed attempts at peace and clarity were further reducing me. No major epiphanies. No significant change in my subconscious. Not only did I *not* feel progress, I felt something else plaguing me. I couldn't verbalize the sense of longing, an emptiness like a giant boulder impeding my path to somewhere both inside and outward. I was freaking out.

Some inner voice was pleading to be heard, held, loved, honored. In my unwavering love for my children and my desire to love my husband in all the ways, apparently, I'd forgotten how to love myself! I needed something more. More time. Space. Help. Guidance. Perhaps hypnosis, or something else drastic.

When powerful women and men spoke about their metamorphoses, they mentioned the deep darkness of the hardest times upon which they eventually sprang forth. They spoke of an epiphany, an "aha" moment of clarity, or an inner voice. I'd experienced none of those. And I envied those women, in particular, who persevered, looked radiant and happy, wore just the right classy-but-not-too-professional ensembles with handmade jewelry. Perfectly coiffed, bouncy hair. White teeth. Expensive shoes. Some seemed pretentious and shallow. But the ones who radiated love and authenticity—I wanted to be like them, not to make a fashion statement, of course, but to be the free-spirited and passionate me, myself, confident in my skin.

In some reading or podcast or passing comment from someone, I was urged to dream big dreams for myself, so I wrote about big dreams. I was told to pretend to be the person I wanted to be (despite the woman I believed I'd become). I pictured myself amongst cosmos or poppies, wearing eco-conscious linen bell-bottoms and a not-too-fitted top that highlighted my post-nursing breasts and broad shoulders. Wore colors that made me feel strong, poised, beautiful. Wore stones that protected my heart. As an expression of myself. Held crystals given to me by spiritual healers and beads by shamans. As symbols of my growth. My inner loving energy illuminated every space I entered. I envisioned myself like that. Wrote about it. Did all the things. Almost every day, something.

One day I sat next to one of those stunning, glowing women at a ladies-only business gathering. Appraising her life-coaching business, I immediately sensed my own inadequacy. Still, I liked her, and I wanted to know how Jacqui had become so confident. The next week, when I saw her flyer for a free consultation, I scheduled an appointment. After our session, in which Jacqui listened attentively to my vision to improve, she referred me to a transformational business coach.

Oooh. Wait. You mean, I can transform my business by getting to the root of who I am AND show up in the world as my true self? It sounded like a way to kill two birds with one stone, without the impossible option of trekking to some remote healing center in the Amazon.

Inner-work therapy to achieve business abundance and rekindle love. Yes! That was what I needed!

The "transformational" pitch sounded perfect, but not so much the idea of being coached (though I'd just sat in session with one, hoping for some positive outcome). Anyway, coaching ads infiltrated every social media outlet; to some of us nutritionists with advanced degrees, the popular (and lucrative) allure of 'health coaching' was competitively scorned. The general public may not know the difference, but I did. I'd just spent six years, copious amounts of money, and an insane amount of time educating myself about the depth of cellular knowledge missing from the both the Western Medical and health-coaching industries. I was not against being coached in general, just not keen to pay for a service in a field that co-opted my own.

And yet... curiosity overcame my resistance. As I sat with the idea, I realized the timing was perfect to hire another guide. Plus, a business coach was different. My obligation with AmeriCorps was ending, I'd just completed all 1,000 hours

Recipe for Divine Intervention

under my nutrition mentor, and my board exam was on the horizon. Soon I'd have only myself keeping me accountable to business growth, and I reasoned that my next step for my career (and, ideally, my marriage) was rooted in my personal growth.

I called the transformational business coach—another impressively authentic woman. Lisa proposed spiritual connection to my true self as the most powerful service to all beings. She reminded me that women who lead with values and speak their truth impact more people; in turn, they reap the rewards of service and invest right back into the richness of life. Doing the work to find myself would be like permaculture to my soul. *Amen!*

I enrolled in Lisa's program. Once again, I was on track to rise up. Over the next couple of months, I dove into my innermost being. Kind of.

It was frustrating. I asked a lot of questions, and the answers either didn't arise at all or were ambiguous. The unclear internal blocks remained. I was going in circles, which I attributed to the pressures I placed on myself. External pressures were to pass my board exam and be a present mother and wife, to make money. Internal pressures were to find my purpose, true joy, and inner peace.

By the new year, all that dang visioning and internal exploration was disappointingly murky. With gentle persuasion, Lisa suggested my *thoughts* could be as toxic to my mind as pesticides were to my body and Earth. Lisa asked, "Jamie, are your thoughts nourishing, like the food you carefully purchase, prepare, and eat with utmost mindfulness?"

Um.... "Wow, Lisa. What do you mean, exactly?"

"Thoughts are intricately connected to our outcomes in life. With *neurolinguistic programming* we can rewire the brain and, as a result, create different results," she explained. Then Lisa led me through an exercise not unlike following the metabolism of nutrients in the cells of my body: I traced my thoughts to my feelings, then to my actions, then to my outcomes. I witnessed how the outcomes, in turn, influenced my thoughts. Cyclical. Energetic. Subconscious. *Oh, yeah, that Law of Attraction concept, coming back around, full circle.*

Now I understood both my rut and my potential for change. Like food altering us on a cellular level, changing who we are from an energetic core (I'm talking nutritional biochemistry) and influencing our brain, behaviors, hormones, and health, our thoughts can do the same. I had faith in the fundamentals of nutrition to guide me on my erratic path and had been nourishing my body with vibrant, nutrient-dense foods to remain healthy. So far, my *body* was, in fact, healthy. All the while, I was psychologically sick because I was wreaking havoc on my mind by demeaning myself. Doubt, unrealistic expectations, loneliness, disappointment, blame, and shame trickled down into my emotional health, contributing to both my fatigue and my unrest. No wonder my energy sucked, and my husband didn't want to come home to me. No wonder my friends stopped calling me. No wonder my mom was worried. I was toxic! I was *poisoning* myself with my thoughts!

There was that damned epiphany, and it was disorienting.

I'd already learned it takes the brain only 21 days to create a new *habit*. Through neurotransformation (aka brain plasticity), we change the way our brain functions. When the brain changes, so does our behavior. Just as food, hydration, supplements, and pharmaceuticals change our biochemical and physical health, our thoughts can change our brain and emotional health. It's all energy, resonating positive and negative ions outward, like radio waves. It's freaking phenomenal!

Always the faithful student determined to evolve, I listened more intently to my thoughts, watched how my thoughts influenced my actions, and recognized the many ways my current life shit was the result of these debilitating patterns. Lisa guided me to notice how I *felt* doing certain things, like yoga, serving clients, cooking, mothering. Wow was I self-deprecating.

Mental habit change would be difficult, and Lisa kept reminding me that the inner work guided the outer work. She challenged me to create a daily practice in the experience of abundance of relief and carefreeness, to create that vibration from the inside, which would resonate outward.

Based on my pitifully haphazard morning practice experience, I needed more accountability for this *daily* work. Thankfully, Lent was a week away. This time, instead of eliminating excess from my food-and-beverage life (the diet psychology for failure and reproach), I decided to invite a new, positive habit into my life (recipe for success). Hence, 40 days of redesigning my thoughts.

On Good Friday, I began reading a book about how abundance is our God-given birthright (more "thought" food?). As I read, the concept seemed like a trick modern religion uses to encourage us to make more money so we can give more money to churches. I read and re-read certain passages about how money is energy and if we just shift our energy, money will come. I shook my head. The only abundances I'd experienced were love and food. Abundance of money (or time) were incomprehensible. But the book did shock me into a parallel *aha!* moment: my thoughts were centered around lack. The absence of something. Lack of joy, trust, love.

Shit. I have to unpack my scarcity mindset, too.

For two weeks I read the book daily, journaled about the concepts, asked more questions, eased my breath, sat painfully in stillness. But then my routine was interrupted by spring break. By day 19 I'd already skipped a day. Then another. I'd failed my Lenten vow, so close to 21 days, and only halfway to 40! Deep down, I'd known it would happen. I'd predicted my failure and I felt ashamed. Perhaps I hadn't truly believed an Abundance Mindset would prevail in 21 days.

My brain downshifted to negative: how ridiculous to think an abundance mindset would just "happen" if I willed it! My heart was emotionally drained, and little was filling it up. My kids, yes, though they were still needing my energy 85% of every waking moment. The meaningful adventures, yes, though they were also stressful. My work, yes, both fulfilling and demanding. My husband...?

I begged—one might say, prayed—to be shown the way out and above the mess I was in. Again, the universe delivered.

At least, *The Universe Has Your Back*, a book by Gabby Bernstein, landed in my hands. I've heard divine things come in threes, so when I was told by three different people I needed to check out the book, of course I had to believe it was for a reason. Gabby's teachings became my anchor, and her meditations my fuel. I was the tiny seed waiting to germinate, and her guidance was the prolific soil holding me so I could root and sprout forth with gusto. I pored over the text with devotion, repeating the mantras and completing every suggested exercise; even signed up to receive recorded guidance. The book prompted readers to replace fear with faith (though I found the word "faith" sticking in my throat like the word "God").

At the end of the book, Gabby reworded faith as love. *Love.* LOVE! Now, that was palatable. Her book became my Love Bible. I read it again, devoting myself to the daily work, making myself accountable to the energies I emitted. The most difficult assignment: recognizing that tough life circumstances presented opportunities when we witnessed them through eyes of love. Everything centered around love. *Can loving my husband in my thoughts and in my actions help cultivate a feeling of love again? In both of us? Simultaneously?*

Then, when three different people suggested I check out the work of John Gottman (note: Godman in German), my nightly reading shifted from food books *Deep Nutrition* and *Why Zebras Don't Get Ulcers* to *The Seven Principles for Making Marriage Work*. I practically begged Chris to read each chapter after I did so we could discuss the ideas, and I was delighted when he read the intro and chapter one. But that was all.

No to reading. No to Friday morning "us" dates. No to spending time together doing what we once loved. No Scrabble. No therapy. He did say yes to a haircut.

"Would you listen to a podcast while I cut your hair?" I asked.

"Sure," Chris gave in, somewhat reluctantly. I pulled up a John Gottman episode about the fundamentals of a fulfilling marriage. As I cut Chris's hair, our bodies were close, but he didn't try to press his lips between my breasts or comment on "the great view," as he used to.

We listened to Gottman describe *contempt*—the most destructive of "The Four Horseman"—as the number one sign of a seriously troubled relationship. Contempt: a variety of negative behaviors toward the other person which made the other person feel *less than*. Disrespect. Sarcasm. Mocking. Eye rolling. Hostile humor. Such contemptuous behaviors permeate psychological, emotional, and physical health, destroying the immune system and causing ill-being. Another viewpoint on negativity, lack, and toxic thoughts followed by contaminated words and embodied in emotional distress.

Good God. That was us.

After years of being called out on my overbearing personality, inflexible opinions, and learned behaviors, I'd come to believe that all the challenges in my life were *my* fault. How often had my husband commented about my "issues," rolled his eyes, and stone-walled me? Suddenly, I understood another of Chris's perspectives: he believed I thought I was better than he was. *Nothing can be further from the truth!*

In all the years of loving Chris and accepting him for who he was, I had believed we co-existed as equals, while he'd been absorbing my words as berating stings and my actions as attacks on his personality. Despite always supporting his passions, acknowledging his gifts, and supporting him to succeed, I'd inadvertently diminished Chris's confidence in other ways. And he mine. We had been chipping away at each other.

RECIPE for DIVINE INTERVENTION

One of my yoga teachers struggled for years with her coffee addiction, but one day she had an epiphany: coffee is a God-given plant food, and when we have a healthy relationship with it, we can find harmony and joy in our ritualistic morning beverage. I don't and will not ever recommend that people give up coffee—that's a decision to be made entirely by an individual. Hence, my ever-changing morning coffee ritual—here's one example, with coffee as toxin-free as one can find.

Muddy Waters
Yield = 1 or more mugs
Total time = 5-15 minutes

Coffee Ingredients
- Swiss water processed whole bean decaf coffee
- Fully caffeinated coffee*
- Whole cardamom pods

Creamer Ingredients
- 1 14-oz can organic, full-fat coconut cream (in a BPA-free can)
- 3 tbsp organic blackstrap molasses (from a glass jar)
- 1 ½ tbsp local raw honey or organic, grade A maple syrup
- 1 tsp ground spice, such as cinnamon, turmeric, more cardamon (optional)

Instructions
1. Grind the beans.
2. To a coffee grinder add 50% decaf beans and 50% regular beans plus 3-5 whole cardamom pods.
3. Grind until well blended and to desired consistency for your coffee maker.
4. If you'd like to make more than one day's worth, transfer ground beans and pods to an airtight container, then repeat until container is full.
5. Make coffee. Using your device of choice (I prefer glass or stainless steel, for toxin-free purposes), make coffee with the ground beans, pods, and water.
6. Make creamer. Add the coconut cream, molasses, and honey or maple syrup to a measuring cup or bowl. Add spices, if you so choose. Whisk well.
7. Make the perfect cup of muddy water.
8. Pour coffee into your favorite mug.
9. Add 2 tbsp or so of your creamer blend.
10. Whisk until well combined.
11. Close your eyes.
12. Sip.
13. Enjoy.
14. Store creamer leftovers in the fridge for up to 3 days.

CHAPTER 39

Recipe for Detoxification

My thoughts were toxic, stress was polluting my well-being, and my relationship with my husband was doomed. Consumed by the mess I was in, I decided to start tidying it all up. My food was already super clean, my eating habits already supported my body's functioning, and my physical environment was relatively free of chemicals. It was my *messy life* I needed to assess.

My nutritionist way to do that was to create a detox program, both for me and for others in need. I called it a "Love Your Liver Detox" for marketing purposes. Of course, it's the liver's *job* to detoxify, yet this crucial organ is absolutely overburdened and needs ongoing support to function well. (I could not know then that I'd be detoxing from a love that no longer served me.)

The basis for a crucially needed detox was, of course, to enhance my own understanding of our highly toxic world and culture. Like so many others, I needed a reset from long-term exposure to almost a hundred thousand human-made chemicals approved by organizations claiming to "watch out" for human and environmental health, and which inundate our soil, air, and water. The parallels between human and planetary sickness undeniable. Even I, who prioritized sustainably grown food and lucky enough to breath clean air, needed a viable excuse to heal myself from a life contaminated with *dis*-ease. I also needed a love reset—love my body, my mind, my career, my clients, my husband.

I packaged the program neatly into five weeks of highly personalized detoxification. Beyond supporting the body's natural detox pathways with nutrients, herbs, hydration, elimination, and reducing toxic load, we would address life habits through eating, mood, mindset, movement, and motivation. Unlike most "cleanses," we'd also address the all-pervading toxic thoughts, relationships, and energy. Finally, we'd focus on prevention from evaluating the innumerable environmental, household, and personal care contaminants. *Whew!*

Until that year, I hadn't yet considered the energetic, emotional, spiritual, psychosocial, neurochemical, soul-sucking toxins. Figuring out "all the ways" to live relatively toxin-free in my own life and sharing it in my work seemed like a purposeful and progressive path. My inner voice was all on board. It was how I could serve, with love. The root of my program was an altruistic desire for every human to live harmoniously with the very nature from which we spring forth and evolve.

On a deeper level, toxic overload was the only explanation I could derive for my sister's endocrine-related cancer. She didn't drink or consume drugs. She grew her own tomatoes and ate wild game. But her house and lawn were toxin-laden, she worked in a public school with chemicals in the copy room, classroom, cafeteria, and on the playground; she lived in a city surrounded by modern agriculture, as well as forests sprayed to eliminate invasive species; and she ate contaminated food. One would never assume her toxic load was any more concentrated than most. I'd never really know.

But I did know that if any human from anywhere could spend a few hours researching the effects of toxins on the planet and their health, most likely they'd change a habit or 10. Show a few reports to a mama and she surely would switch out plastic toys for unpainted wooden blocks; highly scented laundry detergent in plastic bottles for soap sheets packaged in paper envelopes or powder sold in cardboard containers; and dryer sheets for essential oils dropped onto wool dryer balls. Besides

Recipe for Detoxification

helping parents and young children avoid toxins early on, creating awareness around the prevalence of toxins would be my main contribution to helping heal the planet. My program would center around gentle liver-clearing herbs, clean food, sweat, better sleep, and swapping out a few beauty and home products.

It must, of course, also focus on supplanting toxic thoughts, relationships, and energy. In fact, I found scientific data about people healing themselves of chronic disease through reshaping their thoughts. *Woah!* I invested every extra ounce of my energy into researching, creating, and marketing this detox program.

Naturally, I joined the program as I led it—how else would I know if it worked? I announced openly to my cohort of participants that I needed a total reset, too.

I don't recall why my husband joined the detox. Chris didn't have many patterns he felt compelled to change, though perhaps he was motivated to run (and sweat) more. I assured him that results from the herbs alone would be noticeable even if everything else in his life stayed the same. From a practical standpoint, it would be helpful to have my partner on board when making my own changes. From a clinical perspective, I was interested in outcomes for someone who took the liver herbs and binder, yet still drank coffee and alcohol, ate his typical diet, had disordered sleep and other life patterns that may not change. Also, I was desperate for Chris to experience my passion for my work, see me in action, and, perhaps, cultivate a modicum of approval for what I did all day.

The detox program began in early April. I chose to give up alcohol (easy and a no-brainer), as well as all sugar (oy), dairy (duh), and caffeine (infinitely more difficult). I stopped taking all supplements except the program's designated botanicals. I committed to a few habit changes, as well. First, to close my computer and put my phone on airplane mode two full hours before bed. Second, a focused morning routine. Third, one additional outside cardio activity each week. I also scheduled a three-hour Ayurvedic lymphatic massage, scheduled time in a full spectrum infrared sauna, carved out time to visit some hot springs, and encouraged my clients to do the same.

I was doing all the work I'd asked my clients to do. Chris was doing *a couple* of things right along with me.

CLEAN FOOD, MESSY LIFE

The first two weeks went swimmingly. In week one: some expected fatigue, dull headaches, and other symptoms of detox plus the challenges of following through on new patterns and recipes. In week two: most of us had found our rhythm and felt marked improvements in energy levels, the ability to make decisions, less irritability, and improved sleep. We'd resumed normal physical activity and were preparing for week three: the week of "clarity".

I'd planned a day excursion for my family to the same hot springs resort where I'd spent my birthday the year before. We would sweat out toxins and squeeze in much-needed time together. To my disappointment, Chris was crabby and "too tired" to go to the hot springs—it wouldn't be worth the effort to drive two hours each way and rush home in time for work.

"Well, geez, I'm busy too!" I retaliated, as I stuffed towels into the swim bag. "What happened to trying to invigorate the family we don't want to split up?" I yelled while leaving the room before Chris could reply. I was pissed. Truly, I was *over* it.

I grabbed the overnight oats I'd prepared for the drive, packed up car snacks I'd gathered for the kids, and added the detox-aligned lunch to eat in the lodge, plus coconut water to hydrate. I tossed in the swim bag, life vests, warm clothes, and cozy hats for the drive home. I remembered to bring an empty vessel to fill with filtered hot springs drinking water. The kids were still half asleep as I buckled them into car seats.

At some point while loading up, Chris agreed to come. *Great.* I threw a tantrum and got what I wanted. But it clearly had become easier and more enjoyable to plan adventures without my husband. Now I had to switch from pouting to pleasing. Alrighty. I could do that. Though I *wanted* him to come, I really wanted *him* to *want* to come.)

The sky was clear and road was dry, which made the prairie portion of the drive extra cold and the hot springs extra enticing. Chris was extra distant. He hardly smiled, not even at the kids.

Something was off. We were off. One of us? Or both?

I was confident in myself. I concluded that being together was more difficult than pretending we would improve. It was clear the effort to connect had become a drag, just as Chris had predicted our day trip might be. For the first time, I felt

RECIPE FOR DETOXIFIC...

uninterested in him. No desire to ask if he was "okay." next few hours in the warm, soft water I soaked up the l minerals while pure and infinite sadness welled up insi On the way home, Chris drove while I cried.

The next day, Sunday "detox soup day," I excused myself from what was supposed to be our only family night that particular week and, instead, attended a cacao ceremony and crystal bowl sound-healing session. I'd never been to one yet felt drawn to rediscover the therapeutic effects of music—not my husband's music. Slipping into a sound-bath might help me feel grounded during the detox. The timing seemed divinely planned.

Quiet, emotionally shaken and slow moving, I showed up merely to experience the energetic sensations. After cacao and before playing the bowls, the healer asked everyone in the room to share names and intentions for the evening. I knew at least half of the people in the room, and they knew me. When it was my turn to speak, my name caught in my throat. My body shook as I fought back tears. I brought my hand to my mouth, as if I could stop the sobbing, all eyes on me. I shook my head in apology and motioned for the woman on my left to speak. I'd never experienced such a loss for speaking.

Over the next hour or so, I lay on my mat, shivering though covered in wool blankets, and heavy with confusion. I tried to absorb the vibrations and follow the healer's words as she worked each bowl, speaking about the different element energies, and guiding us along the sound journey.

One word resonated: "Surrender." *Surrender to what?*

As the reverberations penetrated my skin, tears flowed down my cheeks in steady streams, moistening my hair and ears. It was an emotional detox from something I didn't yet understand. Remembering to *feel* before conscious *thought*, I ached to let go fully. Muffled by the sound of the bowls, I continued to weep.

As if being awakened from a dream, we were welcomed back into the room and there may have been more sharing or perhaps just gratitude—I'm not really sure. I sat up slowly, gingerly, and wondered what to do next. What had just happened? To what did I surrender, exactly?

I was positioned closest to the door and, quite unlike my usually social self, I wanted to leave rather than engage in conversation with anyone. As I put on my shoes and coat, an acquaintance from the local food movement came into the foyer. Directing the conversation to her, I asked about her efforts toward creating a more thriving food culture—something we both endeavored to cultivate in our community.

Surprisingly, her answer gave me the clarity I'd been seeking. "There is such a lack of passion." She was referring to food creation and sourcing. "I can sense it in the way they speak and in the food itself. It doesn't make sense to eat food created without love—what's the use in that? What kind of energy am I taking in?" She concluded, with a sigh, that she'd grown tired of trying to incite passion when it just wasn't there. She was exhausted working toward something that may not exist. She needed to move on.

Though she was speaking about the chefs and restauranteurs in town, what I heard was: my marriage was passionless, indifferent, energy depleting. I, too, was exhausted trying to reignite something that no longer existed.

The message of surrender was crystal clear: it was time to let go.

RECIPE for DETOXIFICATION

I recommend this soup for a winter detox, but its easily digestible nutrients always will support liver function. The specific veggies offer vitamins and minerals essential for phase 1 and 2 detoxification, and the broth helps move the bowels along (phase 3). Obviously, pesticide-free ingredients raised with love are ideal.

Vegetarian Detox Soup
Yield = 6 servings
Prep time = 8 hours if soaking lentils + 15 minutes veggie prep
Total time = 45-60 minutes (not including soaking lentils)

Ingredients
- 1 c dried brown, green, or black lentils
- 2 tbsp extra virgin olive oil
- 1 yellow onion
- 6 cloves garlic
- 2 tsp chopped fresh rosemary
- 1 stalk celery
- 1 medium carrot
- 1 head cauliflower
- 1 head kale
- 1 c chopped fresh parsley
- 6 c low-sodium veggie (or bone) broth, ideally homemade
- Splash of apple cider vinegar
- Sea salt and black pepper to taste

Instructions
1. Pre-soak the lentils in the morning to make the soup in the evening.
2. Prepare the veggies & herbs. Dice the onion. Mince the garlic. Mince the rosemary leaves. Dice the celery and carrots. Chop the cauliflower stems and florets. Remove the ribs from kale, then chop the leaves. Chop the parsley and save a few sprigs as garnish.
3. Make the soup. Heat the olive oil in a large pot, ideally cast iron, on medium heat. Add the onion and cover, stirring every minute or so, until onion becomes translucent, about 3 minutes. Add the garlic and rosemary. Stir for 30 seconds. Add all veggies and broth.
4. If you soaked the lentils, strain, and rinse them thoroughly, then add to the pot. Bring the soup to a boil, then reduce to simmer. Cover, and cook for 20-25 minutes, stirring frequently. Check the consistency of the lentils—if they're soft, they're finished. Otherwise, cook longer. Add more broth or water if lentils soak up too much liquid.
5. When the lentils and veggies are thoroughly cooked, remove from heat, add a splash of apple cider vinegar, and stir. Taste the soup, then season with salt and pepper.
6. Serve hot, garnished with a few sprigs of fresh parsley.
7. Pause to find gratitude for your meal and your body.

CHAPTER 40

Recipe for Divorce

Finances and infidelity destroy marriages, but I'll argue that a good detox program can be just as effective.

I'd opened some kind of portal into the cosmos of vulnerability and clarity. I must have emitted that energy because the next day, Tax Day, I was hacked. It seemed like I'd allowed it to happen because I was so distracted. Yes, I was neck deep in notes on environmental, household, and personal care toxins for the detox program, but my brain was fixated on the end of my marriage. While I witnessed someone accessing files on my computer, I texted my cousin, an ex-FBI agent who worked in cyber security, for advice and managed not to freak out. I stayed cool as a cucumber. *Somehow, I asked for this.* So, instead of processing the lifechanging conversation I vowed to hold that night, I devoted the day to saving my identity.

My identity. For years I'd been slowly rediscovering crumbs of who I was, and that evening I'd be asserting to the true breadth of my individuality.

After our kids were asleep and Chris had returned home early from a slow night at work, Chris and I sat on our respective sides in bed, looking out the windows over the darkening valley. No skin touching, no eye contact. It was time. I turned toward him and, with certainty, simply said, "Chris, I love you, but I can no longer be your wife." I quickly continued, "We are living two separate lives. I think we both know our children are not a platform for finding happiness together. I cannot raise them in a tense, cheerless household of avoidance and while seeking joy outside our marriage. I don't want to blame you or myself for our ongoing discontent and disconnect."

I paused. Without hesitation, Chris agreed with me. "Trup, I've been thinking the same for a while."

I burst into tears. Over the years, I'd cried a lot, but these tears flowed from deep inside my core as immense pain compressed my heart. I grabbed several tissues. Blew my nose many times. Sopped up my drenched face. Dropped crumpled Kleenex onto the floor. One after another. In only a few minutes, as if I'd released all the water I'd been treading, no more tears came.

Chris patiently waited for me to finish yet continued to look toward somewhere beyond our room. Then he described a vision for our life apart that was more detailed, more specific, and more thorough than any vision I'd asked him (literally, for *years*) to create about what our *together* life could be like. "I respect you as a mother, but I agree—I don't think we can be happy together again."

He shared how we might be in the not-too-distant future as individuals who held each other in high esteem. Separately. "I want to see you around town and say, 'That's the mother of my children' and feel proud of you. I *want* to be proud of your accomplishments, but I can't feel that way like this...." He painted us re-coupled with new partners, all *four* of us attending our kids' birthday parties and soccer games. Me making the cake and bringing the healthy snacks. We'd show up happily. Together, apart. He wanted to raise our children with love and affection, not in a house silent with irritability, snide comments, and cool distance.

"If we don't split up now, we might end up hating each other," he finished.

I didn't know how long ago his light had fully extinguished, but evidently our small efforts over the past year had resulted in the same clarity for both of us. We wanted a relationship more loving than the one we'd created. It had illuminated inside me only the night before, yet he was already thinking about happiness with someone else.

I rallied the courage to ask once again, "*Is* there someone else?"

"No, Trup. I just don't share your dreams and no longer wanted to be a part of them."

Wow.

In the long pause that followed, I wondered whether he'd had a singular moment of lucidity, like the one I'd experienced in the sound healing session, or whether our dysfunction had built up over time. I concluded that it really didn't matter. Our life together was over. Sixteen years of dedication, and though we'd disconnected, we'd be forever entwined beyond what I could have imagined with any other human because our children had been conceived from our love. That sobering moment was one I'd never imagined.

Looking over at him, I sighed and asked, "What do we do now?"

We held each other and slept.

In the morning, instead of working I chose to make our family's favorite comfort-food breakfast. It was the most loving thing I could do. Dutch babies never failed to receive oohs and ahhs from everyone, myself included. It was unclear how many more meals we'd be able to share together.

RECIPE for DIVORCE

This simple, crowd-pleasing meal is adorned with seasonal fruits and favorite toppings. Please note that I've tried seemingly every possible combination of gluten-free, dairy-free, and egg-free—exactly none of them turn out as fluffy, delish, or comforting as the traditional recipe. Experiment, but don't get your hopes up. The suggested topping are my family's favorites—try your own combinations, too!

Dutch Babies
Yield = 4 servings
Prep time = 5 minutes
Total time = 25 minutes

Ingredients
- ¼ c salted, grass-fed butter
- 4 eggs from pasture-raised hens
- 1 c whole organic milk
- 1 c organic gluten-containing flour combination of choice

Toppings
- Whole, plain yogurt or cottage cheese
- Granola
- Fresh fruit or fruit compote
- Maple syrup or ginger syrup

Instructions
1. Preheat the oven to 400 degrees F.
2. Cut the butter into cubes and place in a 9x13-inch glass or ceramic casserole dish. Place dish in the oven to melt and brown the butter, while you prepare the batter.
3. In a medium bowl, crack the eggs and whisk them until combined.
4. Whisk in the milk and then the flour until no (or few) lumps remain.
5. When oven has heated to 400 degrees, remove the dish with the melted butter and place on a hot pad. Carefully pour batter evenly into dish over the butter. Return to the oven and bake for 20 minutes.
6. Gather toppings.
7. Prepare the fruit. If you're making a berry compote (so easy on the stovetop from frozen berries with a few spices), prepare it now.
8. Pull out yogurt, granola, and maple syrup. Kids love to help with this part.
9. Ask your kids to set the table—most are eager to do so because they're so excited for Dutch babies!
10. When the oven timer dings, invite your kids to check out the fluffiness of the Dutch babies. Like a soufflé, the puffiness will fall within a few minutes.
11. While hot, cut into 8 pieces and place a piece on each plate. Add toppings and enjoy.

CHAPTER 41

Recipe for Dissolution

Divorce is like death, only no one brings a casserole. Nothing soothes. Not chocolate or coffee, hemp or ashwagandha, meditation or asana. I thought a "divorce party" might serve the double objective of lightening the mood and informing our friends but, not surprisingly, Chris was not interested.

Regardless, once the divorce decision was made, everything dissolved quickly into a muddy mess of ironies chopping through separation like a butcher knife, slicing up unequal pieces of the pie. Where disagreements had ruled, now we had to communicate—with compassion—about every detail. Where flexibility and understanding had been key ingredients, now they triggered logistical headaches. Who would move out and to where and when? How to tell the kids? How to make the transition a smooth one? How to release attachment to material objects when they mean something to you?

I knew my adrenals were on hyperdrive when I craved brownies smothered in peanut butter and sea salt (for every meal).

With so much division battling in our minds and hearts, we had to concentrate on each step. The first big focus: Separate into two spaces. It was a no-brainer that I didn't want to stay in our house. Plus, I'd moved at least 30 times in my life already—over a dozen times before graduating high school, nine times during college and before "us," another nine times together. That number didn't include all the house-sitting or between-move moves; clearly, I was a well-seasoned mover. Something in me inherently resisted putting down roots. Since moving into that house seemed to have marked the beginning of our end, I was eager to flee from it. Also shaken. Our family home. *Sniff.*

Chris wanted me *out* as soon as possible. Without a solid plan, I resisted. I needed assurance I could afford to be on my own. Time to find a decent place during a crazy-tight housing market in Hailey, where I wanted to become part of the pulse of life. Where everything was within a 20-minute walk of my home, where Aylee went to preschool, and equidistant from Avery's elementary school. Where people walked their dogs, biked to the grocery store, caught the bus. Where my friends could stop by to say hello on their way home from the bank, bookstore, or bakery. Where I would be part of a community.

Between episodes of emotional distress, I started looking for rental homes and found only a handful of options. Crappy, tiny apartments with no storage required exorbitant rent. After visiting just one of them, I stubbornly opposed considering an apartment as an option. Not only did I work from home, but I was also no longer a college student who could squeeze into a trashy shoebox with a car full of clothes. I was a mom with two young kids. And I loved to cook. I had a desk; they had toys. How could I roll out my yoga mat on moldy carpet? I would not begin my new life sacrificing certain standards. But wow. In our resort valley, the only viable rental options were twice what I penciled out I could afford, not including utilities. Our separation was difficult enough in a small town where divorce was unusual, but more apparent than our anomaly was the vast chasm between the wealthy and the working class.

Chris urged me to rent one of the few available cookie-cutter, run-down, over-priced houses; I refused. I was free to manifest what I wanted, and I trusted I would do just that. Where I was typically reactive, I knew patience and perseverance would prevail. Where he was typically realistic, his haste to be rid of me seemed to defy logic. We really were so different.

Recipe for Dissolution

During my morning routine, I became fixated on creating a vision for myself and for my kids with their single mama. While sipping my matcha, I calculated my income and my needs. Energized by my second beverage (coffee, honey, and nut-based creamer), I sent emails to my community describing my specific housing desires. While nourishing myself with a triple chocolate brownie with peanut butter and sea salt (for breakfast), I clarified my goal of moving into a spacious home with a big kitchen by the time school started in the fall. I'd have four months to figure it all out.

During those months, we decided to split the house each week according to Chris's night-work schedule—I'd stay there 4–5 days with the kids, then leave for 2–3 days when he had the kids. In that scenario, our kids would be at home and as stable as possible during our transition. I'd secured nine places to rest my head over the 12-week summer while house-, dog- and cat-sitting. It would be a lot of shuffling stuff around for me but, hey, I was up for the adventure!

Next, tell our children.

The Sunday before school was out for the summer, Chris and I took our coffees out to the front porch swing. I looked out at the peaceful view that would no longer be mine, and I looked at the husband who would no longer be mine. He was so comfortable in that house, in that life, and I was the one messing it up for him. I'd be giving him the house he'd always wanted, his dream. Living true to myself meant rediscovering my own dreams. Still, my stomach sank. We were really doing this.

I asked Chris, "Are we ready?"

Before he could answer, a hummingbird flew toward us, paused within a few feet, buzzed until it was sure we knew what it was doing there, then flew away. My sister Jessica had come to me many times since her death as a hummingbird. That day, both Chris and I felt sure it was her nudge of approval.

"I think that's a pretty good sign it's time," Chris said, as if reading my thoughts.

When the kids were outside with us, we told them we had something important to share. Avery, who had just turned seven, looked eager to learn of some new gift or adventure. Aylee, at four, was fixated on her stuffies and sitting right between Mama and Daddy.

I started. "You know how Mama has always wanted to live in Hailey? And you know how Dad works nights? Well, Mama is going to look for a house in town and you'll say with me on the nights Dad works. Then, on Dad's nights off, you'll come back and live with him in this house."

Aylee hardly blinked at the news. Avery immediately said, "Mom, it would be cool if you could find a house near the skate park!" He was excited to have two houses. We reminded him of one of his friends who had two houses. Then he asked, "Where will our kitty go?"

"Lulu will stay here," Chris replied, though we hadn't really talked about it. She had always been Chris's cat.

"Can I have two bikes?" Avery continued.

"We'll have to see about that…" I answered.

"Can we go back inside now and play?" Aylee inquired.

"Of course!" I said. And that was that.

Over the next few chaotic months, as we bounced around (nine homes in twelve weeks), I started the process of separating our things. I wrote a list of the stuff we *needed* to live and a list of the stuff we coveted. It was a lot to process. I googled what I *should* be taking with me, according to the state: anything purchased during marriage is common property, and anything purchased before marriage belongs to the person who bought the item. Gifts belonged to the person gifted the item.

Chris disagreed with the state's outline. Still, I was surprised when he insisted on keeping, well, all the furniture (seriously, all of it). He wanted all the beds and linens, side tables and dressers, the entertainment center and TV, the dining room table, the kitchen stools, and the three special lights we'd purchased together: the lighthouse fog light from the Oregon coast; the farmhouse dining room fixture from our first condo in Portland; the vintage round globe we brought home from LA which we dubbed "the moon." He wanted me to take the pink couch our new neighbors had recently given to him instead of my favorite leather one with rivets or the one I'd had special-made in LA by Rosa's company (which employed US citizens at fare wages and utilized toxin-free materials).

Recipe for Dissolution

I was surprised when he didn't want to give up the old, real-wood bookshelf, which housed 123 of my books and three of his. Strangely, he wanted my desk. He didn't want the baby grand piano that Avery had been playing all school year– apparently, Chris thought it was too big for the living room and, besides, he didn't like the color. *Okaaaay.* I supposed it wouldn't be too much to hire people to move it repeatedly until I could afford to buy my own home. (I added to my rental house requirements and vision: a space big enough for a baby grand. *Sheesh.*)

On top of everything else, he pleaded to keep one of my favorite pieces of artwork, a large black-and-white framed photograph I'd purchased from an artist friend around the time Chris and I had met. Weary and overwhelmed, I relented (and have missed it dearly).

I also left pieces of our family life, like framed photos and crafts our kids and I had made together. I didn't *want* to leave them, but I thought I should. To keep the peace. For some stupid reason, I even left half of my plants, which I'd potted, nurtured, and adored.

His resistance to my needs was my cue to ask for and expect much less than half. I would sleep on a mattress on the floor rather than argue about a bed, bookshelves, or sheets and towels for myself and our kids. I took my books, my clothes, my bins of photographs, but not a single other piece of memorabilia from our life together. I left gifts Chris had given to me: the painted steer skull hanging over the fireplace; the popcorn machine. I took the kids' vintage play kitchen and art easel, both of which Chris thought cluttered up the house. Dividing up camping, skiing, and other recreational items would become contentious later.

I couldn't function without my kitchen being fully stocked. Separating the kitchen proved to be a more difficult task than I'd imagined. Though the kitchen had felt like my space, suddenly everything felt like his. Plus, Chris was fully capable of cooking, and I knew he'd soon have to cook more than he ever had before. So, we'd both need operational items. Almost daily I used the VitaMix, Cuisinart and immersion blender. Could Chris prepare food without those appliances? He said he could.

Clean Food, Messy Life

On the nights I spent at the house with our kids, I started making a list of every kitchen item so it would be easy to pack up whenever I signed a lease. I took stock of the non-useful items. A vintage Osterizer blender I knew Chris liked to look at on the counter, though it didn't work very well. He was happy to have it. The bread box. I loved that red bread box. We bought it at the annual 4th of July antique fair for one of our anniversaries. I knew Chris would want it because it fit perfectly on the counter and contrasted nicely against the white subway tiles he'd installed. I forced myself to remember I was letting go of things I didn't need.

He would keep the plates—I'd already decided to purchase some kitchen items and write them off against my business since I used them in photographs for my website, social media, and group programs.

But the bowls—the vintage milk glass bowls—were mine. The handmade ceramic wide bowl—my sourdough mixing bowl purchased at a Sun Valley art fair before we married—that was mine. The white ceramic casserole dishes of all sizes and shapes with the iconic blue floral print—a dime a dozen at thrift stores, but Jessica had rescued some of those pieces from our parents' house after their divorce, and several of the small bowls came from each of our grandmothers after they'd died. Those were mine, too. Also the family heirloom hand-mixer (useless), wooden spoons (splintered and scorched), and aluminum bakeware (which I was sure contributed to Alzheimer's disease and never used), I had to take with me. Because, well, they were mine.

The cast iron pots and pans—we'd purchased a refurbished one each year while vintage shopping in Portland. Was it okay to take them all? Which did I use most? Definitely the Dutch oven. Our other pots and pans were just okay—stainless steel, but not my fave. *Can I afford to buy a new set, the super pricey ones that met my toxin-free standards?*

The goddamn spatulas. I had my favorites. *Does Chris know that? Should I take them?*

The coffee grinder, the French press, the glass container with the pheasant logo I'd purchased from our favorite coffee roaster in Portland. I could leave those, I suppose. *Does that seem fair?*

Recipe for Dissolution

Vulnerable, and with rising fear about how I'd pay for a house all on my own and furnish it with everything I needed...I opened the pantry to a wonderland of food reserves. I was relieved to witness the abundances I'd procured and stored; it renewed my hopes to see such plenitude at my fingertips.

Oh, my. Was I ever prepared for the apocalypse! I'd done a damn good job of ensuring we had back-ups of pretty much every food staple and luxury edible item one could possibly need (for three months). This was my version of food security—if we'd had enough cans of tomatoes and dried beans and rice in the pantry, our family could survive anything.

And so could I. On my own. A divorced woman with two kids in a small, exorbitant mountain valley. I was a capable and independent. That notion may have been problematic in our marriage, but it would serve me well in the uncertain times to come. Plus, I knew how and when to ask for help.

Certainly, I didn't need help dividing up the pantry. Chris surely didn't realize how many foods were housed in there. I would leave items for meals I assumed he might prepare.

I took bulk beans from a local farmer and cans of beans (many varieties) for when I didn't have time to soak and cook them myself; two cans of corn (why did we have canned corn?); a box of organic soup; olives in jars; most of the diced tomatoes and tomato paste; kid snacks (Mom-approved bars, seaweed, dried fruit, plus a couple of Annie's fruit bunny snacks and Peter Rabbit squeezy packs leftover from Easter baskets); trail mix; my own adult bars for hiking plus a couple of those keto buffalo jerky things for outdoor back-up food. Several bags of apples that I'd dried, plus figs and mangoes from Costco. Bulk oats, steel-cut oats, oatmeal packets for camping. Canned mackerel, sardines, salmon. Jars of grape juice from my dad; jam, peaches, pickles, and elderberry syrup from Jaclyn; onion conserves and salsa from Jessica's widowed husband's wife. Peanut butter, almond butter, chocolate-peanut-coconut butter (yeah, I'd be taking that one, thank you very much).

Let's see, starchy foods: I divided up the pasta—penne, orzo, maifun, soba, gluten-free something-or-other, and more; bulk bags of quinoa, brown rice, popcorn kernels; several types of seeded and sea-salted crackers in boxes. *Chips? Chris can keep those*. Organic flour—unbleached white, whole wheat, semolina, spelt, buckwheat; white rice, brown rice, quinoa, oat, coconut, almond, garbanzo bean, pumpkin seed, and corn meal. *Does he need any of those?* I surmised he wouldn't.

On the floor of the pantry was sparkling water in glass bottles (my back-up water supply). Also mango and lemon juice in plastic bottles from Costco (he could have those). Local potatoes and onions and garlic (I took half). A six pack of beer (his).

For now, my husband might keep the full chest freezer, a gift from my dad (if I couldn't find a house with a garage). It was full of food we'd been given thanks to a healthy harvest, or meals I'd batch-cooked and saved; Ziploc bags of frozen raspberries, blackberries, strawberries, grapes and green beans from my dad and his wife; apple pie filling, apple sauce and plum sauce I'd made from the fruit off our trees; pureed squash, shredded zucchini, and whole tomatoes from last season's bounty. Jars of pesto I'd made (unlabeled). Stacks of yogurt containers labeled as turkey or chicken stock or homemade veggie broth. Soup galore, soaked and cooked black and pinto beans, meatballs, and red sauce I'd prepared. We had super-size-me Costco bags of frozen peas, broccoli, berries, wild-caught salmon burgers. There was duck breast from a client who thoughtfully gifted it to me after a healthy hunt. Elk and venison—ground, sausage, brats, and steak—from my sister and her husband. A couple of organic, pasture-raised (expensive) chickens from my favorite farmers.

I took inventory and divided it all up and felt guilty for the imbalance, as my side of the food list was quite a bit longer than his. I was unsure how much space I'd have in the freezer in the new home (wherever that would be). Plus, I hadn't peeked into the small freezer in the kitchen, home to the frozen foods I'd used most, where I'd also noticed the silicone ice cubes and the beer steins, which reminded me to divide up the liquor cabinet.

Hmm. Somehow, over the years, the liquor cabinet had expanded, with specialty bottles of who-knows-what for some kind of drink I'd never heard of. It made me rather nostalgic to think that we'd once had just bourbon, vodka, Kahlúa, and a couple of mixers. I wondered when Chris had bought those other specialty liquors, and why I'd chosen not to notice. I wasn't really drinking, but I wanted some bourbon (at least!) on hand

Recipe for Dissolution

to share with my friends who might come over unexpectedly in my new home.

In the cabinet next to the liquor were the cookbooks. I left the three that were not mine—cooking soups, making salsas, and one describing how to fold napkins into fancy shapes. I also left a Thai cookbook from our travels, and an original copy of my aunt's backcountry cookbook (in case Chris would want to try his hand at Dutch babies).

Finally, the jars of dried goods, a focal point on the open kitchen shelves. These were my go-to jars, easy to grab while food-prepping. Neat and colorful in both contemporary and old-school Mason jars, I'd organized kidney beans, black beans, small white beans, black-eyed peas, split peas, yellow lentils, bulgur, and popcorn kernels. On the shelf above those, more Mason jars of quinoa, jasmine rice, arborio rice, brown rice, forbidden rice, farro, buckwheat groats, rolled oats, and polenta. I started packing them up and, to my surprise, Chris protested! Though he never cooked with them, he liked the way they looked on the shelves. *Alrighty.* I divided half of each jar into an empty one (of which I had plenty), so we could both have some.

In all the dividing, I realized that every single item in our home meant something to him, or me, or us. We were not frivolous; we'd filled up our home with meaningful objects or well-made functional gadgets, making it difficult to remain neutral; every decision was thoughtful.

Still, I felt I had to justify my reasons for taking some of the stuff on my list, even when the lines of demarcation seemed obvious. I felt ashamed for wanting to possess certain functional items, and guilt for taking others. I felt like I was begging for some furniture when there was such excess; that I was looting the walls of treasured artwork, which, in reality, was almost all mine. While I didn't want to leave holes in the life we'd built together, it was inevitable as we consciously widened the gap between us.

To assuage my guilt, I replaced a few items I'd be taking. I found an upright, black piano (the color he'd wanted), and persuaded Chris (and others) to help move the baby grand when it came time. I purchased a new, round cast-iron skillet, some white serving bowls, a small food processor, and a few spatulas.

Ultimately, I took what cluttered up his life, and less than what I needed. He may have had most of the pie, but I had the essentials for cooking and working. I would have my kids more nights than not. I had my values and my dreams. Other than our kids and a desire to come back to myself, that was all I needed to start my new life.

RECIPE for DISSOLUTION

When we crave chocolate, fat, sweets, and salt, likely our adrenals are on overdrive and our cells need energy pronto—this is a normal survival reaction to acute stress. Therefore, these nutrient-rich brownies are well-balanced and super delish! If possible, enjoy the process of making them, eat mindfully, and appreciate that you are momentarily nourished.

Triple Chocolate Brownies with Peanut Butter & Sea Salt
Yield = 1 (though it's wise to share)
Prep time = 15 minutes
Total time = 45 minutes

Ingredients
- 1 ½ oz dark chocolate
- ½ c butter or coconut oil
- ½ c peanut butter (I like chunky)
- ¼ c turbinado sugar or other raw sugar
- ½ c pure maple syrup
- ½ tsp vanilla paste or 1 tsp pure vanilla extract
- 1 packet instant coffee or 1 tsp coffee grounds (optional)
- ½ c whole wheat flour
- ¼ c pumpkin seed flour (or coconut flour)
- ¼ c cocoa powder
- 1 tsp ground cinnamon
- 1 tsp baking soda
- ½ tsp sea salt
- 2 eggs from pasture-raised hens
- 1/3 c unsweetened shredded coconut flakes
- 1/3 c dark chocolate chips

Instructions
1. Preheat oven to 350 degrees F.
2. Prepare an 8x8-inch baking dish by greasing it with some butter or coconut oil. Set aside.
3. Melt chocolate, butter or coconut oil, peanut butter, sugar, maple syrup, vanilla, and coffee in a small pot on low heat. Stir until thoroughly combined, then remove from heat.
4. In a medium bowl, add flour, cocoa powder, cinnamon, baking soda, salt and stir to combine.
5. In a small bowl, whisk eggs together, then combine with the chocolate/peanut butter mixture, which should be cool enough that it won't cook the eggs.
6. Pour wet ingredients into the dry ingredients and combine well.
7. Fold in the shredded coconut and chocolate chips.
8. Pour the batter into the dish and bake for 30-35 minutes, until the edges begin to pull away from the sides of the pan and a toothpick comes clean after being inserted into the middle.
9. Let cool for about half an hour (if you can wait that long!) before cutting into squares and gobbling it up.

Thank You!

There are so many people who have helped me write this book thanks to their presence in my life, which helped create the story I lived.

My mom, Iny Day-Truppi, who witnessed much of this story as it unfolded in real time and, upon reading about some rather reckless events she knew nothing about, chose to love me anyway. She's always been my biggest supporter. She still corrects my grammar and word usage. She surprises me with matcha lattes. She's also my copy editor.

My dad, George Truppi, for being as book-obsessed as my mom. History books, mostly, but books, nevertheless. His love of nature and gardening helped develop my connection to the earth and my food values.

My ex-husband, for telling me I had a good idea about a book when we were still married. It was supposed to be a funny parody, you know, to lighten the mood. He endured my food obsessions until they became too much. His impact on my life is indescribable and, of course, I'm eternally grateful he helped bring my two favorite people into the world.

My children, Avery and Aylee, for being my guides and inspiring me to be a better version of myself. Avery, for his enthusiasm for my book and assurance that his mama is going to be a famous author. Aylee, for climbing into my lap many mornings as I wrote and reminding me to take breaks to just be with her.

My friends, many of whom are in this book, described by their real names. You are the abundant wildflowers on my life's journey. Many of you have supported me through the writing process and reminded me I am more than who I think I am. My food system friends. Fellow yogis. Nutritionist colleagues, professors, mentors, and clients. Extended family. Community. Coaches, guides, therapists. You were part of my story, yet your names and presence may not have made it into the book. I'm grateful for you, too.

My content editor, Maraya Loza Koxahn, who gave me honest, detailed advice that helped me in my numerous rounds of edits (yeah, I know, 6 rounds…).

Finally, the amazing folks at Self-Publishing School who have endured this tumultuous path with me. You've inspired and encouraged me; you've held me up. I probably wouldn't have written this book without y'all. My very patient coach, Ellaine, who has never seen another author pine over edits as I have. I hope I've made you all proud.

Made in the USA
Middletown, DE
17 December 2022